STUDIES IN MAJOR LITERARY AUTHORS

Edited by

William E. Cain

Professor of English
Wellesley College

A ROUTLEDGE SERIES

Studies in Major Literary Authors

William E. Cain, *General Editor*

Gerard Manley Hopkins and Victorian Catholicism
Jill Muller

George Orwell, Doubleness, and the Value of Decency
Anthony Stewart

Progress and Identity in the Plays of W. B. Yeats
Barbara A. Seuss

Frederick Douglass's Curious Audiences
Ethos in the Age of the Consumable Subject
Terry Baxter

The Artist, Society & Sexuality in Virginia Woolf's Novels
Ann Ronchetti

T. S. Eliot's Civilized Savage
Religious Eroticism and Poetics
Laurie J. MacDiarmid

Worlding Forster
The Passage from Pastoral
Stuart Christie

William Dean Howells and the Ends of Realism
Paul Abeln

Whitman's Ecstatic Union
Conversion and Ideology in Leaves of Grass
Michael Sowder

Ready to Trample on All Human Law
Financial Capitalism in the Fiction of Charles Dickens
Paul A. Jarvie

Pynchon and History
Metahistorical Rhetoric and Postmodern Narrative Form in the Novels of Thomas Pynchon
Shawn Smith

A Singing Contest
Conventions of Sound in the Poetry of Seamus Heaney
Meg Tyler

Edith Wharton as Spatial Activist and Analyst
Reneé Somers

Queer Impressions
Henry James's Art of Fiction
Elaine Pigeon

"No Image There and the Gaze Remains"
The Visual in the Work of Jorie Graham
Catherine Sona Karagueuzian

"Somewhat on the Community-System"
Fourierism in the Works of Nathaniel Hawthorne
Andrew Loman

Colonialism and the Modernist Moment in the Early Novels of Jean Rhys
Carol Dell'Amico

Melville's Monumental Imagination
Ian S. Maloney

Writing "Out of All the Camps"
J. M. Coetzee's Narratives of Displacement
Laura Wright

Here and Now
The Politics of Social Space in D. H. Lawrence and Virginia Woolf
Youngjoo Son

HERE AND NOW

The Politics of Social Space in
D. H. Lawrence and Virginia Woolf

Youngjoo Son

Routledge
New York & London

Published in 2006 by
Routledge
Taylor & Francis Group
270 Madison Avenue
New York, NY 10016

Published in Great Britain by
Routledge
Taylor & Francis Group
2 Park Square
Milton Park, Abingdon
Oxon OX14 4RN

Printed in the United States of America on acid-free paper
10 9 8 7 6 5 4 3 2 1

International Standard Book Number-10: 0-415-97540-9 (Hardcover)
International Standard Book Number-13: 978-0-415-97540-7 (Hardcover)

Library of Congress Cataloging-in-Publication Data

Catalog record is available from the Library of Congress

Taylor & Francis Group
is the Academic Division of Informa plc.

Visit the Taylor & Francis Web site at
http://www.taylorandfrancis.com

and the Routledge Web site at
http://www.routledge-ny.com

For Genie and Jenny

Contents

Permissions   ix

Introduction   1

PART ONE: REWRITING PRIVATE AND PUBLIC SPACES   17

Part One Introduction   19

Chapter One   27

Chapter Two   57

PART TWO: REMOLDING HOME AND NATION   83

Part Two Introduction   85

Chapter Three   93

Chapter Four   117

PART THREE: UTOPIC SPACES HERE AND NOW   141

Part Three Introduction   143

Chapter Five   153

Chapter Six   175

Conclusion   205

Notes   209

Bibliography 235

Index 249

Permissions

Introduction

This study investigates the political implications of the works of D. H. Lawrence and Virginia Woolf through the lens of the concept of social space. At first glance, the combination of Lawrence and Woolf seems rather unusual. Critics have hardly discussed these writers together, and when they have, their focus has fallen mainly on differences between them. Reading through essays, letters, diaries, and fictions of Lawrence and Woolf, we are often struck by radical contrasts in style, aims, temperament, and background. Lawrence never went along with the contemporary modernist "movements" promoted in his lifetime by such figures as T. S. Eliot, James Joyce, Ezra Pound, Wyndham Lewis, and Virginia Woolf.[1] He refused to follow theories of aesthetic autonomy and impersonality and mercilessly mocked the "critical twiddle-twaddle about style, and form, all this pseudo-scientific classifying and analysing of books" ("John Galsworthy," *Phoenix* 539). Lawrence's frequent attacks on literary experimentalism point to his self-willed dissociation from the high modernism with which Woolf is often linked. His attitude toward gender and sexuality is another key feature that has led scholars to regard him in opposition to Woolf.[2] In contrast with Woolf's feminism and advocacy of androgyny, Lawrence evinced a determined misogyny, evident, for example in the notorious *Fantasia of the Unconscious* and presented homosexuality as one of the most hideous diseases afflicting modern society.

Critical assessments of Lawrence and Woolf seem to have made the differences between them even more prominent. While Lawrence, a son of a miner, became a working class hero in the hands of critics like F.R. Leavis during the 1960s, Woolf, with an upper-middle class background, was somewhat dismissed or stigmatized as a snob. By the end of the century, however, Lawrence's reputation in literary criticism is less secure than that of Woolf. Unlike Woolf, now considered one of the major figures of English modernism, feminism, and pacifism, Lawrence is known as the priest of a cult of the phallus, a view initiated by Kate Millett's *Sexual Politics* (1971). Feminist critics have interpreted Lawrence and Woolf's contrasting attitudes towards the m/other in light of the patriarchal construction of the male self with its related anti-feminism. They argue that Lawrence's desire to escape from the devouring mother reveals his misogyny and his wish to establish masculine autonomy and integrity, reflecting his troubled relationships with women and his anxiety in the face of women's growing claim for independence.

Critics have further associated the divergent gender politics of Lawrence and Woolf with different worldviews, arguing that where Lawrence's stress on boundaries and distinctions is entwined with his male-centered, exclusive vision of society, Woolf's penchant for fusion is evident in her more inclusive, web-like vision of the world. Furthermore, critics' indictment of Lawrence's proto-fascist leaning has put him in diametric opposition to Woolf, who attacked fascism along with her battle with patriarchal, nationalist, and imperial ideologies. Lawrence criticism, however, has taken another direction over the past few years. The drift towards more interdisciplinary approaches to modernism as well as a more flexible concept of gender has transformed the study of Lawrence. A growing number of scholars have attempted to reconsider Lawrence's position with regard to modernism and gender politics, while broaching new issues of race, ethnicity, and nationality as well.

And yet, the connection between Lawrence and Woolf has hardly drawn detailed critical attention.[3] Interestingly, it was Woolf who was most keenly aware of similarities between Lawrence and herself. In a 1932 diary entry, she writes, "he and I have too much in common" (*The Diary of Virginia Woolf* 4: 126). Although the context suggests that Woolf's recognition of affinity with him primarily derives from her insight into Lawrence's choking egotism, a quality that she herself shared, her life-long interest in and her increasingly positive evaluation of Lawrence indicate that her recognition of something "too much in common" between them goes beyond the shared preoccupation with self.[4]

While I am aware of both the differences between Woolf and Lawrence and of the complexity of each, my study aims to excavate less observed similarities between them through a reading that takes up recent concerns with space in regard to modernism and modernity that have been developed by both literary critics and by other scholars from various fields. The issue of space in studies of modernism is not new. Since Joseph Frank's 1948 essay, "Spatial Form in Modern Literature," the concern with space has long been crucial to understanding modernist formal aspects of juxtaposition, montage, or collage that inscribe an overall unity of artwork and society within the representation of a fragmented society. In the essay, Frank maintains that modernist narratives unfold through the spatial juxtaposition of images instead of the conventional temporal frame of linear development. Despite its importance, Frank's view of space has the limitation of confining modernism to formal innovations. Aligning space with image, form, style, fictional order, and artistic autonomy, Frank's work has contributed to characterizing the cultural phenomena of modernism in terms of the preoccupation with the interior space—e.g., the consciousness, psychological state, and subjective rendering of reality—and the subsequent dissociation from exterior reality and space.[5]

Of course, my stress on space does not deny the importance of the subjective and psychological dimension in modernist aesthetics. Nor does it simply aim to pay attention to an external reality that is understood to be in opposition to the interior realm of consciousness, assuming a neat dichotomy between the interior and the exterior—a binary that both Lawrence and Woolf consistently interrogated as much as they were fascinated with the human psyche. Instead, by drawing upon the notion of social space, my study attempts to reapproach this binary underpinning the longstanding view of modernism, illuminating how Lawrence and Woolf, each in their own ways, were actively engaged in social life. More importantly, my study shows how the political implications of Lawrence's treatment of space converge with those of Woolf's.

My concern with space owes much to theorists who have addressed the issue of space with reference to modernity. In the late 1960s, for instance, Michel Foucault brought discursive and physical space into a discourse of modernity. According to him, "space was treated as the dead, the fixed, the undialectical, the immobile. Time, on the contrary, was richness, fecundity, life, dialectic" ("Questions on Geography," *Power/Knowledge* 70). Interrogating the devaluation of space throughout history Foucault argues for the essential conjunction of time and space in the formation of modernity, power, and knowledge. He characterizes modernity in light of the adoption of new disciplinary mechanisms that reformulate physical spaces as well as discursive and conceptual spaces, mechanisms that have normalized and reconstituted the human subject. Henri Lefebvre is another key figure who has triggered a new understanding of modernity and everyday life through a reconceptualization of social space.

Attention to the complex terrain of space and time aligned with the experience of modernity helps us address spatial forms in modernist arts from a new angle. Note the similar language that appears in Frank and Foucault. Defining the present epoch as "the epoch of space," Foucault states, "we are in the epoch of simultaneity; we are in the epoch of juxtaposition, the epoch of the near and far, of the side-by-side, of the dispersed." Foucault goes on to define our experience of the world in the present time as "less that of a long life developing through time than that of a network that connects points and intersects with its own skein" ("Of Other Spaces" 22), a phrase that is again akin to Frank's contention that modernist narrative unfolds through spatial juxtaposition of images instead of the conventional temporal frame of linear development.

Although Foucault does not refer to the heyday of English modernism here, his observations enable us to look at modernist spatial concerns from a different perspective. Taking a cue from Foucault's observations that relate simultaneity, juxtaposition, and networks to socio-geographical experiences of the proximity and conjuncture of heterogeneous relations and beings, we may argue that the predominant spatial forms are not necessarily linked to a timeless artistic order separated from experiences of physical space. Instead, the spatial concerns of modernist art can also be seen as a reflection of socio-geographical and psychological experiences that dramatically reorient space and time—experiences that are induced by the tremendous spatio-temporal changes of the era. As a matter of fact, avant-garde American writer Gertrude Stein detected the connection between modernist spatial aesthetics and the contemporary geographical experiences in her book *Picasso* (1938). As Gillian Beer points out, Stein's comments on the formal reordering of the earth brought by the aeroplane mark a new sense of space and nationhood that questions centrality and borders.[6] According to Stein, the experience of flight over the world during the First World War significantly changed the spatial experience of the era, part of which is reflected in some formal aspects of modernist artwork. The war, Stein writes, "was not a composition in which there was one man in the center surrounded by a lot of other men but a composition that had neither a beginning nor an end, a composition of which one corner was as important as another corner, in fact the composition of cubism" (qtd. in Beer, *Virginia Woolf* 150).

The decline of new criticism and the increasing interdisciplinarity of modernist studies have redirected spatial concerns to a more complicated terrain of corporeal reality, power relations, political practices, and cognitive structures. Stephen Kern addresses the experience of modernity and modernist aesthetics in light of a changing "culture of time and space." According to Kern, the years from 1880 to 1918 in the West are marked by "new modes of thinking about and experiencing time and space" generated by the advancement of modern technologies of travel, communication, capital, and medicine (1). Kern argues that these drastic changes brought about particular artistic responses such as the prominence of "spatial forms" in cubism, futurism, and the stream of consciousness novel. In a similar vein, literary critic Marshall Berman has centered his understanding of modernism in modernity's tremendous transformation of spatio-temporal perspectives and experiences. Roger Friedland and Deirdre Boden also maintain that the transformations of the meanings of space and time that were integral to the organization of modernity affected modernist visual arts and narrative forms.

As contemporaries in the early decades of the twentieth century, Lawrence and Woolf lived through the epistemological, physical, and psychological changes of spatio-temporal perspectives and experiences that were affected by urbanization, industrialization, and the Great War. Compared with Woolf, Lawrence seldom drew upon spatial forms. And yet, his essays, letters, and fictions certainly reflect important insights into the changed sense of time and space that contemporary aesthetics suggested. He was as attentive to current spatial discourses embodied in aesthetic experiments as Woolf was. For example, his concern with socio-cultural space drove him to turn to the concept of the fourth dimension that frequently appeared in aesthetic discourses of modernism influenced by contemporary scientific discourses[7]—such as cubism, post-impressionism, and futurism—so as to advance his own vision of an alternative space: a multifaceted terrain of relations, contacts, and co-existence of heterogeneous things and beings near and far away. In a number of instances, space in Lawrence features as an open and dynamic site that calls for tolerance of differences, changes, and conflicts, a vision of space which overlaps with Woolf's. Lawrence and Woolf appropriate the political significance of the cultural spatial reorientation and artistic responses to it. Borrowing Kern's words, the new view of space in Lawrence and Woolf as "active," "full," and "dynamic" rather than inert, empty, and passive, assailed the traditional hierarchies and sanctuaries of privilege, power, and holiness, and evaluated the entire dominant social order (152, 154, 180).

The affinity between Lawrence and Woolf in their treatment of space comes not only from their shared exposure to the contemporary spatio-temporal transformation, but also from their marginality. Both writers felt themselves to be outsiders, living on the margins of their society—Lawrence because of his social class, and Woolf because of her sex. Keenly aware of oppressive social systems and unequal power relations operating in seemingly natural practices and discourses revolving around geographical locations or territories, they critiqued the contemporary ways of producing, conceptualizing, and representing various spaces. They recorded with approving eyes the gradual collapse of Victorian conceptual and physical *topoi* and heralded the construction of new ones.

To elaborate this argument, my study integrates recent theories of social space into interdisciplinary concerns with space both in and outside literary criticism. My use of the term "social space" is built primarily upon Lefebvre's influential book, *The Production of Space*.[8] Lefebvre's account of the production of space is based on his critical dialogue with contemporary theoretical discourses such as (post) structuralism, psychoanalysis, semiotics, and deconstruction along with his efforts to incorporate a Nietzschean perspective into a Marxist framework. Combining Nietzschean genealogy and an emphasis on the body (the physical) with the Marxist debates over fragmentation, abstraction, alienation, and fetishization in capitalism, Lefebvre maintains that our understanding of space as a naturally given homogeneous locus is in fact socially, historically, and ideologically constructed. Far from being a neutral background, Lefebvre argues, "any space implies, contains, and dissimulates social relationships" (82–83). Like products subject to fetishization in capitalist society, social space simultaneously embodies and conceals the process of social production.

Lefebvre's theory pushes the Marxist frame a step further by critically reappropriating the concept of production, endowing social space with a generative force. Arguing that the concept of "production" has been distorted and abused as it has been reduced to a mere act of generating goods, ideologies, or knowledge, Lefebvre seeks to broaden it "to include the production of space as a process whose product—space—itself" embraces both things and "a productive process" (129, 137). That is to say, when Lefebvre speaks of social space as a product, he refers not merely to a fixed "outcome of past actions" but also to something that "permits fresh actions to occur" (73). "At once a result and cause, product and producer" of social relations and power (142), social space, therefore, is not entirely subsumed to power. No space is fully fetishized, and no social relationships can be totally obscured, for every space retains "forces" and "differences" that "can never be totally quieted" (23). In short, social space is "not . . . an empty and neutral milieu occupied by dead objects" but "a field of force full of tensions and distortions" (145). Social space is a reification of power structures and social relations, and yet it is anything but a deterministic structure or an inert object. Instead, it is a dynamic site that is at once oppressive and emancipating, open to new uses and practices.

Along with Lefebvre's spatial theory, there has been an interdisciplinary surge of concern with space and cultural geography from various fields such as sociology (Anthony Giddens, Pierre Bourdieu), geography (Edward Soja, David Harvey), feminist geography (Gillian Rose, Linda McDowell, Doreen Massey), urban studies, and cultural studies of everyday life (Michel de

Certeau). These studies have shed new light on our understanding of the relationship between spatial regimentation, power, and political agency. What links the diverse projects of these theories together is their shared challenge to the classical notion of space as a homogeneous, objective, empty container in which culture and history unfold. Although their focus may differ, theorists generally agree that social space is both a product and producer of human goals, motivations, powers, and practices, all of which differ according to gender, class, race, nationality, or sexual orientation. Triggered by these recent interests in space, critics have reshaped our understanding of literary presentation of spatial locations and discourses. Critics such as Franco Moretti and Susan Stanford Friedman, for example, have argued for the generative roles of space, contending that space in both actual life and in literary works should be understood as a dynamic site replete with overdetermined cultural meanings rather than an inert and empty background where culture and narrative take place.

Following recent critics' creative and critical adoption of recent concerns with space, my project investigates the limitations and contradictions as well as the usefulness of spatial theories in reading Woolf and Lawrence. One of the flaws in Lefebvre, for example, is his tendency to underestimate the critical force of literature, a tendency which is bound up with his implicit hierarchical dichotomy between language and reality. Contradicting his own effort to go beyond the divisions between the material, the discursive, and the mental aspects of space, Lefebvre's Marxist impulse to prioritize materiality at times drives him to underscore that space first and foremost belongs to the physical realm, an argument that involves a rather simplistic relation between space and its literary representation. According to Lefebvre, one of the blunders made by previous theorists and historians of space is their tendency to reduce space to "ideals and discourse about space" (116) or "a literary language of texts" (136). "Its [space's] mode of existence, its practical 'reality,'" he states, however, "differs radically from the reality (or being-there) of something written, such as a book" (142).[9] Here, Lefebvre's division between space and discourse about space, or between object and cognition, undercuts his own critical strength that issues from his demand that we should not separate mental from physical space, but rather understand space as simultaneously conceived, perceived, represented, and lived.[10]

Lefebvre's implicit but persistent attack on semiology is another case in point. Criticizing semiological "reading" of space, Lefebvre claims that space is "produced before being read" (143). Here, this remark seems to define space as something that exists before the act of reading or writing.[11] But if, following Lefebvre's own definitions, social space is not a static and fixed object but something at once physical and discursive, something active, dynamic, and generative, how could it be possible that space exists in advance of hermeneutic activities or re-presentation? Furthermore, Lefebvre's hierarchal division between reality/materiality and language leads him to underestimate literature. Of course, his critique of literary language is leveled against a specific kind of language that seeks to convey a false picture of the world by concealing its constructedness through the illusion of reality, a criticism which Lawrence and Woolf made as well. The problem when reading Lefebvre, however, is that it is hard to resist the impression that he undervalues literature in general under that homogenizing label, "verbal," and that he in fact sees all kinds of discourses as being trapped into an ideological, false conceptualization of space. Discussing the relation between language and space, Lefebvre holds that space "cannot be reduced either to an everyday discourse or to a literary language of texts" (136). Lefebvre's view of literature as a reductive verbal artwork goes to such an extent that he sets up a hierarchal distinction between (literary) "text" and space as "texture" (118), with the former associated with something intellectual and ideological and the latter with something relational and multifaceted. It is no wonder that Lefebvre primarily ascribes the spatial politics that produces alternative social space either to the reappropriation of material space or to theoretical thinking, while dismissing the subversive potential that literary works can perform.

Confronting the above problem, my study seeks to use Lefebvre's insightful understanding of space in reading literary texts in a more productive way. One of the central assumptions that underlie my project is that language and space are interconnected and mutually constitutive. Indeed, one of the important contributions made by poststructuralist, semiotic, or deconstructive theories about literary texts is their initiation of a new understanding of the relation between language and reality, or discourse and practice. As these theories have shown, reality is not something that exists before language; nor is language a mere copy of reality. Language and reality are not separable but mutually constitutive of each other. Ironically, it is Lefebvre's own theory of space that points to the nexus between space/reality and its discursive practices. If, as Lefebvre notes, social space is not a mere result of production but a multiple network open to multidirectional reproductions of new spaces (117)—i.e., something that is represented, experienced, and produced through multifaceted spatial codes—it should be also noted that there is no unidirectional intervention of ideologies and ideological codes or language into the production of space or vice versa. Both space and language are at once subject to and rebellious against power.

Furthermore, Lefebvre's concept of spatial code helps us to illuminate the spatial politics that the works of Lawrence and Woolf achieve. As Lefebvre suggests, the production of social space is inseparable from a process of signification, namely, a spatial code. Each society and culture has produced particular codifications of space that vary according to historical periods as well as to individuals within the same society. Through these specific spatial codes individuals of a particular society accede at once "to *their* space and to their status as 'subjects' acting within that space" and "comprehending it" (17, emphasis in original). Spatial codes are several and heterogeneous; some are dominant and others are marginalized; they have their rises, specific roles, and demises. A spatial code is a kind of signifier where ideological discourses and practices constantly clash with rebellious ones. For example, "home" is a complex signifier; it refers to a material dwelling place and invokes various connotations that diverge according to cultures and histories, as well as to individual experiences associated with gender and other social standings. As feminist scholars have noted, patriarchal society has produced a male-centered physical structure and mental representation of home—home as a paradisal place for rest, nurturing, and harmony. This dominant spatial code has naturalized and reinforced the exploitation of labor and the subjugation of women and/or lower class people in domestic space, obscuring the perception and experience of marginalized others. However, the predominance of an ideological discourse of the home that reflects and reproduces the dominant socio-spatial order does not preclude room for resistance and change. People have articulated different perspectives and experiences in and about the home and developed diverse practices that challenge the dominant social order. As being itself a particular kind of spatial code, literature can unveil the existence of the marginalized and suppressed discourses and practices about home, destabilize its ideological discursive and physical structure by exposing its constructedness, and envision less oppressive homes. As such, a spatial code is "not simply a means of reading or interpreting space: rather it is a means of living in that space, of understanding it, and of producing it" (Lefebvre, *The Production of Space* 47–48).

In short, in this study the term "social space" refers neither to a purely physical nor to an entirely psychological concept. It designates the material, mental, and discursive spaces that produce and are produced by power structures and social relations. For the purpose of my study, the production of social space in reference to spatial codes is particularly important. Social spaces and spatial codes are mutually constitutive, and similar in their ambiguous relationships with power. Their fundamental heterogeneity, ambiguity, and alterability make them resistant to socio-cultural hegemonies, even as they reflect and reproduce them. In this sense, social space is "both the geographical site of action and the social possibility for engaging in action" (Gottdiener 123).

The landscape of social space thus includes utopia—a better place coming into being here and now—as well. My move to bring together the notion of utopia with that of social space is inspired by the new approach to utopia that has been proposed by some recent scholars. Contending that utopian thought and writing cannot be simplified as an expression of a reactionary and escapist desire for stasis and homogeneity, these theorists have endeavored to broaden the very concept of utopia so as to reconsider the politics of utopia. Instead of confining utopia to a completed ideal world located in a remote time and space, they stress a dynamic and subversive process that dismantles the status quo, a process that broaches infinite possibilities for change. In this view, utopia refers to the other place that emerges through the discrepancy between the ideal and the real, present and future, a differentiated space coming into being within the very structure of the present. This new concept of utopia involves a spatio-temporal reorientation, conceiving and engendering a new kind of here and now that is incomplete and open to perpetual restructuration.

Understood in this way, utopia shares interesting affinities with social space. Indeed, for Lefebvre, the open-ended character of social space makes it a site for the creation of "a differential space" that dismantles the status quo (Lefebvre 302). Like the new concept of utopia, moreover, the notion of social space cannot be taken out of time. Far from being governed by a purely abstract and mechanical temporality, social space is the place where people experience the present as offering infinite possibilities for the transformation of past, future, self, and social relations. It is in this sense that Lefebvre regards urban space—as a typical social space—as an apt place for the eruption of utopian "moments" to take place.

Reading Woolf and Lawrence in terms of social space, thus, goes further than examining the significance of diverse locations. Focusing on the ways in which these writers employ and rewrite spatial codes my study explores various ways of conceiving, perceiving, and representing space that "uncover the social relationships" (Lefebvre 89). Anticipating recent spatial theories, space in Lawrence and Woolf functions not merely as a neutral background where human activities and narrative take place but also as a generative force for their production. It is cultural and historical social space open to competing conceptualizations and human interventions. Space in Lawrence and Woolf raises issues of borders and movements, belonging and exclusion, limits and expansions, and enclosure and mobility. Through these writers, we witness that no space is equally accessible to all. Characters have different memories, thoughts, or images of distinct spaces, and their behaviors vary from one space to another. Their spatial perceptions and experiences are tied up with multifaceted spatial codes. Spatial codes in these writers reveal heterogeneous spatial experiences and practices in and about space, which differ from individual to individual according to their class, gender, or nationality. Through the enactment of insurmountable tensions and conflicts of social relations and spatial codes, Lawrence and Woolf simultaneously expose and disrupt the dominant social order that governs the ways in which people construct, live, and imagine space, making dominant spatial paradigms unstable and open to change.

My project aims to contribute to recent scholars' attempts to restore the socio-historical contexts that have often been dismissed by the emphasis on the "inward" turn in modernist texts. Despite the increasing efforts of literary critics, some scholars still tend to view modernist literature in light of interiorization and the subsequent disengagement from social terrain. In Soja's view, for example, the increasing interiorization and the attendant disappearance of setting or space in certain modernist fictions went hand in hand with the subordination of the spatial problematic in social theory (31–35). This statement becomes especially problematic when we note how profoundly Woolf—who is one of the most prominent representatives of the modernist preoccupation with consciousness and interior reality—spatializes her politics through her use of devices different from those of traditional narrative whose spatial politics relies much on literal description of physical places and backgrounds.

Focusing on social space when reading Woolf and Lawrence enables us to look at the often-neglected similarities between them, and more importantly, to better understand the complex politics of their works. It also provides us with a new way to interpret these writers' visions of epiphanic moments; far from seeing them as one of the modernist symptoms of transcendence and dissociation from ordinary life, I propose that these moments mark an active engagement with everyday life. Critically unveiling an oppressive power system whose ideologies are embodied and reproduced by conventional spatial codes, Lawrence and Woolf offer alternative visions of space and spatial codes, paving the way to restructure gender, class, national identities, social relations, and human geography in general.

CHAPTER OUTLINE

This study is composed of three parts that explore different aspects of social space—social spaces in private and public domains, in the national imaginary, and in utopian spaces. I discuss Lawrence's and Woolf's well-known novels as well as less discussed short stories, essays, and letters. Part I focuses on how Lawrence and Woolf challenge the dominant ways of conceptualizing and representing private and public spaces. I begin by arguing that although some aspects of private/domestic space in Lawrence and Woolf reflect patriarchal experiences and discourses, these writers are not trapped into the ideological limits that constrain Victorian intellectuals like John Ruskin and recent theorists like Gaston Bachelard and Lefebvre. I demonstrate that where Ruskin, Bachelard, and Lefebvre tend to dehistoricize and naturalize private/domestic space, Lawrence and Woolf challenge their problematic spatial codes. Fighting the ideological rendering of domestic space—which works to maintain the patriarchal, class-stratified social order by promoting a homogenized vision of the home as free of domination, conflicts, and resistance—these writers picture domestic space as multifaceted and dynamic. For them, space is oppressive and yet alterable. They excavate the often-muted experiences and perspectives of the marginalized, while reflecting and subverting the dominant socio-spatial order at the same time. These writers challenge conventional practices and discourses surrounding public space as well. They critically expose the gendered division of space and the restrictions on women's entrance into the male-dominated public sphere, and call for the reconceptualization and restructuration of public space through rigorous interrogation of the cultural myth of public space as a place for self-realization and emancipation.

Chapter One of Part One begins by discussing how Lawrence shatters the cultural myth of home. I contend that the dominant image of home as a harmonious, immutable, maternal haven is replaced by a picture of highly contested domestic space in works like "Discord in Childhood," "Master in His House," and *Sons and Lovers*. Moving on to *The Rainbow* I argue that various private and public spaces in the novel play a crucial role in reversing patriarchal discourses about gender and space and ultimately in advancing social criticism. In Chapter Two, I make a similar point about Woolf's critical approach to private and public spaces. Analyzing Woolf's essay, "Great Men's House," *A Sketch of the Past,* and *Mrs. Dalloway,* I demonstrate the ways in which Woolf exposes gender and class relations materialized in physical and discursive private spaces. Taking *Three Guineas* and two essays, "The Docks of London" and "Oxford Street Tide" from *The London Scene* as examples, my discussion proceeds to show how Woolf's feminist agenda is intertwined with other political issues of nationalism, militarism, and class-stratified society with a specific emphasis on spatial politics that interrogates problematic assumptions about public spaces.

In Part II, I explore another aspect of social space at work in the national imaginary. Around the end of the nineteenth century, England saw the growing urge to build national identity through the metonymic association of nation with home. The Victorian picture of home as an enclosed, safe haven fit well into a cultural trope of the nation as an island. I argue that Lawrence and Woolf's awareness of the power imbalances operating in the domestic space of the home expands to a critical insight into the exclusive impulses that set up the physical and mental border between inside and outside, constructing the self/insider as being moral and sound and the Other/outsider as being morally degenerated and dangerous, thus justifying the subjugation or exclusion of the latter. I contend that Lawrence and Woolf's critical analyses of power relations and nationalist ideologies implicated in the home-nation analogy lead to a blurring of borders, transforming dividing walls into thresholds for contact with others, and remolding a more inclusive space of home/nation.

In Chapter Three, I discuss a couple of Lawrence's autobiographical pieces, a short story, "England, My England," a novella, *The Virgin and the Gipsy,* and *Kangaroo.* These works critically analyze egotistic and exclusive drives surrounding the contemporary association of the physical and psychological territories of home and nation. The protagonists repudiate or abandon their home/nation whose claustrophobic atmosphere precludes them from building sound relationships with others. They cross over borders to make contact with others, seeking a permeable home/nation. Chapter Four uses a short story, "The Journal of Mistress Joan Martyn," to explore Woolf's critique of the impulse to subjugate and exclude the Other that is embedded in the association of home and nation through the image of an island. Woolf's critique of the ideological association of home and nation develops further in *The Waves,* I argue, as evidenced by the challenge to the imperial nation delivered through a critical rendering of the trope of the English family house. Examining characters' use of the discourse of self, home, and nation, I contend that the novel destabilizes the imperial home and nation from within. Reading *The Years,* I argue that the Pargiter family's move from single family houses to flats can be interpreted as a step toward a more inclusive space of home and nation that is tolerant of and even willing to live together with marginalized others.

Part III investigates utopian spaces in Lawrence and Woolf, drawing upon recent scholars' redefinition of utopia together with Lefebvre's view of social space as "differential space" emerging through utopian "moments." Defining utopia as a different/other space that disrupts dominant spatial practices and discourses, we can see that the previous chapters have already touched on the utopian aspects of social space in one way or another. Part III extends the discussion of the previous chapters by focusing on the ways in which Lawrence and Woolf respond critically to the ideological lure of changelessness and homogeneity embedded in the vision of traditional utopian thinking and writing, and envision alternative utopian spaces that emerge through a radical reformulation of time, space, and social being. As in Lefebvre, these writers' view of space as being replete with conflicts and contradictions, thus open to perpetual changes, goes hand in hand with the reconceptualization of time as well. Both Lawrence and Woolf engender subversive utopian spaces emerging through the eruption of epiphanic transformative moments—such as the "urgent, insurgent Now" in Lawrence or "moments of being" in Woolf. In these moments, the self abandons socially imposed selfhood and reconstructs a new one and builds both a more dynamic and fluid self and more open relationships with others. Far from locating a vision of a better world in an unreal, distant realm, these writers see utopia coming into being through an active interaction with, intervention into, and transformation of the here and now. To put it differently, the alternative utopian spaces surface not so much through the systematic depiction of a blueprint for an ideal society as through epiphanic moments and open-ended, dynamic social spaces, which rupture any kind of imagined closures.

Chapter Five begins by tracing young Lawrence's preoccupation with and growing criticism of his own utopian vision of an ideal society, Rananim, as well as of socialist utopianisms by examining his letters, a short story, "The Man Who Loved Islands," and an essay-fiction, "A Dream of Life." I argue that Lawrence's constitutional antipathy to a deterministic and static view of self and the world drove him to seek his own vision of utopian "living space" and "insurgent Now," as illustrated by several essays such as his writings on apocalypse, "Democracy," and "Morality and the Novel." Through a reading of *The Rainbow* and *Women in Love* I further demonstrate that Lawrence's alternative utopias are located in the productive chronotope wherein protagonists undergo a destruction of culturally prescribed selfhood and relationships with others and formulate more fluid, dynamic, related ones.

Chapter Six investigates Woolf's vision of alternative utopias. Reading Woolf's essays such as "The Memories of a Working Women's Guild" and *Three Guineas,* I demonstrate that these writings indicate instances when Woolf turned toward traditional utopian visions, especially during the years of the 30s when she was directly involved with political writings and activities. A close look at *Mrs. Dalloway,* however, suggests that from early on in her career Woolf was resistant to any static vision of self, time, and society and persistently sought out more dynamic utopian visions. I contend that the novel presents a vision of alternative utopia, as seen in the depiction of

London as a dynamic, ambiguous social space and Clarissa's epiphanic moments, both of which challenge the ideological limits of socialist, escapist, and totalitarian urbanist utopianisms at that time. Finally, I examine Woolf's concept of "moments of being" in reference to her essay "The Moment: Summer's Night" and her final novel *Between the Acts*. My argument is that as in Lawrence, these writings offer visions of an alternative utopia which emerges through disruptive moments "here and now" that shatter the illusory stability of self, social order, and the relationship between beings and things.

Part One

Rewriting Private and Public Spaces

Part One Introduction

As recent scholars have noted, every society has prevalent ways of structuring, producing, and conceptualizing space that reflect its dominant ideologies and social order. The physical and conceptual division between private/domestic and public spaces, for example, has been integral to maintaining the patriarchal social order. Whereas places outside the home have been used and viewed as basically places for men, domestic space has been regarded as the place where women should be. This spatial dichotomy has justified patriarchal oppression by restricting women's access to public space and legitimizing the exploitation of women's labor in private/domestic space.

In this section, I investigate the ways in which Lawrence and Woolf criticize or reverse the conventional conceptualization and representation of public and private spaces.[1] Most simply, by private and public space in this section I mean domestic/familial and extra-domestic/familial spaces respectively. By analyzing Lawrence's and Woolf's treatment of various places through the concepts of social space and spatial code, I demonstrate that the spatial politics in their writings is closely connected with gender and class politics, and social criticism in general.

At first glance, it seems that the gap between Lawrence' and Woolf's attitudes toward the patriarchal discourses about private and public spaces could not be wider. Roughly speaking, whereas Woolf interrogates and challenges the cultural connotations and ideological implications embedded in these terms, Lawrence, especially at his worst, appears to take them for granted and even reinforce them. In contrast to Woolf who criticizes the ideology of separate spaces, Lawrence—even when his problematic gender politics is not blatant— makes occasional observations that may provoke outcry from feminist readers. In his essay, "Matriarchy," for example, the anonymous narrator's attack on bullying husbands' obsession with asserting masculine authority at home takes a curious turn as it leads to rather a condescending admonition for men to stop fussing over all too little (i.e., the desire to be master at home) and instead, to seek to develop their "social cravings" and freedom by simply giving women their independence as "mothers and heads of the family" (552). Thus, the initial criticism of man's preoccupation with authority which the writer attributes to man's jealousy and fear of women's growing advancement into the social world, turns out to be no better than a trap to confine women to the female zone of home so that men can develop their "social instinct" in their proper place—the public/social realm of "clubs and public-houses . . . free from the tight littleness of family" (552).[2]

Nevertheless, there are similarities in Lawrence's and Woolf's treatment of space. In particular, in exploring the psychological state of their childhood, both Lawrence and Woolf often unite home and the mother through the image of a provider of comfort, harmony, and stability. For example, in *A Sketch of the Past*, Woolf's most extended autobiographical writing, much of her recollection of the early years centers on the childhood home bound up with the mother. She writes of her mother: "Certainly there she was, in the very center of that great Cathedral space which was childhood; there she was from the very first" (81). In the memoir, her mother permeates the entire house to such a degree that the maternal body is nearly identified with the house: "[A]nd of course she was central. I suspect the word 'central' gets closest to the general feeling I had of living so completely in her atmosphere that one never got far enough away from her to see her as a person. . . . She was the whole thing; Talland House was full of her; Hyde Park Gate was full of her" (83). Similarly, in *Sons and Lovers* which was based on Lawrence's own experience, the protagonist's childhood life and his gradual initiation out of it revolve around the solid ground/home/mother—the "one place in the world that stood solid and did not melt into unreality: the place where his mother was" (273).

In a sense, the association between home, mother, and the sense of stability in Lawrence and Woolf is not exceptional. Victorian intellectuals such as John Ruskin often likened the house to a container of childhood memories revolving around the relationship with the mother and the power of resisting the vicissitudes of life.[3] The psychological dimension of domestic space that is tied up with the childhood experience of the maternal body also reverberates in the French philosopher Gaston Bachelard's book, *The Poetics of Space*—a phenomenological study of "intimate places." Using the image of the house that appears in literary texts as a "tool for analysis of the human soul," Bachelard shows how the house—especially when it is evoked in relation to childhood—functions as an indicator of a psychic state (xxxiii, 72). Noting that "the poetics of the house" points to the value of the intimate space that provides protection from mutability and "illusions of stability," Bachelard contends that the house not only contains but also constitutes the memory of childhood and that its virtue as a shelter and refuge has been often aligned with the comforting maternal body (19, 5). Quoting a line from O. V. de Milosz' poem, "Melancholy"—"I say Mother. And my thoughts are of you, oh, House. / House of the lovely dark summers of my childhood"—Bachelard notes how "the mother image and the House image are united" (45).

As scholars like Doreen Massey have suggested, despite their emphasis on psychological aspects, patriarchal discourses about home are socio-cultural products. As a matter of fact, the association of the childhood home with the maternal and a sense of stability that we see in Lawrence, Woolf, Ruskin, and Bachelard, is an outcome of a patriarchal society where early child-rearing is almost entirely in the hands of women, a society founded on a gendered division of space and labor. Indeed, Massey observes that "the place called home in Western culture" has often been framed around women who have been forced to stay behind and to take the role of providing stability and security for men (166–67). As we shall see, however, what makes the similarities between Lawrence's and Woolf's treatment of space so intriguing is not so much their shared adoption of dominant spatial codes as their challenges to them. Indeed, in a number of instances, Lawrence and Woolf reveal their keen awareness that the current picture and discourse of domestic space is a socio-cultural construction subservient to the dominant social order, an awareness that enables them to mock, interrogate, and challenge ideological implications embedded in conventional spatial discourses and practices, thus overcoming the ideological limits of Ruskin and Bachelard.

One of the most problematic aspects of the image of home as a maternal space in patriarchal discourse is that it helped to confine women to domesticity, naturalized their labor in home, and erased their individuality. Within this space, a woman became a "ghostly figure of desire [with] no place to occupy in the social order," losing her identity and fading into the man's house (Armstrong 186). Indeed, in Bachelard we witness the ways in which the name of "builder" of home that is granted to women works to erase their suffering and even eulogize their drudgery. According to Bachelard, the harmonious home is "built" by "the housewife" who "awakens furniture" by ceaseless polishing while her husband "build[s] a house from the outside" without knowing about this "wax civilization"(68). In addition to naturalizing the division between female/interior and male/exterior, Bachelard suppresses women's labor in the household by asserting that this housewifery is beneficial even for women because it "cheers" their "heart" instead of exhausting their mind and body (81). In this respect, we can see that Bachelard's valorization of domestic space in terms of timelessness, stasis, order, and maternity (79) at once reflects and transmits a male-dominant cultural heritage.

In addition, the image of home as a private, changeless, safe haven that prevails in Ruskin and Bachelard (contrasting with the image of changeable, social, and historical public space) has served to maintain unequal power relations not only between different genders but also between different classes by naturalizing or obscuring the social relations, conflicts, and tensions that exist in domestic space. For a theorist like Henri Lefebvre—who insists that every space is a social space entangled with specific material, and historical contexts—Bachelard's theory of domestic space thus manifests one of the deplorable symptoms of a modernity that has obscured the materiality of space and the social relations of production (*The Production of Space* 94). Criticizing the tendency to dismiss the materiality and historicity of space, Lefebvre endeavors to locate "lived" space in the realm of culture and history (39, 46).

Anticipating Lefebvre's theory of social space, Lawrence and Woolf disrupt the equation of private/domestic space with maternity, femininity, harmony, and changelessness. Fighting the dominant spatial discourse that erases the exploitation of the marginalized in domestic space, these writers constantly bring to the fore the incessant and unrewarded toil of women and/or working class people, the confinement of women, and the conflicts that issue from unequal relations and domination. At the same time, Lawrence and Woolf excavate the multiple meanings of domestic space, refusing to offer a homogenized vision of it—that might render domestic space static and unalterable. In Woolf, the home is a place from which she felt estranged because of the privilege of the male member of the family. It is also a place of confinement—the place where she had to remain while her brothers left home for education. At the same time, it is a place divided by class where her mother as a Victorian matron supervised and dictated to lower class people, a place that opened Woolf's eyes to class disparities and her own class privileges. Similarly, domestic space in Lawrence is a socio-cultural place ridden with conflicts between different genders and classes, a heterogeneous place of nurture, feminine subjugation, masculine violence, and resistance.

Even when Lawrence and Woolf take recourse in the comforting maternal domestic space as an ontological ground and a resource for their artistic imaginations, their private/domestic spaces do not end up being an entirely harmonious, ahistorical, and changeless realm. In Woolf, for example, there are instances where even the most maternal space of stability is interrupted by moments of change and unsettlement. In *A Sketch of the Past*, for example, the moment when the domestic/maternal space of childhood expands to "vast space" or "a great hall" is immediately disrupted by a vision of movement and change: "A great hall I could liken it [childhood] to; with windows letting in strange lights; and murmurs and spaces of deep silence. But somehow that picture must be brought, too, the sense of movement and change. Nothing remained stable long" (79). In a similar vein, Lawrence reverses the conventional association of home and mother with stability and stasis in a work like *The Rainbow* by aligning them with a vision of perpetual journey and movement. By excavating the so-far muted spatial code of the marginalized, Lawrence and Woolf offer a corrective to the dominant picture of home that mainly reflects the perspective and the experience of the privileged.

Interestingly, the ways in which Lawrence and Woolf render domestic space as being dynamic, multifaceted, and open invite us to look critically at the ideological limits of Lefebvre's view of domestic space. Despite his apt criticism of Bachelard, Lefebvre also tends to depoliticize and dehistoricize domestic space. For example, Lefebvre views domestic space as an example of what he terms "appropriated space"—space of resistance and emancipation that challenges the dictate of the state.[1] What is problematic here is Lefebvre's rather romanticized view of domestic space founded on the assumption that domestic space is inherently independent of and immune to the power imbalances and oppressive social relations operative in the space outside of the home. Lefebvre's association of domestic space with nature, interiority, and enclosure further confirms my point. He advocates for the "natural space" of home or "the indoor space of family life," as if the home were a natural space free of domination and conflicts in contrast with the "outside space of the community" (117, 166). Moreover, Lefebvre sticks to the division between the private and the public by drawing on the language that is akin to the Victorian ideology of separate spheres. "The real requirements of the present situation," he states, are that "[t]he sphere of private life ought to be enclosed, and have a finite, or finished aspect. Public space, by contrast, ought to be an opening outwards" (147). In this respect, Lefebvre's valorization of domestic space shares Bachelard's blunder of dehistoricizing and depoliticizing the home by rendering it as natural, independent, closed, and static. In contrast, Lawrence and Woolf neither idealize private space as a place of resistance and emancipation nor relegate it to a purely oppressive domain. In their writings both private and public spaces are multifaceted and dynamic social spaces that are filled with unequal social relations and yet open to resistance and changes.

The similarities and complexities of private/domestic space in Lawrence and Woolf hold true for their depictions of public space as well. Both Lawrence and Woolf are keenly aware of the cultural connotations and ideological implications embedded in the physical and conceptual referent of public space. Their challenges to the conventional practices and conceptualizations surrounding public space are multifold. To begin with, these writers critically show the monopolization of public space by men and the limited access of women to the world of politics, education, profession, and so forth. Lawrence and Woolf understand that the advancement of women's status requires their equal access to public space. And yet, they do not see women's entrance into public space as desirable nor do they believe that such an entrance would immediately bring about women's independence and self-realization, since they detected problems and dangers in the way public space was produced, used, and conceptualized. Going beyond criticizing the male monopolization of public space, therefore, these writers seek a more radical intervention into the production of public space. They argue for the need to reshape the very conceptual and physical ground of public space by exposing various ideologies that have supported and legitimized the production of the space—space which society has called "public" and privileged over private space as a place of self-realization and emancipation. Woolf's feminist demand that woman share all the benefits that public space promises, for instance, is frequently accompanied by her rigorous attack on problems associated with that very space. Likewise, despite his occasional limits, Lawrence does not always represent public space as an ideal alternative to the stifling home. He also offers a penetrating criticism of the male-centered public space as a construct which represses both men's and women's individuality and sound relationships with other people. Pointing out how the male-centered space has cultivated and justified nationalism, imperialism, and militarism, as well as dehumanizing institutionalization and industrialization, both Lawrence and Woolf press for a restructuring and reconceptualization of public space. For these writers, public space, like private space, is a dynamic, multifaceted, and alterable space open to change and resistance; it is a space that is not reducible to either a purely oppressive or liberating structure but remains at once an oppressive and emancipating social space.

In sum, my argument in Part I is that Lawrence and Woolf disrupt the dominant socio-spatial order by refiguring private and public spaces. These writers locate both private and public spaces in a historical and cultural realm by featuring them "not as an empty and neutral milieu occupied by dead objects but rather as a field of force full of tensions and distortions" (Lefebvre 145). They echo and adopt dominant spatial discourses, but they also interrogate and reverse them. In this sense, the terms private and public spaces in Lawrence and

Woolf are highly complex ones that are under constant interrogation and reconfiguration rather than referring to something socially and culturally fixed. While Lawrence and Woolf were keenly aware of the negative impact of the conceptual and physical production of private and public spaces and the ideological division between them, they also knew that such spatial productions and conceptualizations are not absolute, but constructed, and thus can always be modified and remolded.

In Chapter One, I argue that much of Lawrence's gender and class politics involves his critical response to the dominant spatial code. His writings frequently uncover the unequal relations between different genders and classes, reversing the patriarchal discourse about gender and space. Such works as "Discord in Childhood," "Master in His House," and *Sons and Lovers,* shatter the current cultural myths of domestic space as a harmonious, safe, maternal haven. Home in these works is a multifaceted socio-cultural space filled with power imbalances between different genders and classes. Instead of providing a stereotypical picture of the home seen from the patriarch's perspective, these works uncover the suffering, labor, and agony that all family members undergo in one way or another. I move on to show that home in Lawrence disrupts the Victorian picture of the home as a maternal space of nurturing, food, and warmth, as evidenced by the violent but caring father haunting the hearth—the "female realm" in a patriarchal household (Lefebvre 247). Addressing space in a larger social, cultural, and historical context, *The Rainbow* invites us to understand Lawrence's gender politics from a new angle. By examining such places as a house, a cottage, a cathedral, a school, or "The Man's World" in this novel I will demonstrate how these places emerge as sites where women's spatial codes and practices challenge and reverse the patriarchal discourse about gender and space.

Chapter Two investigates the political significance of Woolf's treatment of domestic and public spaces. Exposing unequal class and gender relations and the contestation between diverse spatial codes and practices, Woolf locates domestic space (such as a dining room, a house, or a party table) in a social and historical realm in *A Sketch of the Past,* "Great Men's Houses," and *Mrs. Dalloway.* Essays like "The Docks of London" and "Oxford Street Tide" from *The London Scene* dismantle the dominant socio-spatial order by employing multiple spatial codes. These essays foreground the experience of the marginalized—women and/or the working class—in the urban landscape and highlight their conflicting spatial codes that challenge authoritative and homogenizing rendering of London. In Woolf as in Lawrence, both domestic and public spaces thus surface as heterogeneous, dynamic, and flexible social spaces open to perpetual remolding and change.

Chapter One

In a number of instances, domestic spaces in Lawrence's writing shatter the Victorian myth of the home as a maternal, timeless, harmonious haven—an ideological rendering that works to maintain the dominant social order by obscuring social relations existing in the home. Going against this cultural picture of domestic space, the home in Lawrence is replete with power imbalances and tensions between family members. Lawrence's little discussed poem, "Discord in Childhood," published in *Amores* (1916), provides an interesting entry point for looking at domestic space in his works.[1] As the title suggests, the poem is about Lawrence's recollection of childhood charged with conflicts and discord.

> Outside the house an ash-tree hung its terrible whips,
> And at night when the wind arose, the lash of the tree
> Shrieked and slashed the wind, as a ship's
> Weird rigging in a storm shrieks hideously.
>
> Within the house two voices arouse in anger, a slender lash
> Whistling delirious rage, and the dreadful sound
> Of a thick lash booming and brushing, until it drowned
> The other voice in a silence of blood 'neath the noise of the ash.
> (*The Complete Poems of D.H. Lawrence* 36)

Several critics have read the poem in light of an early form of the Lawrentian philosophy of the opposition in human relationships or a painful recollection of his unhappy experience of parental conflicts.[2] Refusing to read the poem in terms of a typical Lawrentian theme, Sandra M. Gilbert stresses the powerful poetic imagination that enhances pure violence to the level of mystery (46). Although these readings have pointed out certain thematic concerns of the poem, they tend to universalize ("human relationships"), to personalize, or to dehistoricize ("mystic power") the home, dismissing its socio-political significance in the poem.

The poem criticizes a conventional idea of home. Depicting home from the perspective of the dominated—women and children, the poem draws our attention to tensions and conflicts that permeate the house. The central image of the (male) "thick" lash that drowns and silences the voice of the (female) "slender" lash restores the history of agony, domestic violence, and power imbalance between husband and wife that the Victorian discourse of home has sought to erase by its emphasis on the sense of stability, timelessness, harmony, and protection. In addition, the poignant sense of the conflicts and violence endemic both inside and outside the house shatters another spatial myth—the division between the chaotic and mutable exterior world and the peaceful and stable interior world. The target of the poem's criticism goes even beyond the Victorian discourse of home. In presenting the image of the ash tree—the age-old symbol of home in its association with stability, protection, shelter, and nurture—as part of a terrifying landscape that corresponds to domestic discord, the poem engages in a critical dialogue with the longstanding Western cultural icon of home as well.[3]

In addition to excavating unequal power relations between man and woman, Lawrence questions the ideological implications embedded in the contemporary patriarchal discourse about domestic space that prescribes woman's nature and place. This observation is important because it exemplifies the complex ways in which Lawrence's critical appropriation of conventional discourse contests patriarchal ideologies, inviting us to look at his gender politics afresh. To some extent, feminist attacks on Lawrence have derived from critics' dissatisfaction with the writer's seemingly uncritical adoption of patriarchal discourse. While there are instances where Lawrence's remarks sound offensive to some feminist readers as in "Matriarchy," there are other less-noted examples that testify to his critical distance from the customary discourses surrounding women and the home. As Nancy Armstrong points out, the English ideal of the household as a self-contained unit has entailed the cultural definition of woman's identity as its moral and managerial center. The imposition of this identity has deprived woman of "representable materiality"(71). Armstrong's argument provides us with a useful vocabulary to illuminate the subtle way of challenging patriarchal spatial discourse that we often witness in Lawrence's texts. Note, for example, how the narrator conveys the Brangwen men's view of wives in a language that obliquely aligns women with a domestic space of stability and morality in the often-cited passage from Lawrence's other novel, *The Rainbow:*

The men placed in her hands their own conscience, they said to her 'Be
my conscience-keeper, be the angel at the doorway guarding my outgo-
ing and my incoming.' And the woman fulfilled her trust, the men
rested implicitly in her, receiving her praise or her blame with pleasure
or with anger, rebelling and storming, but never for a moment really
escaping in their own souls from her prerogative. They depended on her
for their stability. Without her, they would have felt like straws in the
wind, to be blown hither and thither at random. She was the anchor
and the security, she was the restraining hand of God, at times highly to
be execrated. (19)[4]

Taking a cue from Armstrong's observations, I propose that the above passage draws our attention to the ideological implications of patriarchal discourse.

As the passage shows, patriarchal discourse binds woman and home
together through the same language—"security" and "stability"—and thus
justifies and naturalizes woman's confinement to domesticity. The seemingly
neutral presentation of the typical patriarchal perspective, however, turns to a
rather abrupt juxtaposition of contrasting but fundamentally related identities of women—the scared being ("the restraining hand of God") and the
condemned (the one "to be execrated") at the end. In this way, the passage
registers the ambiguous response of patriarchal discourse to the cultural construction of women's identity and the consequent loss of their individuality.
A careful reading suggests even further that the passage challenges the
authority of the male perspective by pointing out that the definition of
woman as a stable and ethical center of the home discloses (and probably
reinforces) the fundamental insufficiency and dependence of man. In other
words, the passage exemplifies the strategic ways in which Lawrence challenges the patriarchal social system through critical adoption of conventional
spatial discourse. Far from naively reproducing patriarchal discourse,
Lawrence subverts its power by making it reveal its own ideological limits
and problems. In the following chapter, I will further demonstrate that the
novel disrupts the current socio-spatial order in its critical investigation of
practices and discourses surrounding woman's and man's space.

"Master in His Own House"—a short journalistic piece dating from
Lawrence's last year and a half of life—confirms my point further. At first
glance, the essay appears rather problematic. Lawrence holds that the current
men's resentment against "overbearing modern women" derives not from
women's intrinsic "bossiness" but from men's fundamental "indifferences" or
"deadness"(548). In spite of the advice for men not to blame women, the

argument becomes disprovable or at least confusing as it develops a rather suspicious argument for the restoration of a genuine masculine mastership by shattering this indifference. Nevertheless, the essay still merits attention as it reveals Lawrence's critical insight into the ways in which patriarchal spatial discourse reflects and reinforces unequal relations between women and men. In the essay, Lawrence argues that men need to stop sticking to "ready-made phrases" or "mass ideas" such as "[a]n Englishman's home is his castle" or "master in his own house" (546). According to him, such phrases reflect and exacerbate men's preoccupation with masculine power, making men either overreactive or totally inert in the face of women's growing social advancement. Anticipating recent scholars' excavation of the cultural hegemony and socio-spatial order inscribed in these well-known phrases of that period,[5] Lawrence points out that such conventional phrases and the related behaviors at home are at once an outcome and a cause of a social order that threatens to erase the individuality of both men and women, as well as to perpetuate the domination of the one over the other. He goes on to argue that only through "individualization," instead of mass thinking—namely, only by rethinking individuals in terms of "Jim" and "Julia" rather than in the generalized terms of husband and wife, for example (547)—can we nullify the desire to dominate others.[6]

As we have seen so far, "Discord in Childhood," *The Rainbow*, and "Master in His Own House" suggest ways to look at the political significance of Lawrence's treatment of space and the dominant spatial code. These works challenge the dominant socio-spatial order by offering alternative pictures of and discourses about space. Going against the ideological rendering of space they foreground unequal social relations, conflicts, and resistance. The spatial politics in Lawrence includes a critical interrogation of the conventional spatial discourses. As we shall see, these aspects apply to Lawrence's critical approach to public space as well.

"THE ANGUISH OF THE HOME DISCORD": REFIGURING DOMESTIC SPACE IN *SONS AND LOVERS*

The conflict and violence that surround home in "Discord in Childhood" found a more complex expression in *Sons and Lovers*. At the beginning of Chapter Four, "The Young Life of Paul," the narrator depicts the house into which the Morel family newly moved in:

> When William was growing up, the family moved from the Bottoms to a house on the brow of the hill, commanding a view of the valley, which

spread out like a convex cockleshell, or a clamp-shell, before it. In front of the house was a huge old ash-tree. The west wind, sweeping from Derbyshire, caught the houses with full force, and the tree shrieked again. Morel liked it. "It's music," he said. "It sends me to sleep." But Paul and Arthur and Annie hated it. To Paul it became almost a demoniacal noise. The winter of their first year in the new house their father was very bad. . . . Having such a great space in front of the house gave the children a feeling of night, of vastness, and of terror. This terror came in from the shrieking of the tree and the anguish of the home discord. (77–78)

As in the poem, the above passage is resistant to the contemporary myth of domestic space as it highlights tension and conflict within the home. Furthermore, it challenges the dominant spatial discourse that privileges the patriarch's perspective and experience of the home by demonstrating that the home is a multifaceted place which each member of the family perceives and experiences differently. Whereas Mr. Morel likes the new home, the children find it detestable. Its bleak and even terrifying surroundings are constant reminders of the father's violent behavior. As the story goes on, we come to realize that the Morel family's distinctive emotional responses to the new home has much to do with the socio-cultural significance that the location of home has brought to the family.[7] The shift in the location—"from the Bottoms to a house on the brow of the hill"—brings the children a new understanding of social relations outside the home and an attendant sense of isolation and inferiority. While "the children of Scargill Street felt quite select," the Morel children living at "the end" of the street were sensitive to their isolation (97): "They all loved the Scargill Street house for its openness, for the great scallop of the world it had in view" (99). The deprivation of the openness of the view, the break with "the great scallop of the world," and the attendant awakening to disparities—through their awareness of poverty and alienation—negatively affect Mrs. Morel as well. The new dwelling place exacerbates her "suffering and disillusion and self-denial" and the feeling that "she had never had her life's fulfillment" (85).[8]

In a sense, the entire narrative of the novel revolves around various aspects of and perspectives on domestic space, exposing diverse ideologies and reversing the power structure implicated in the dominant discourse about home. Fighting the patriarchal discourse of home, the novel highlights rather than obscures women's existence, labor, and suffering, while suggesting how women perceive and experience home differently from men. Despite her ceaseless labor to create a resting place for the family, the wife/mother is deprived of any ownership of the house and is bullied by the husband. At one time, Mr. Morel shouts at his wife, "get out of it [the house]. . . . It's mine house, not thine," and literally shuts her out (33). Far from giving a sense of comfort, the home for Mrs. Morel is a prison where she is bound to feminine duties. Mr. Morel deals with his wife as if she were a servant (52) and forces her to "wait on a man" (53). Unlike Mr. Morel, who freely claims his right to take a rest at home and enjoy the world outside, she should be inside, suffering: "It galled her bitterly to think he [Mr. Morel] should be out taking his pleasure and spending money, whilst she remained at home, harassed" (28). For Miriam—Paul's friend—too, the home signifies restrictions imposed on women. Suppressing her zeal for learning, she has to remain at home while her brothers are at school (157). She lives unnoticed by her brothers and is frequently silenced by her mother (158, 183).

In addition to foregrounding women's suffering and labor, the novel disrupts the patriarchal spatial code by critically rewriting it through a woman's perspective. In Mrs. Morel's view, for example, the idea of stability and changelessness of home that is predominant in Victorian discourse takes on negative meanings. For her, the house that "stands behind her, fixed and stable" arouses an intolerable sense of suffocation and confinement instead of the sense of security and protection men would enjoy. At the sight of the house, she feels "buried alive" and horrified by the idea that "things were never going to alter" (12–13).[9] In the novel, however, Mrs. Morel is not the only person who suffers and toils in the home. As a matter of fact, for Walter, a miner married to a woman with a higher social standing, home is not the place where he can freely rest and dictate as a master of the house, as the patriarchal idea of home usually presumes. On the contrary, he is the most isolated figure in the house. Far from securing his identity, domestic space—where the children explicitly and implicitly comply with their mother's ethics and her valorization of middle-class values over working class ways of life—constantly threatens Mr. Morel's selfhood.[10] As an "outsider" at home, Walter finds "his real self" only when he "enter[s] again into the life of his own people" (82). Estranged from the home, he keeps seeking a surrogate home in the pit or a pub: "For him, the Palmerstone would be cosier" [than home] (45). Juxtaposed with the power imbalance between the violent and loud husband and the agonized and muted wife, the class conflicts surrounding the home complicate the politics of the novel, undercutting the legitimacy of Mrs. Morel's perspective.

Drawing our attention to class and gender conflicts that the conventional discourse of home usually leaves out, the home in the novel shatters another cultural myth of home as a place built by the mother's care and nurturing. In the novel, it is the father, not the mother, who is more closely associated with food, nurturing, and the hearth—the place that the patriarchal society usually regards as a feminine realm. Walter brings food such as gingerbread and coconut, rakes the fire while Mrs. Morel goes to bed (14), makes the meal (55), and nurtures the sick children. Although Paul's Oedipal feelings keep suppressing his explicit affection for the father's warmth—in contrast with the rather cold mother—these episodes reverse the typical association of gender and space, home and mother, through the powerfully caring figure of the father.

Through complex aspects of Mr. and Mrs. Morel's roles and feelings the novel presents the home as a social space where "the imaginary relation between self and other is performed" (Rose 61); it is a place where people are at once bound and resistant to the socio-cultural imperatives imposed on them. That the cultural imposition of roles and identities are simultaneously manifested and challenged in the domestic space becomes all the more salient when a visitor from outside the family enters into the Morel house. When William, the eldest son, brings his girlfriend, Louisa—who is socially superior to the Morel family—to the house, the working class family house immediately emerges as a social terrain that awakens both the visitor and the Morel family to class-consciousness and socially expected spatial performances. Note the recurrent idea of "role-playing" that points to performativity and constructedness of class-identities and behaviors played out in the house. In Louisa's presence, William's sister, Annie "played the part of maid" (145) and Mr. Morel is willing to offer her his arm-chair—"the place of honour" (146), signaling the shift in the center of power from the working class patriarch to the lady from the city. "Play[ing] the grand lady" (149) among her "inferiors," Louisa fails to "realize them as people," or if she does, she gives notice to what they say as if "a servant had spoken" (146). [11] In this dynamics of class relations, it seems that the individuality of the entire lower class family has faded into their own house, a situation that usually happens to women or servants. [12]

Going beyond portraying the class system that operates in domestic space, the novel implies the possibility of establishing different socio-spatial practices through the sense of uneasiness or anger of those who live the space. William, for instance, got angry at Louisa's making a servant of his sister (150), and Mrs. Morel felt "hurt and humiliated" (147). On Louisa's side, the Morel house, unlike her Aunt's, makes her feel "nervous," awkward, and fearful (147). She has difficulty in adjusting herself to her expected role and interacting with others in this unfamiliar social milieu. That is to say, Louisa's visit clearly demonstrates how home is always a social space—a space where people are compelled to "put on" culturally imposed roles, feeling at

times awkward or resistant to them (148). The dominant social order, therefore, is always subject to challenge. Note for example the passage that destabilizes Louisa's authority by suggesting that it is contingent upon a specific
location rather than being inherently hers. We are told: "And yet she [Louisa]
was not so grand. For a year now she had been a sort of secretary or clerk in a
London office. But while she was with the Morels she queened it. She sat
and let Annie or Paul wait on her as if they were her servants" (149). Cultural
expectations in the house are shattered, and Louisa finally ceases to assume
the role of the lady. She "chang[es] her tune" (149), and along with this, the
Morel household surfaces as a social space wherein people at once perform
and subvert the "imagined relations" imposed by the society.

Domestic space in *Sons and Lovers* is simultaneously social, cultural,
and psychological space that each of the Morel family perceives and lives differently; it is a multifaceted and dynamic social space that cannot be reduced
to any single authoritative perspective and experience. It is a place of tremendous maternal power, ceaseless battle between masculine, physical violence
and maternal, frigid Puritanism, fights between different classes and genders,
as well as a place of warmth, rest, and nurture. The complex aspects of
domestic space help us read Paul's final decision to leave the home after the
mother's death from a new perspective. Many critics have interpreted the
ending scene in light of Paul's repudiation of mother and home, unwittingly
following the patriarchal identification of the two that the novel in fact
destabilizes.[13] What Paul really wants to leave behind, I believe, is the complex psychological, geographical, and cultural dimensions that the home
embodies: the poignant sense of class disparities, the lack of cultural nurturing for the would-be artist, the conflicts between working and middle-class
values, violence and domination, as well as his infant psychology and
dependence bound up with his Oedipal feelings for the parents.

In short, far from being a neutral background, domestic space plays a central role in the development of the class and gender politics in *Sons and Lovers*.
Fighting the ideological rendering of home as an ahistorical, permanent, and
harmonious place, the novel grounds it in a concrete socio-cultural context, critically excavating domination and resistance in the conflicts between different
classes and genders. As such, domestic space in the novel emerges not so much
as an unalterable structure of oppression as a dynamic and flexible social space.

REVERSING GENDER AND SPACE IN *THE RAINBOW*

The Rainbow, a family chronicle of three generations written between 1913
and 1915, revolves not only around a temporal axis but also around a spatial

one, as the titles of the chapters like "They Live at the Marsh," "Wedding at the Marsh," "The Cathedral," and "The Man's World" suggest. Although several critics have noted the spatial aspects of the novel, they have usually dismissed the material, social, and historical significance of the various places in the novel. Even those critics attentive to the socio-historical significance of space offer rather limited readings because they tend to ignore the context of women's history and thus fail to recognize the crucial role that various places play in advancing the gender politics of the novel.

For example, Scott Sanders states that the movement from generation to generation in the novel involves a progressive widening of consciousness on the part of the characters along with a physical movement away from the isolated Marsh Farm into the industrial city. According to Sanders, the less successful man-woman relationship of later generations comes from Lawrence's own failure to explore the possibilities of living within an urban and industrial world (89). Sanders contends that Lawrence's division between society and nature cannot help but make the novel fundamentally "anti-social," as evidenced by the author's endorsement of nature as an alternative to the corrupted society (213). Drawing on a schematic division between nature and society, Sanders reduces the significance of space to the two broad categories of nature and society, a reductionism that fails to illuminate the complex social and cultural meanings that various places in the novel deliver. Drawing upon multiple meanings of the word "space," Robert Kiely argues that the novel's "dominant structural as well as thematic and metaphorical concern is spatial"(98).[14] Notwithstanding Kiely's unusual interest in Lawrence's "treatment of space"(109), his interpretation also becomes problematic as he translates specific locations into symbolic, conceptual, or linguistic spaces. In a sense, the evaporation of social, cultural, and material space that we see in Kiely is a corollary to his core proposition that modern fiction is about an escape from Romantic egotism, "a movement from the individual and local to the relational and universal" (6). Reading Joyce, Lawrence, and Woolf in light of the issue of relationships, Kiely states that Bloom's Dublin, Mrs. Dalloway's London, and the Notthinghamshire of the Morels and the Brangwens turn into "universal space"(13).

F.R. Leavis and Raymond Williams raise the issue of space in a more concrete historical context, and yet their readings are also limited in that they leave out the issue of gender that is in fact deeply related to the issues of history and space in the novel. Leavis investigates how Lawrence as a "social historian" (145) expands and relates his personal experiences to a remarkable study of historical circumstances by recording faithfully the gradual intrusion of the modern industrial age into rural life. Concerned with class relations, Raymond Williams also reads the novel in terms of the historical conditions revolving around a "cultural border" (264) between rural and urban spaces. Although these readings rightly underscore some of the social and historical conditions to which the novel depicts and responds, they still lead to rather a limited understanding of the novel, for both of them neglect another side of history that the novel investigates: the history of women's search for independence and the production of private and public space in a patriarchal society.

The novel opens with the famous depiction of the traditional way of life at the Marsh Farm during the days when harmony with nature was still possible in the rural area. But the evocation of the settled continuity of life immediately yields to a suggestion of the momentous changes brought by the growth of industrialism to the valley around 1840. As critics have suggested, the opening pages are a kind of concentrated, introductory statement of the novel's themes or concerns—the fundamental desires of men and women (Daleski), the invasion of modern industrial society into nature (Sanders), the moment of the mixture of the old and the new worlds that took place on a cultural border between mine/farm and the opening world of education and art (Williams), and so forth. But these readings have usually dismissed another crucial theme that the opening passages presage: woman's revolt against the traditional spatial divisions and discourses and their search for alternative ones. From the outset, the novel suggests that the different modes of life, perspectives, and desires between men and women are tied up with divided spaces. Note the following:

> The women were different. . . . [T]he women looked out from the heated, blind intercourse of farm-life, to the spoken world beyond. They were aware of the lips and the mind of the world speaking and giving utterance, they heard the sound in the distance, and they strained to listen. It was enough for the men, that the earth heaved and opened its furrows to them. . . . [T]hey lived full and surcharged. . . . But the woman wanted another form of life than this, something that was not blood-intimacy. Her house faced out from the farm-buildings and fields, looked out to the road and the village with church and Hall and the world beyond. She stood to see the far-off world of cities and governments and the active scope of man, the magic land to her, where secrets were made known and desires fulfilled. She faced outwards to where men moved dominant and creative, having turned their back on the pulsing heat of creation, and with this behind them, were set out to discover what was beyond, to enlarge their own scope and range and freedom; whereas the Brangwen men faced inwards to the teeming life

of creation, which poured unresolved into their veins. Looking out, as she must, from the front of her house towards the activity of man in the world at large, whilst her husband looked out to the back at sky and harvest and beast and land, she strained her eyes to see what man had done in fighting outwards to knowledge, she strained to hear how he uttered himself in this conquest, her deepest desire hung on the battle that she heard, far off, being waged on the edge of the unknown. She also wanted to know, and to be of the fighting host. (8–9)

In the passage Lawrence locates the different desires of the Brangwen man and woman in a specific historical and cultural context of the production of gendered space. In a sense, the Brangwen men's concord with the farming life without seething anxiety for the world beyond is made possible in part through their cultural privilege over women in terms of space: their right to claim ownership of or inhabit any place. The road from here (the Marsh Farm) to there (the city) might be much wider for them than for women. Reminiscent of Miriam's forced silence at Willy Farm or Mrs. Morel's anguished sense of unfulfillment of the self in *Sons and Lovers,* the fact that women are deprived of the language and opportunity to realize their social yearnings makes them dream of the "active scope of men," the "spoken world," the world of freedom and self-fulfillment. The passage historicizes distinctive psychological states between men and women by relating them to their different experiences and conceptualizations of diverse places. It records women's double alienation from both the rural and the urban area, while men dominate and conquer both. Indeed, from the beginning the narrative underscores the divided sense of home as a resting place for men, and a working place for women: "the men sat by the fire in the house where the women moved about" (8), a division that appears again in the phrase, "Brangwen could sit silent, smoking in his chair, the mother could move about" (105).

In sum, the passage pictures an era that saw women's growing dissatisfaction at the gendered distribution of space, a discontent about to shatter the traditional spatial arrangements and unequal relations between men and women. Here the predominant divisions between the feminine and the masculine, the domestic and the public sphere are investigated, interrogated, and transgressed through women's frustrations and longings rather than simply naturalized and reinscribed. Grounded and cultivated in specific spatio-cultural circumstances, the Brangwen women's yearnings function as a prelude to one of the major themes of the novel—a critical investigation of male-centered domestic and public spaces primarily delivered from women's perspectives.

As we shall see, the focus on space sheds new light on the search for independence of Ursula, the main female protagonist in the novel. Many Lawrence scholars such as Leavis, Williams, and H. M. Daleski have viewed Ursula as a kind of a female successor to the task left with Paul at the end of *Sons and Lovers:* the initiation into adulthood, independence, and the public world. As a prototype of a modern woman, they suggest, Ursula seeks independence and fullness of being through repudiation of mother, domesticity, and home. In Millett's view, despite Lawrence's initial sympathy with Ursula's effort to transcend the confining traditional world, he ultimately fails to suppress his jealousy and intolerance of the emancipation of women of his generation, as exemplified by his decision to have Ursula fail to survive in the "man's world" by keeping her from getting a degree from the university (262).

Despite their contrasting interpretations about the significance of Ursula's quest, the above readings share a common problem in that they tend to take for granted both the division between the confining/feminine/domestic space and liberating/masculine/public space, and the contrast between the former generations of the Brangwen women like Lydia and Anna, who are bound up with domesticity, maternity, and home, and Ursula, who endeavors to transcend them.[15] Founded on these assumed contrasts and divisions, these readings seem to imply that women's emancipation could be realized simply by becoming a member of the "man's world," thus privileging the man's world over the woman's world and reinforcing the hierarchical division of gendered space, an ideology that the novel in fact strives to dismantle.

Reading against the grain, I propose that the novel binds the three Brangwen women, Lydia, Anna, and Ursula, together through their critical reactions to dominant spatial codes and practices. While the degree to which these women achieve subversive potential may differ, they share the rebellious spirit to interrogate and dismantle the ideological implications embedded in the male discourses and practices surrounding domestic and public spaces. In the novel, various places such as the house, the cottage, the cathedral, the school, or the "man's world" of war, nationalism, and politics, play a crucial role in the performance of social criticism, inviting us to look at gender politics from a new perspective as well. As we shall see, these places are highly contested social spaces where women's spatial perspectives and practices constantly challenge and reverse those of men. Through the clash between women's and men's spatial codes, the novel exposes various forms of domination and resistance that are embedded in spatial discourses and practices, an exposure that grounds both domestic and public spaces in a social and historical realm open to restructuration and reconceptualization.

CONFLICTING SPATIAL CODES: ANNA AND WILL IN THE YEW COTTAGE AND LINCOLN CATHEDRAL

Critical interpretations of the relation between Anna and Will have been divided. Some scholars have read it as one of the "the most difficult" but intriguing parts of the novel (Leavis 123), stressing the remarkable narrative "detachment" (Kiely 106) that delivers the devastating battle between the couple that erupts first in the Yew Cottage and then culminates in Lincoln Cathedral. Others have contended that Lawrence explicitly takes sides with the male character; the episodes indict Anna for Pyrrhic victory over the male, a triumph that ravages both Will and herself. In these readings, the significance of the cottage and the cathedral has hardly been noted except for occasional observations concerning their symbolic, abstract, or metaphorical meanings in relation to the characters' psychology. In addition, Anna's challenges to Will have usually been either considered simply in terms of the insurmountable antithesis between female and male psychology or denigrated as evidence of a destructive female will-to-power.

However, close attention to the significance of the two locations—the Yew Cottage and Lincoln Cathedral—enables us to look at the battle between Anna and Will from a new perspective. To begin with, much of the conflict between Anna and Will derives from their different spatial codes regarding domestic (the cottage) and public (the cathedral) spaces. As we shall see, these places feature in the episodes as heterogeneous social spaces that these characters perceive and experience differently. More importantly, Anna's challenge to Will can be read as a subversive spatial code that unveils and attacks the ideological implications of Will's conventional spatial codes.

The first few honeymoon days at the Yew Cottage bring Anna and Will a break with conventional time and space. "Severed from the world" (144), the couple arranges their life apart from the conventional activities governed by the church-clock (144). Instead of providing the couple with the same sense of happiness or freedom, however, this new chronotope brings out conflicts between them caused by their distinctive psychological and behavioral responses, responses that are founded on sets of divisions between the personal and the social, the domestic and the public, and the feminine and the masculine spheres.

In the cottage Will "could not get rid of a culpable sense of licence," the "guilty" feeling that he neglects "some duty outside" (144). He is "troubled" by this severance from the outer world and feels "ashamed" and "unmanly" (147), confronting the fact that he does not follow the "established rule of things," the rule that demands "man ought to get up in the morning and wash oneself and be a decent social being" (149). The narrative here reveals how deeply the dominant spatio-temporal distinctions between night and day, inside and outside, home and society, private and public, and womanly and manly forms of life have been instilled in Will's psyche. As time passes, however, Will's initial anxiety, shame, and uneasiness take a curious turn toward an opposite pole: the joy of utter isolation from the outer world. After the early "confounding experience" (149), he begins to value the cottage life in terms of eternity, perfect freedom, and reality while associating the public world outside with lies, destruction, and death (150–51). In a sense, however, this change is not that surprising. Both the initial guilty feelings and the blind attachment to an entirely isolated private life come from the same root: the absolute breach between the interior/private and the exterior/public world.

On the contrary, Anna shows a different way of "living" in the cottage, a mode which is linked to her distinctive perspective and experience of domestic space as a woman. The unconventional time-space of the cottage allows Anna the freedom to manage time according to her own needs and desires, enabling her to enjoy the cottage life "more quickly to her fullness" than Will (150). At the same time, Anna seems to have a keener understanding of the cottage as a socio-cultural space that demands socially expected performances rather than as a purely personal and private place. Thus, when Anna's father visits the couple, she immediately "assumed another character" (149) while Will is at a loss at this unexpected invasion of the social world. More importantly, for Anna the cottage life does not mean an entire break with the social world: "She was less hampered than he, so she came more quickly to her fullness, and was sooner ready to enjoy again a return to the outside world" (150). Unlike Will, who sinks into the abstract realm of privacy where "there was no world, no time" (157), Anna prepares for a tea-party that may balance her private and social instincts, rebelling against any "ready-made duty" and seeking to realize "her *self*" (157). In sum, Will and Anna's distinct responses to the domestic space of the cottage reveal their different relations to the dominant spatio-temporal order, destabilizing the patriarchal prescriptions about the gendered roles and spatial divisions between the private/feminine/domestic and social/masculine/public spheres.

The above instances show that whereas Will follows conventional spatial order, Anna challenges and reverses it. Far from condemning Anna—as some critics would suggest–the novel positively reinforces her critical stance.

Indeed, the episodes of Anna and Will within and about the cottage favor Anna's "less hampered mind" and "independence" that challenges Will's conventional discourse of home (150, 151). The criticism that the narrator mounts on Will confirms this point. Will is enslaved by "maxims," "rules" or the "conventional mind," and his "unquestioned concepts" forces him to "[do] foolish things"(149, 171). Anticipating the essay, "The Master in His Own House," the novel exposes the problematic male psyche lying behind the patriarchal spatial code and its potential harm for both man and woman. Oscillating between the false choices founded upon the spatial binaries, Will fails to adjust himself flexibly to the new circumstances that the cottage introduces. Abandoning the social world, Will tries to compensate this self-willed loss by claiming his authority in domestic space, threatening to dominate and subjugate Anna. Enthralled to his egotistic, patriarchal self, Will "asserted himself on his rights" and "arrogated the old position of master of the house"(173). He "asserted his position as the captain of the ship. . . . He wanted to loom important as master of one of the innumerable domestic craft that make up the great fleet of society" (174). To apply Lawrence's argument in "The Master in His Own House," the above passages point to the connection between the patriarchal discourse of domestic space and the formation of the patriarchal, masculine self—insecure, dependent, hence bullying; Will's recourse to the dominant spatial code results from his lack of selfhood in the first place and the attendant dependence on his wife.[16] Confronting the increasingly bullying husband, Anna fights back by shattering the authority of the patriarchal spatial code. Anna "felt no belief" in and "jeered at" Will's "master-of-the-house idea" (174).

Despite Anna's constant challenge, however, the huge cultural force that has long formulated the discursive and material patriarchal home is not something that she can shatter once and for all.[17] In the face of the growing patriarchal prerogatives, Anna in the cottage "was not safe" any more (181). Even worse, the constant burden of childbirth keeps weakening Anna's subversive potential, "because she must stay at home now" (195). The cottage that has been a place for an alternative space and time now seems to return to a conventional site for motherhood, forcing Anna to settle in "her builded house" (195).

And yet, the chapter ends neither by mocking Anna's power that is incapable of going beyond the boundaries of the home nor by worshiping a triumph of the matriarch. Instead, the text constantly points to Anna's uneasy, forced compromise with the socio-cultural regime, leaving her subversive desires unquenched. The process of Anna's domestication keeps being interrupted by her recurrent desire to go beyond her domestic confinement, a desire that she inherited from her ancestress' yearning for the world beyond the home portrayed at the beginning of the novel. Anna "had a slight expectant feeling, as of a door half opened," "strain[ing] her eyes to something beyond" (195). The chapter ends by describing the insurmountable tension between the patriarchal order and her subversive desire, the on-going clashes between the two spatial codes that take place within the psyche of Anna under the increasing pressure of motherhood. Anna keeps turning to the "hope, the promise" of journey that she finds in the rainbow, while continuous childbearing compels her to lapse into "vague content" of being settled down. Far from having Anna capitulate to the dominant socio-spatial order, the text persistently highlights the would-be "wayfarer" Anna's quenchless desire for travel, movement, and far away horizons that contrasts with Will's focus on home and stasis, thus reversing the typical association of gender and space. Lawrence writes, "still her doors opened under the arch of the rainbow, her threshold reflected the passing of the sun and moon, the great travelers, her house was full of the echo of journeying. She was a door and a threshold" (196). Here, the phrase goes against the patriarchal discourse that prescribes the nature of women's identity and that of domestic space in static and fixed terms. The phrase puts both Anna's selfhood and the home in dynamic and flexible terms through the images of "a threshold" and "a door," images that signify perpetual comings and goings, openings and closings.

The images of the door and the rainbow in the above are noteworthy in that they suggest the connection between the women of three generations—Anna, her mother Lydia, and her daughter, Ursula. As I shall discuss further on, Lydia had retreated in disillusionment to the home from the public world of man. However, the home that Lydia created through her second marriage to Tom is not a conventional one. It is a different kind of home built out of her critical response to the male-dominant world, a space where she experiences both "bonds" and "liberty." She transforms the home, her self, and her marital relation into a "doorway": "They [Tom and Lydia] had passed through the doorway into the further space, where movement was so big, that it contained bonds and constraints and labours, and still was complete liberty. She was the doorway to him, he to her" (95). The image of the doorway here defines both Lydia's home and her identity in terms of perpetual movement and journeying, reversing the patriarchal discourse and preparing for the images of "a door" and "a threshold" that we have seen in the case of Anna and Will. Anna's battle presents many more difficulties and tensions than in her mother's generation, but it delivers an increased sense of critical intensity and subversive potential as well. Anna's daughter, Ursula, takes over the task of the adventurer in the next generation. Refusing to be

subsumed either by the house or by the "man's world," she struggles continuously to create her own self and place through the vision of the rainbow.

Before I explore the politics of gender and space in Ursula's story, let
me examine the quarrel between Anna and Will in and about Lincoln Cathedral, an incident that revolves around two conflicting spatial codes about
public space, preparing us for a clearer understanding of the significance of
Ursula's challenge to the "Man's World." The conflict between Anna and
Will culminates in the seventh chapter, "The Cathedral." Leavis reads this
chapter in light of the fight between Anna's "destructive rationalism" and
Will's religious ecstasy (124), a conflict that shows the failure of fulfillment
in marriage (127). For Daniel J. Schneider, although the "sympathetic
union" is more difficult in this couple than in the previous generation, the
fact that the cathedral that Will worships is female is a positive sign for their
relationship because it indicates Will's inheritance of the ancestral adoration
of matriarchy that Lawrence endorses (119). In Millett's view, however,
Will's very fascination with the female/womb/cathedral is no better than a
latent animosity to the power of the womb, prefiguring Lawrence's conversion to a doctrinaire male-supremacist ethic (257). "So entirely does the
womb dominate the book," Millett writes, "that it becomes a symbol, in the
arch of Lincoln Cathedral, or in the moon, of the spiritual and the supernatural. The womb is so portentous and enviable an organ that the men in the
book make some effort to participate in the marvel" (258, 259).

In spite of the differences in their perspectives, these readings share a
similar problem. They unquestioningly accept Will's perspective of what the
cathedral stands for—its symbolic power on the one hand, and its identification with the woman on the other—either dismissing Anna's alternative view
of the place or reducing her objection to Will's view to a malignant and
destructive feminine will. [18] Leavis' sympathetic understanding of Will's
experience of transcendence indicts Anna's opposition as a sign of her inability to reach such a psychic state, or even worse, her "destructive rationalism."
In Millett, Anna is hardly mentioned. Kiely brings up the significance of the
cathedral in relation to the issues of language and communication, stressing
Lawrence's balance between Will's and Anna's ideas of space (106). But
unfortunately, Kiely himself seems to lose this balance, as he attributes "the
collapse of his [Will's] marriage" to a "malicious" Anna, whose every word is
"calculated to destroy his pleasure" (107).

The conflict between the couple revolves around different spatial codes
with their attendant viewpoints about self, other, and space that affect and
have been shaped by the experience of space. Through this conflict, the
cathedral surfaces not so much as a pure idea of the absolute/mother but as a

heterogeneous place experienced and conceived differently. Instead of reading Will's "transports and ecstasies" (201) in the cathedral as a neutral depiction of what the cathedral really means for him and for the reader as well, let
us look at the ways in which the text demonstrates how this transcendental
experience is bound up with what Will believes this space to be. For Will, the
cathedral is an "absolute" "symbol" of "eternity" and "timeless consummation" (206, 202):

> He looked up to the lovely unfolding of the stone. He was to pass
> within to the perfect womb. . . . Away from time, always outside of
> time! Between east and west, between dawn and sunset, the church lay
> like a sea in silence, dark before germination, silenced after death. Con-
> taining birth and death, potential with all the noise and transition of
> life, the cathedral remained hushed. . . . Brangwen came to his consum-
> mation. (201–02)

The passage discloses the ideological implications embedded in Will's experience and perspective of the cathedral. It demonstrates how the feminization of
the cathedral space—operating in Will's spatial code—is intertwined with the
masculine impulse to define, silence, or control woman's body and identity.
Turning the cathedral into the womb, Will's discourse deprives the
space/woman of history ("outside of time") and language ("silenced,"
"hushed"). The feminization of the cathedral goes hand in hand with Will's
contradictory but fundamentally interrelated desires for unification and domination. Note his impulse to dominate this feminine space/body—intimated by
the image of the cathedral passively laying, silenced while Will reaching "consummation"—mixed with his wish to be merged into the maternal space.
    Anna immediately detects and challenges the ideological implications
operative in Will's spatial code. She refutes the feminization of the cathedral:
"The 'she' irritated her. Why 'she'? It was 'it'" (200). She repudiates Will's
view and experience of the cathedral not because she is unable to reach a
transcendental dimension but because she senses that it works to restrict her
freedom and individuality in the name of a virtue and perfection which are
subservient to male desire and need. "[M]istrusting the culmination of the
altar" and fighting with the "sense of being rooted in," Anna "claimed
another right"—"the right to freedom above her, higher than the roof"
(203). Refusing to be confined in "a great roof that closed her in," Anna
wanted to "rise from it as a bird rises with wet, limp feet from the sea . . . [to]
tear herself away like a bird on wings, and in the open space where there is
clarity, rise up above the fixed, surcharged motion" (203).

The significance of Anna's imaginary flight is two-fold. Firstly, it symbolizes her resistance to Will's masculinist spatial code. Secondly, it challenges another—but related—problematic impulse implicated in Will's spatial code: the self-centered vision of the space and the attendant negation or underestimation of the other. For Will, the cathedral was the "absolute" place that "he wanted" to "satisfy his blind passion" (205, 206). Such an egotistic bent is combined with an illusionary binarism as well. Reminiscent of his holding on to the division between the private and the public in the cottage scene, Will believes in the dichotomy between the two worlds—the world inside of cathedral, that is, the world of "a reality, an order, an absolute," and the world outside, that is, an unreal world, "a meaningless confusion" (205), a binarism that privileges the former over the latter. Thus, Will's experience of transcendental rapture in the cathedral is accompanied by an act of negating numerous conflicts, sufferings, and contradictions with which people in the real world live, an act that he needs to create a totally gratifying place of his own.

In contrast with the rapture that transposes Will into a world of his own, Anna's flight takes an opposing direction. Whereas the cathedral for Will signifies an exclusive space of his own that satisfies his desire and secures his masculine selfhood, for Anna it is a place where she discovers the existence of other beings and their anger, laughter, and agony. In the midst of the imaginary flight, Anna suddenly "caught sight of the wicked, odd little faces carved in stone. And she stood before them arrested." The passage continues:

These sly little faces peeped out of the grand tide of the cathedral like something that knew better. They knew quite well, these little imps that retorted on man's own illusion, that the cathedral was not absolute. They winked and leered, giving suggestion of the many things that had been left out of the great concept of the church. "However much there is inside here, there's a good deal they haven't got in," the little faces mocked. Apart from the lift and spring of the great impulse towards the altar, these little faces had separate wills, separate motions, separate knowledge, which replied back in defiance of the tide, and laughed in triumph of their own very littleness. "Oh look!" cried Anna, "Oh look, how adorable, the faces! Look at her." Brangwen looked unwillingly. This was the voice of the serpent in his Eden. She pointed him to a plump, sly, malicious little face carved in stone. "He knew her, the man who carved her," said Anna. "I'm sure she was his wife." "It isn't a woman at all, it's a man," said Brangwen curtly." "Do you think so— No! That isn't a man. That is no man's face." Her voice sounded rather

jeering. . . . She was spoiling his passionate intercourse with the cathedral. (204)

The above passage can be read as an example of Anna's challenge to Will's
ideological spatial code, a code that is bound up with the production of what
Lefebvre termed "abstract space." Roughly speaking, in Lefebvre's theory the
production of an abstract space like a church goes hand in hand with that of
ideological spatial codes that seek to disseminate illusory views of self, other,
and reality by eliminating differences, conflicts, sufferings, labor, and contradictions that exist in the space. Abstract space is forced to function more like
a symbol, losing its grip with the material, socio-historical context with
which it in fact occupies, reifies, and interacts.[19] In relation to Lefebvre's
observation, the cathedral mediated by Will's perspective is an example of
abstract space. Above all, Will would not allow any disturbing existence of
the other in "his Eden." He denies any alien element that might disrupt his
own territory, the "symbol" of the absolute world that is to gratify his passion
(205). In contrast, Anna directs her gaze at the material and mundane existence of other inhabitants, bridging the worlds inside and outside of the
cathedral, thus dismantling Will's illusory division between the two. She
excavates "little things" that had been left out of "the great concept of the
church," that is to say, those many things that have been made invisible or
effaced by Will's spatial code.

From this perspective, Anna's mistrust of Will's enthusiasm is an attack
on the complicity between a masculinist, dogmatic impetus and an abstract,
fetishized vision of the cathedral. Anna's antipathy to Will's rapture therefore
cannot be reduced to malicious feminine will or destructive rationalism.
Instead it should be understood as a subversive spatial code that "retort[s] on
man's own illusion," that is, an attack on the feminization and the abstrac-
tion/fetishization of the cathedral space that marginalizes, subjugates, and
excludes the other, including women. It is a challenge to the ideological limits implicated in Will's transcendental, religious rapture, a seemingly innocent feeling that in effect complies with the ideological production of the
cathedral.[20] Anna's disturbing spatial code—her "profane" mockery and jeering—brings Will a sense of disillusionment and loss (205). He lost his
"beloved realities" and the "absolute" (206, 207).

Privileging Will's experience and view of the cathedral over those of
Anna, critics have usually interpreted Will's loss as a lamentable defeat by a
malicious Anna. What this reading has usually neglected is the ambivalence
of the narrator, who at once laments and celebrates Will's loss. Lawrence's
penetrating description of Will's painful sense of loss and disillusionment is

followed by a passage that intimates some benefits that Will's fight with Anna in the cathedral has brought to him: a better knowledge of the cathedral, human relations, and reality. Leaving the cathedral, Will realizes the narrowness and falsity of the doorway of the cathedral. "[S]adly and disillusioned," Will realizes that

> the doorway was no doorway. It was too narrow, it was too false. Outside the cathedral were many flying spirits that could never be sifted through the yellow gloom. He had lost his absolute. He listened to the thrushes in the gardens and heard a note which the cathedrals did not include: something free and careless and joyous. He crossed a field that was all yellow with dandelions, on his way to work, and the bath of yellow glowing was something at once so sumptuous and so fresh, that he was glad he was away from his shadowy cathedral. (206)

The passage registers a moment when Will accepts the falsity of his dichotomy that excludes those various "flying spirits," "free," "careless" and "joyous" vitality of life from his "shadowy cathedral."

As in the previous chapter, however, the conflict between the two spatial codes does not lead to a simplistic solution such as a sudden self-realization or perfect reconciliation. Will's awakening to the corporeal reality that his mystified cathedral world has excluded is temporary. His "inadequacy" and the "limitation of his being" made him "unready for fulfillment" (209, 210). He gradually turns his back away from "the outer world" for a even more fetishized cathedral: "It was the church *building* he cared for. . . . To keep the church fabric and the church-ritual intact was his business; to have the intimate sacred building utterly in his own hands. . . . The church was false, but he served it the more attentively" (209, emphasis in original). In Anna's case, the growing demand of motherhood and domesticity keeps her from fully developing her subversive spatial politics. But Ursula inherits her mother's legacy and pushes its political potential a step further.

As we have seen so far, the cottage and Lincoln Cathedral are the examples of the ways in which domestic and public spaces function as social space—a multifaceted space simultaneously material and discursive—that produces and is produced by different perspectives, discourses, and experiences, space that at once embodies and subverts dominant ideologies and social relations.[21] As a contested, heterogeneous place where different spatial codes clash with each other, these places bring out Anna's and Will's different responses to dominant spatial codes, interrogating the legitimacy of the dominant practices and perspectives surrounding domestic and public spaces. In this respect, we may argue, the cottage and the cathedral are central to the novel's challenge to ideologies embedded in dominant spatial codes, rather than merely a neutral background or a purely abstract symbol.

FIGHT WITH THE "MAN'S WORLD" AND THE SEARCH FOR AN ALTERNATIVE SELF AND SPACE

The issue of space is central to Ursula's search for independence and individuality.[22] Inheriting and substantiating her mother and grandmother's discontents at home and aspirations for the world beyond the domestic boundary, Ursula grows to be an ardent seeker of her own space, first at home and then in the "Man's World." Repudiating the patriarchal home that would not allow her individuality and independence, Ursula launches into the public world—the city, the world of language, self-fulfillment, and freedom. But what she confronts is an even worse masculinist space that threatens to annihilate the individuality and independence of both woman and man under the reign of industrialization, institutionalization, imperialist nationalism, and war. The novel ends with Ursula's search for a third space built out of a radical interrogation of the dominant socio-spatial order.[23] To put it differently, Ursula's critical response to and interaction with dominant conceptualizations, discourses, and practices surrounding domestic and public spaces—whose landscape includes home, schools, universities, industrialized cities and towns, the world of war, politics, patriotism, namely, the "man's world"—are central to her search for individuality and emancipation. Along with Ursula's growth, the attack on patriarchal spatial regimentation merges into social criticism, as it exposes various ideological limits and problems embodied by what the society has produced in the name of the "Man's World."

Born to a late Victorian family in a small mining town, from an early age, Ursula finds her home to be "a nightmare," a "bedlam" that fetters woman by the ceaseless demands of maternity and domestic duties (264, 265). Ursula's quest for her selfhood begins with her craving for a private space of her own within this nightmarish domestic space—with children running everywhere and the cleaning-woman "grumbl[ing] and scold[ing]" (265)—a yearning that is constantly shattered or forcefully prohibited. Like Miriam in *Sons and Lovers,* Ursula wishes to escape from the sisterly duties that her "ubiquitous" siblings demand and locks herself in to read. But she soon realizes that claiming her private space and time in the house is not pardonable or even conceivable. For a woman to do this nearly amounts to death. When she would not answer to the annoying knocks on the door, her siblings instantly yell, "she is dead" (266). In the end, "she must open the door" and return to the world of woman's laborious duties, as intimated by the first sound that she hears as soon as she steps out of the momentary space and time of privacy—"the screech of the bucket downstairs dragged across the flag-stones as the woman washed the kitchen floor" (266). After the children's interruption, Ursula moves to the parish room. But at this time, her claim to her own space brings her an even more painful experience of being brutally expelled by her father. Intolerant of the idea that Ursula should occupy his place, her father rushes to her immersed in reading in the parish room with a duster in his hand. Crying in anger, "[w]ho the deuce opened the door?," he "turned and flapped the cloth hard across the girl's face," and Ursula, stunned, went away (267). The battle between father and daughter in the parish room points to the domination of masculinist and patriarchal power in domestic space. Indeed, watching Ursula go, Will feels "a sense of triumph and easy power, followed immediately by acute pity" (267).

The parish room episode functions as a kind of a springboard for Ursula's turning toward space outside the home as a ground for self-fulfillment. Ursula's launching into the public world further substantiates the complex aspect of the spatial politics of the novel, exposing various problems embedded in the physical and conceptual domain of public space. Like the earlier Brangwen women, Ursula imagines public space as a world of self-realization and emancipation, but what she first confronts is the fact that it is a man's place, a place that restricts woman's entrance. The novel then pushes its attack on the gendered division of space one step further by shattering the very ground of the production of public space. It does this by suggesting that the association of the man's world with liberation and self-realization is another form of what Rob Shield would call "place myth."[24] What Ursula really should overcome, the novel implies, is not only the physical barrier that the society sets up but also the very cultural myth of public space internalized within Ursula herself—the myth of public space as the space of self-expression, individuality, freedom, and fulfillment of which the Brangwen women have long dreamed. Contrary to the contemporary myth of public space, what Ursula confronts within the "Man's World" is the dehumanizing social, cultural, and economic forces—such as industrialization, institutionalization, mechanization, capitalism, patriotism, militarism, and so on—that instill false beliefs of self, other, and social relations in the name of freedom, the Whole, or the nation. By showing that what the society produces and defines as "public space" is harmful to both woman and man, the novel makes a strong claim for remolding the conceptual and physical ground of public space.

Ursula's launching into the public world begins with her entrance into the Grammar School in Nottingham. Her "illusion of school" as a liberating place, however, is soon shattered as the school proves to be a place that produces "the average Self" through fearful authority (271). The next significant experience of the public world that Ursula has is mediated through her relationship with her first love, Anton Skrebensky. Ursula's "strong sense of the outer world" that the cousin brings to her here is depicted as a promising world of self-realization, individuality, and freedom (290), pointing to the internalized cultural myth of the public world. As time passes however, Ursula begins to doubt such a vision of the public world, as illustrated by the following conversation between Ursula and Skrebensky about war and nation. Challenging Skrebensky's mechanical complacency about his duty to fight for the nation, Ursula asserts an individuality that is not to be subjugated to the interest of the nation or other grand causes:

> "Well, if everybody said it, there wouldn't be a nation. But I should still be myself," she asserted brilliantly.
> "You wouldn't be yourself if there were no nation."
> "Why not?"
> "Because you'd just be a prey to everybody and anybody. . . ."
> "What do you fight for, really?"
> "I would fight for the nation."
> "For all that, you aren't the nation. What would you do for your self?"
> "I belong to the nation and must do my duty by the nation."
> "But when it didn't need your services in particular—when there *is* no fighting? What would you do then?"
> He was irritated.
> "I would do what everybody else does."
> "What?"
> "Nothing. I would be in readiness for when I was needed."
> The answer came in exasperation.
> "It seems to me," she answered, "as if you weren't anybody—as if there weren't anybody there, where you are. Are you anybody, really? You seem like nothing to me." (311)[25]

This conversation points to Ursula's awareness of the danger of the public sphere that seeks to eradicate individuality in the name of the nation.

In a sense, the public world that threatens one's integral selfhood had been already prefigured by the public world of men to which Ursula's grandmother,

Lydia, had once been exposed and from which she had retreated. After the death of her second husband, Tom, Lydia becomes close to Ursula. Frequenting her grandmother's bedroom, Ursula listens to her story about her life, a story that opens her eyes to the man's world and its threat to individuality. Lydia's first marriage to a Polish surgeon and revolutionary brought her an experience of the man's world outside the home. Charged with revolutionary fervor, Lydia served her husband and his "ideas of nationalism, of liberty, of science" (257). But Lydia soon confronted the contradictions and problems of the world of politics, action, and nationalism. First of all, it was gendered space; although it helped Lydia step beyond of the narrow borders of domesticity, it did not give her any sense of fulfillment or independence. As in the home, where she toiled like a "slave" to her husband, in the public world Lydia was deprived of her identity and liberty (257). For her, the exterior world turned out to be no better than a larger structure of the male-centered home, as suggested by the attitude of her husband—a representative of the man's world—to her, an attitude that Lydia resents to this day: "[h]e incorporated her in his ideas as if she were not a person herself, as if she were just his aide-de-camp, or part of his baggage, or one among his surgical appliances" (256).

In addition to instrumentalizing and subjugating women, the public world proved to be even more dangerous in that it tended to annihilate the individuality and integral selfhood of both women and men in the name of responsibility, activity, and the benefit of the Whole. Anticipating Ursula's insight into Skrebensky's existential void, Lydia notices the loss of self that results from her husband's blind subscription to the cause of the man's world: "She, Lydia Brangwen, was sorry for him now. He was dead—he had scarcely lived. . . . [h]e had never lived" (258). Through her second marriage to Tom, Lydia retreats to domestic space, but this does not mean a regressive return to a place that enslaves her. Lydia's relation with Tom enabled her to find "her place" in the new home. Through mutual effort, both Tom and Lydia achieve a certain degree of "liberty" (95). "She was the doorway to him, he to her" (95), and she "was very glad she had come to her own self" (259). Lydia's story prefigures Ursula's search for individuality and independence tied up with her revolt against oppressive places, both domestic and public, building a strong bond between Lydia and her granddaughter. Ursula and Lydia "seemed to understand the same language" (254), we are told, and Lydia opened for Ursula "the door . . . on to the greater space . . . a vast horizon. That was a great relief, to know the tiny importance of the individual, within the great past" (260).

The dawning awareness of the problems of public space becomes clearer as Ursula starts working in a public school and then resumes her relationship with Skrebensky. After her futile efforts to "have a place in the house," "to insist, in her own home, on the right of women to take equal place with men in the field of action and work," Ursula finally realizes that "she could not go on living at home . . . without place or meaning or worth" (354, 357). The chapter titled "The Man's World" deals with Ursula's square confrontation with the "outer, greater world of activity, the man-made world"(361) as a schoolteacher. Once again, Ursula's initial expectations about the man's world are disappointed. What Ursula really encounters in the school is a mechanical world of will that trammels self-realization. The school reminds her of "the church's architecture" that embodies "the purpose of domineering, like a gesture of vulgar authority"(369). In Ursula's eyes, the school appears to be a "timeless" "empty prison" (369, 370). She is frightened by the schoolmaster's "mechanical ignoring of her" and feels as if "she were addressing a machine" (370). As in the home, she feels "non-existent" (370), "hav[ing] no place nor being" (377). This does not mean, however, that the school is a liberating place for men, either. In the school, even one of the most powerful men like the schoolmaster loses his independence and integrity: "Imprisoned in a task too small and petty for him," he "always suppress[ed] himself" until he became "so little, and vulgar, out of place" (387–88).

In this respect, it is important to note that Ursula's search for emancipation goes beyond simply a matter of joining the man's world. Of course, the cultural lure surrounding public space as a site for freedom and fulfillment affects Ursula's psyche to the extent that she still at times considers the man's world as a necessary ground for her self-realization. The school makes her realize that "the man's world was too strong for her" to "take her place in it" (387), but she would not give up her effort to "hold her place" in "the world of work and man's convention," to be "a recognized member with full right there" (396, 406, 410). But her wish to be a member of the man's world gradually yields to a more radical spatial politics. Along with her prior direct or indirect experiences of public space—through her days in the Grammar School and her grandmother's story, as well as her relation with Skrebensky—her experience of the public school helps her realize that the existing man's world is not an option for her emancipation and self-fulfillment.

Ursula's renewed relationship with Skrebensky after his six-year absence puts her revolt against public space into the larger context of social criticism. Echoing Lydia's story of her first husband and confirming Ursula's intuition about Skrebensky's inner deadness six years ago, the man's world of militarism and imperialism for which Skrebensky works as a patriotic servant has further eradicated his individuality. In Ursula's eyes, Skrebensky returns with a frightening touch of "self-effacing diffidence" and looks as if "he wished to be unseen" (442). Ursula immediately detects that the world of imperialism has produced Skrebensky's mechanical and abstract subjectivity while endowing him with power in the name of civilization:

> She could see him so well out there, in India—one of the governing class, superimposed upon an old civilization, lord and master of a clumsier civilization than his own. . . . He would become again an aristocrat, invested with authority and responsibility, having a great helpless populace beneath him. One of the ruling class, his whole being would be given over to the fulfilling and the executing of the better idea of the state. And in India, there would be real work to do. The country did need the civilization which he himself represented; it did need his roads and bridges, and the enlightenment of which he was part. He would go to India. But that was not her road. (444)

The road that Skrebensky takes cannot be Ursula's because she refuses to be a part of the world that he represents and belongs to—the exploitive, imperial, mechanical man's world of brutal power. Ursula says to Skrebensky:

> "You think the Indians are simpler than us, and so you'll enjoy being near them and being a lord over them . . . And you'll feel so righteous, governing them for their own good. . . . Your governing stinks. . . . It's all such a nothingness, what you feel and what you don't feel. . . . I'm against you, and all your old, dead things" (444).

For Skrebensky, Ursula's remarks seemed to "strike the flag that he kept flying" (462). Ursula's revolt against the man's world here expands to a criticism of militarism, imperialism, and nationalism, and even of a larger masculinist social system that has instrumentalized human beings.

Ursula's observations mark a new dimension in her spatial politics. They point to her realization that being an equal member of the man's world does not emancipate her; on the contrary, it might mean her implication in a horrible dehumanizing and tyrannical system. In this sense, far from being an alternative option for domestic space, the public world of men turns out to be another oppressive structure to fight with, to restructure. Ursula's quest for individuality gains its critical force neither through a mere integration into the man's world nor through an entire denial of it, but through the creation of a critical third space within the male-dominated space. To some extent, Ursula's revolt against the school adumbrates this possibility. Ursula neither subscribes to the world outside the home nor entirely breaks with it, as her critical distance from her friend Maggie intimates. Unlike Maggie—a suffragist teacher whose revolt against the man's world ends with her withdrawal to an enclosed life in a cottage—Ursula would not "escape" from the "dry, tyrannical man-world" (410). Instead, her spatial politics operates in a way that it destabilizes the system from within: "His [the headmaster's] system, which was his very life in school, the outcome of his bodily movement, was attacked and threatened at the point where Ursula was included. She was the danger that threatened his body with a blow, a fall" (391).

Shattering her "bondage to Skrebensky and Skrebensky's world" (492), Ursula finally grounds her quest for independence and the fullness of being in a third space, an in-between space, as the passage from "The Rainbow" chapter sums up. During her illness—a kind of a prelude to her spiritual rebirth—Ursula asserts her will to disengage herself from the conventional world to create her own place: "I have no father nor mother nor lover, I have no allocated place in the world of things, I do not belong to Beldover nor to Nottingham nor to England nor to this world. They none of them exist, I am trammeled and entangled in them, but they are all unreal. I must break out of it, like a nut from its shell which is an unreality" (493). This Joycean drive to emancipate her self from the conventional world while not entirely denying her fundamental involvement with it, leads to a radical spatial politics. Subverting the overwhelming force of the man's world to turn a human being into "a shadow ever dissolving" (479), Ursula imagines the world itself, not herself, to be non-existent. But at the same time, Ursula is aware of the limits of a simple reversal and the impossibility of total negation of the man's world:

> . . . to her feverish brain, came the vivid reality of acorns in February lying on the floor of a wood with their shells burst and discarded and the kernel issued naked to put itself forth. She was the naked, clear kernel thrusting forth the clear, powerful shoot. . . . When she opened her eyes in the afternoon and saw the window of her room and the faint, smoky landscape beyond, this was all husk and shell lying by, all husk and shell, she could see nothing else, she was enclosed still, but loosely enclosed. There was a space between her and the shell. It was burst, there was a rift in it." (493)

Reading the image of the ubiquitous husks and shells as a metaphor for the man's world in which Ursula "is loosely enclosed," I would argue that the above passage dramatizes a moment when Ursula realizes that her independence can come only through the creation of a critical third space within the dominant world, through an on-going intervention into the man's world. To put it differently, her spatial politics is at work in a "rift" "between her and the shell," namely, a space that disrupts the man's world from within. However oppressive public space might be, it emerges here as a fundamentally dynamic and alterable social space—a site for restriction and confinement, on the one hand, and for negotiation and resistance, on the other, open to change and restructuration.

As we have seen, Ursula rejects both domestic and public spaces as they have been constituted in her time and place. What the rejection of domestic space indicates, however, is not so much her antipathy to the home or to her mother's capitulation to domesticity as her repudiation of the oppressive patriarchal home that would deny woman's identity and place, a home against which her mother, Anna, also fiercely rebelled, though with a limited success due to the huge cultural burden of motherhood and domesticity. Ursula's endeavor to realize her mother and grandmother's dream of entering into the public world of man brings her only a series of disillusionments and alienations, leading her to the final declaration of independence from the man's world. Yet, Ursula's rejection of the public world does not indicate Lawrence's inability to cope with the modern industrial world and the attendant anti-social temperament that privileges nature over society. What Ursula turns away from is not society in general but a specific form of society that threatens to annihilate integral selfhood and individuality, a form of the public sphere that Lydia, Ursula's grandmother, had once entered into and retreated from with anger and criticism. In this sense, Millett's contention that Ursula fails does not hold true either. Contrary to Millet's suggestion that the man's world rejects Ursula—an argument that dismisses Lawrence's criticism of the man's world—it is Ursula who rejects the man's world.

In sum, the spatial politics in *The Rainbow* are central to the novel's gender politics and social criticism. The novel challenges the conceptual and physical production of domestic and public spaces in contemporary society by various devices. First, the novel fights the patriarchal picture of domestic space that tends to naturalize or erase the unequal relation between women and men by bringing the exploitation of woman's labor in the home to the surface. In relation to this, the novel critically demonstrates how the conceptual and physical division between feminine/private and masculine/public spaces in a patriarchal society has restricted women's access to public space and their search for independence and self-realization, as well as reinforced the domination of man over woman both in domestic and public spaces. Far from making domestic and public spaces a purely oppressive structure, however, the novel envisions these places as sites of resistance and change as well.

Both domestic and public spaces in the novel surface as contested, dynamic, and multifaceted social spaces where women's spatial codes constantly expose and challenge the ideological implications of men's. In addition, by disrupting the place myth of public space as a world of emancipation and independence, the novel unveils various ideological limits and conditions that in fact annihilate integral selfhood and preclude self-realization. In these ways, the novel strives to destroy oppressive domestic and public spaces and to remold a vision of more liberating ones.

Chapter Two

As in Lawrence, domestic space in Woolf is a multifaceted, dynamic social space that individuals perceive and experience differently according to gender and class. Going against the Victorian picture of domestic space that mainly reflects the patriarch's perspective and experience, such works as *A Sketch of the Past,* "Great Men's Houses," and *Mrs. Dalloway* feature domestic places like a dining room, a drawing room, or a party table as a socio-historical arena produced by the labor of women and/or the working class. Although Woolf persistently exposes unequal power relations between different genders and classes in domestic space, she does not turn the space into a pure determinant of human life. Instead, she destabilizes its seemingly rigid structure and envisions the possibility of remolding it by foregrounding the often-obscured practices and spatial codes of the marginalized.

Similarly, public spaces in Woolf function as a critical tool for gender and class politics. As feminist critics have noted, public space in Woolf is usually associated with what the patriarchal society deprived women of: emancipation and professional life. But again as in Lawrence, Woolf's feminist spatial politics seeks woman's emancipation not through their participation in the man's world but rather through a more radical challenge to it, exposing problems like violence, inequality, and dehumanization, as evidenced by *Three Guineas.* While Woolf does not use the word "public" directly, there are a number of significant places outside domestic space in her works, opening a possibility to redefine and reshape public space. For example, the less-discussed work, *The London Scene,* unsettles the definitional and physical domain of public space from within by uncovering its fundamental constructedness, as well as the conflicts between different genders and classes.

REFIGURING DOMESTIC SPACE: *A SKETCH OF THE PAST* AND *MRS. DALLOWAY*

In her memoir *A Sketch of the Past* much of Woolf's childhood memory revolves around her family's alternating dwelling places, 22 Hyde Park Gate in London and Talland House in Cornwall. As shown briefly before, the domestic surroundings in the memoir—especially in the earliest memories of childhood that she likens to "a vast space" (78)—disclose the writer's psychological and emotional state through the association of domestic space with the ubiquitous, comforting maternal body, an association that is in line with the current discourse of the home. The portrayal of domestic space as a place of maternal nurture and harmony, however, is frequently disrupted, and the social and cultural context becomes increasingly prevailing, mirroring the shifting perspectives in Virginia's experience of domestic space along with her growth.

As Woolf's recollection moves on, 22 Hyde Park Gate—where she was born and lived for twenty two years—surfaces as a multifaceted site filled with complex networks of gender and class relations, "a complete model of Victorian society" (147). To begin with, it is a microcosm of the patriarchal society that exploits women's labor and annihilates their individuality through the ceaseless demand of housewifely duties. For example, Woolf points out how the mother's enormous burden to keep "the panoply of life," to satisfy her husband and seven children's needs makes her life "an extended surface," making her "a general present rather than a particular person" (83). It is also the place where Woolf first learned the Victorian training of feminine decorum, and confronted and fought with various cultural strictures on her social and intellectual aspirations as a woman. The house was like "a cage" where young Virginia had to "be shut up" while her brothers left home for school (116).

Rather than being a unified, harmonious haven, the family house in Woolf's memoir is a contested battleground for different genders and generations, a multifaceted site for oppression and resistance. Woolf writes: "Two different ages confronted each other in the drawing room at Hyde Park Gate. The Victorian age and the Edwardian age"(147). Indeed, the drawing room in the memoir features as one of the most conflicted places where two different temporalities and values—the father and the brothers living in 1860 and Virginia and her sister, Vanessa, living in 1910—constantly waged "bitter" and "violent" war (147), as epitomized by the green dress episode. According to Woolf's memory, when she turned up in the drawing room in her green dress, her brother George humiliated her by ordering her to "tear it up"

(151). As Woolf speculates, George's intolerance for the green dress goes beyond "aesthetic disapproval." His "enraged male voice" designates a furious interdiction against a possible "insurrection," or "defiance of his accepted standards." It is expression of "a serious displeasure" at the "infringement of a code" (151). The drawing room here functions as a socio-cultural space replete with tensions and conflicts, staging both the oppressive power of the dominant social code and the resistance to it.

It is important to note that it is in this oppressive drawing room that Woolf developed her critical perspective on gendered society—a precious asset for her future career as a feminist social critic. In this drawing room, a microcosm of a Victorian social system, Virginia felt "the outsider's feeling." She continues:

> I felt as a gipsy or a child feels who stands at the flap of the tent and sees the circus going on inside. I stood in the drawing room at Hyde Park Gate, and saw society in full swing. I saw George as an acrobat jumping through hoops. . . . The patriarchal society of the Victorian age was in full swing in our drawing room. It had of course many different parts. Vanessa and I were not called upon to take part in some of those acts. We were only asked to admire and applaud when our male relations went through the different figures of the intellectual game. (153).

The passage once again demonstrates how Woolf turns the drawing room into a site for challenge and resistance while documenting patriarchal oppression. Woolf was clearly aware of the subversive potential of the outsider's feeling informed by the experiences in the drawing room—the capability to question the authority of dominant social order. Subtly shifting the focus of the meaning of the outsider—from someone who is expelled to someone who is distant from, and thus critically "observant" of the center, as the word "spectator" in the following further confirms—Woolf transforms the drawing room from a site of oppression and exclusion into one of opposition and critical investigation. The outsider's feeling, she writes, "gave my attitude to George a queer twist. I must obey because he had force—age, wealth, tradition—behind him. But even while I obeyed, I marveled—how could anyone believe what George believed? There was a spectator in me who, even while I squirmed and obeyed, remained observant, note taking for some future revision" (154).

The domestic space of 22 Hyde Park Gate is replete with tensions and conflicts between different classes as well. In this place, Woolf began to sense and view critically her class privilege as a member of an upper-middle class family. In the memoir, Woolf shows how the class disparities instilled in the upper-middle class psyche are materialized by the very architecture of the house. For example, her father's great study with three windows at the top of the house (119) is not only an indicator of the patriarch's privilege—independence and privacy—but also a materialized sign of the hierarchical divisions between the classes. Visualizing the vertical structure of the house, Woolf takes a journey from the dark servants' sitting room, through the "very Victorian" dining room and the tea table—"the center of Victorian family life—to her father's great study, the "brain of the house" (116–19).

Instead of naturalizing class divisions embodied in the very structure of the house, Woolf questions their legitimacy by bringing latent tensions and conflicts between the classes to the fore. Note the following incident triggered by the inferior living condition of the servants within the house that took place in the dining room. Woolf recalls:

> The basement was a dark insanitary place for seven maids to live in. "It's like hell," one of them burst out to my mother as we sat at lessons in the dining room. My mother at once assumed the frozen dignity of the Victorian matron; and said (perhaps): "Leave the room"; and she (unfortunate girl) vanished behind the red plush curtain which, hooped round a semi-circular wire, and anchored by a great gold knob, hid the door that led from the dining room to the pantry. (116–17)

The passage is notable for a couple of reasons. The maid's complaint points to the unequal class relations materialized by the house. In addition, it illustrates the ways in which the dining room functions as a social space—a heterogeneous place that two classes use differently. It is a place for liberal education for the Stephen children and a work place for servants. It is also a place of both oppression and resistance in a similar way that the drawing room that we have seen was. The maid's potentially subversive voice is immediately silenced by the upper-middle class matron, and yet the episode still interrogates the power imbalance between the two classes in the Victorian household. As a matter of fact, in the passage Woolf keeps a critical distance from the oppressive power that both the mother and the house embody, while not entirely denying her own implication in the dominant socio-spatial system. She subtly inserts her critical view of the Victorian social order by exposing the cultural unconscious of the upper-middle class and its architectural manifestations. Note for example the seemingly passing remark about the plush curtain that "hid[es]" the passageway leading "from the dining room to the pantry." In my view, Woolf's description of the curtain's function in terms of "hiding" points to her critical awareness of the upper-middle class impulse to preserve the illusion of the homogeneous space of the dining room by "hiding" the reliance on servant's labor that the passageway leading to the pantry designates.

The following passage further illuminates the complexity of Woolf's spatial politics. Recollecting that "there were different smells on different landings of that tall dark house" (118), Woolf moves on to a memory of a visitor's unexpected "penetrat[ion]" into the servants' shabby bedrooms that caused her mother's embarrassment. She writes:

> My mother, I noted, seemed a little "provoked," a little perhaps ashamed, that he had seen what must have been their rather shabby rooms. My father's great study . . . was a fine big room, very high, three windowed, and entirely booklined. His old rocking chair covered in American cloth was the center of the room which was the brain of the house. (119)

Woolf's use of the words like "seemed" or "perhaps" draws our attention to the present writer's act of reading her mother's psyche, a psyche that Woolf was able to read because she, as a daughter of the upper-middle-class family, to some extent shares it with her mother. But at the same time those words suggest Woolf's distance from her mother as a critical observer, as further evidenced by her foregrounding of the "I" who self-consciously "noted" (and now recollects) the incident. That is, Woolf's report of the Victorian matron's embarrassment at the exposure of the shabby room points to her own sense of shame at the very existence of the inferior living condition of the servants. At the same time, it conveys Woolf's insight into the Victorian cultural psyche that was fundamentally ashamed of and wished to cover the shabby bases on which they built their selfhood, as intimated by the abrupt transition from the exposure of the servants' room to the father's study, representative of proud Victorian selfhood. Thus, the text foregrounds the spatially structured collective selfhood of the Victorian upper-middle class, constructed on the disparities and divisions between a dark, lower, and bodily place and a bright, higher, and intellectual one—as suggested by the comparison of the father's study to the "brain." To put it differently, the text bespeaks what Frederic Jameson termed the "political unconscious"—in the sense that it excavates the dominant cultural principle of division, the buried shame at disparities, and the fundamental connectedness between two spaces and classes that Woolf wishes at once to hide and to dig up.

Woolf's treatment of domestic space helps us look at the relation between gender and class politics in her works from a new angle. Woolf's class politics in relation to her feminism has generated divided responses from critics. To risk some simplification, critics like Jane Marcus have viewed Woolf's class politics as socialist, praising her inclusion of the class issue within the feminist agenda. For others, however, the very conflation of class and gender is problematic because it ultimately tends to obscure the class issue by subsuming it to the issue of gender. Arguing for the fundamental discrepancy between the fight with patriarchy and the critique of the class system, these critics contend that the attempt to combine these two is in danger of trivializing or neglecting the power imbalance between women of different social standings in the name of feminism.[1]

However, Woolf's treatment of domestic space in the memoir suggests that the class and gender politics of her writing is more complicated than the above debates assume. In my view, the above arguments—whether defensive or hostile to Woolf—fail to capture how Woolf changes her strategies, at times combining and at times differentiating the issues of gender and class. In other words, Woolf's concerns with women and/or the working class in regard to domestic space at times merge and at times diverge, depending on contexts and situations. Woolf's varying strategies, I believe, come from her understanding that to fight patriarchal tyranny in the house, it may be more effective to think through connections rather than disparities between the middle-class woman and servants in the name of the outsider, producer, and the obscured. Indeed, as we have seen in the memoir, when the focus falls on the privilege of men in the house, Woolf unites the mother and the maids through their ceaseless toil and labor, instead of highlighting power relations between these women. However, there are certainly other moments when Woolf differentiates lower class women from domineering (upper) middle-class women in terms of unequal social relations of exploitation and domination, as evidenced by the dining room scene where her mother is aligned with oppressive power.

"Great Men's Houses" and *Mrs. Dalloway* illustrate the significance of Woolf's treatment of domestic space in relation to the class and gender politics. To speak briefly in advance, in "Great Men's Houses" the overriding concern with the privilege of men in domestic space leads the writer to connect upper and lower class women through their labor and suffering in the house instead of differentiating them through class disparities. In the party scenes of *Mrs. Dalloway*, however, the focus falls on class relations as constituent of domestic space. Furthermore, the latter is notable because it suggests that when the issue of class is at stake, Woolf's political strategy becomes the more complicated, probably because of her self-consciousness of her own class privilege and reluctance to assume a naïve or hypocritical critical position as if she stood outside the class system. As exemplified by the dining room scene in the memoir, the party scenes in the novel play out interesting narrative strategies that demonstrate Woolf's careful exposure of class ideologies surrounding domestic space. While I am mindful of the varied emphases and strategies, I will try to demonstrate that domestic space in both works challenge the conventional picture of home and its ideological implications.

Woolf's essay "Great Men's Houses," which first appeared as one of the six articles published in *Good Housekeeping,* challenges the Victorian male discourses of home through the depiction of the house of two male literary figures—Thomas Carlyle and John Keats. The essay begins with a sketch of Carlyle's house that goes against the conventional tendency to erase women's labor in domestic space by emphasizing their ceaseless toil and suffering. In addition to the counter-cultural depiction of home, the essay is also notable in that it exemplifies a Woolfian strategic connection between women from different classes, a strategy that fits well the feminist fight with the patriarch's privilege in domestic space. The essay then proceeds to attack another cultural myth of home that has produced an illusion of domestic space as an enclosed haven entirely isolated from public space.

Beginning with an ironic statement that points to the male-centered city space, "London, happily, is becoming full of great men's houses," the narrator observes how a male writer like Carlyle enjoyed the private intellectual space "up in the attic under a skylight" while his wife and servants worked to provide a comfortable home for him (23). The essay offers a corrective to contemporary Victorian discourse by portraying the home from the perspective of women who provide men with the opportunity to pursue artistic and intellectual activities through their labor. Far from being a place for rest or intellectual activities, for women the house is a work place. While Carlyle "wrestl[es] with history," the house reverberates with "the voice of pumping and scrubbing, of coughing and groaning" (24). "Thus," the narrator continues, "number 5 Cheyne Row is not so much a dwelling place as a battlefield—the scene of labour, effort and perpetual struggle" (25). From the viewpoint of those exploited even the garden functions differently: for the man of letters, it is "a place of rest and recreation" but for Mrs. Carlyle and servants, it is no better than "another smaller battlefield" (25). Looking at the picture of Mrs. Carlyle, the narrator once again highlights woman's suffering and hard working in the man's house: "Her cheeks are hollow; bitterness and suffering mingle in the half-tender, half-tortured expression of the eyes. Such is the effect of a pump in the basement and a yellow tin bath up three pairs of stairs" (25). The stress on the patriarch's privilege in the house leads the narrator to bind women across different classes as the marginalized and exploited. Mrs. Carlyle and the "unfortunate" maids are connected through their common suffering and labor on the one hand, and through the image of the producer of the domestic space, on the other: "All through the mid-Victorian age the house was necessarily a battlefield where daily, summer and winter, mistress and maid fought against dirt and cold for cleanliness and warmth. The stairs, carved as they are and wide and dignified, seem worn by the feet of harassed women carrying tin cans" (24).

The essay goes on to challenge another myth of domestic space—a place of seclusion. Although the narrator depicts Keats—who was sick and poor—with much more sympathy, she disrupts the seemingly naïve romantic discourse that presumes home to be a perfectly isolated space. Subtly mocking "an air of heroic equanimity" that surrounds this poet's house, the narrator rather abruptly draws our attention to life "that goes on outside the window." She continues, "[l]ife goes on outside the wooden paling, when we shut the gate upon the grass and the tree where the nightingale sang we find, quite rightly, the butcher delivering his meat from a small red motor van at the house next door" (28). Through the image of the butcher outside the poet's house, the narrator suggests that domestic space can never be an entirely secluded, asocial haven, thus pointing to the fundamental interconnection between domestic/private and public spaces as well.

The challenge to the dominant spatial code finds a more complex expression as it touches on class relations in *Mrs. Dalloway*. To borrow Lefebvre's theory, two party scenes, Lady Bruton's party and Clarissa's party, in the novel advance the spatial politics that destabilizes the "fetishization" of domestic space by critically exposing the upper class psyche that is oblivious to the existence of the working class as a producer of space. To elaborate Lefebvre's theory further, one of Lefebvre's political projects that he wishes to achieve through the notion of social space is to shatter the fetishization of space, and ultimately the status quo. According to Lefebvre, a society has tried to maintain the status quo by obscuring "productive labor" and social relations that have generated space, thus, making us believe space to be a neutral background and take the dominant social order for granted. Lefebvre writes: "[P]roductive labour is sometimes forgotten altogether, and it is this 'forgetfulness'—or this mystification—that makes possible . . . fetishism"(113). In this respect, spatial politics in Lefebvre involves a fight with a forgetfulness that has worked to misrepresent, naturalize, or obscure the existence of labor and social relations involved in the production of social space. Anticipating Lefebvre, the depiction of Lady Bruton's party fights the fetishization of domestic space by drawing our attention to the working class labor while critically exposing the upper class psyche that upholds the dominant socio-spatial order. After unveiling the dominant spatial code and recuperating the existence of the generative force of the working class through Lady Bruton's party scene, the novel foregrounds the spatial code of the marginalized; it opens Clarissa's party scene with the gaze of the maids, a gaze that challenges the dominant social order.

To get a piece of advice on a letter concerning the issue of emigration that she intends to send to the Times, Lady Bruton invites Hugh Whitbread and Richard Dalloway along with other upper class acquaintances to her lunch. The luncheon party scene begins with an interesting depiction of the luncheon table. The matron's nearly godlike voice announces the start, giving an invitation to the guests on the one hand, and ordering servants' labor on the other:

> "But let us eat first," she [Lady Bruton] said. And so there began a soundless and exquisite passing to and fro through swing doors of aproned white-capped maids, handmaidens not of necessity, but adepts in a mystery or grand deception practised by hostesses in Mayfair from one-thirty to two, when, with a wave of the hand, the traffic ceases, and there rises instead this profound illusion in the first place about the food—how it is not paid for; and then that the table spreads itself voluntarily with glass and silver, little mats, saucers of red fruit; films of brown cream mask turbot; in casseroles severed chickens swim; coloured, undomestic, the fire burns; and with the wine and the coffee (not paid for) rise jocund visions before musing eyes; gently speculative eyes; eyes to whom life appears musical, mysterious; eyes now kindled to observe genially the beauty of the red carnations which Lady Bruton (whose movements were always angular) had laid beside her plate, so that Hugh Whitbread," feeling at peace with the entire universe and at the same time completely sure of his standing, said, resting his fork, "Wouldn't they look charming against your lace?" Miss Brush resented this familiarity intensely. She thought him an underbred fellow. She made Lady Bruton laugh. (104–05)

The luncheon table here is a social space. It appears as a heterogeneous place divided into labor and leisure. As Alex Zwerdling puts it, the passage exposes an entire social system "based on the power and wealth of one class and the drudgery of another," revealing how in this system the labor of the other is "easily ignored by master and servant alike" (126). Indeed, the passage shows that the servants are reduced to mere automatons directed by "a wave of the hand" in the very place they are maintaining and producing.

Furthermore, the passage demonstrates that the upper class has a psychological, conceptual, and physical experience of the space that is akin to what Lefebvre termed the fetishization of space. Note for example, the image of the nearly anthropomorphized table that "spreads itself voluntarily with glass and silver." The phrase bespeaks the upper class view of the luncheon table as something mysteriously given, a view that dismisses the labor of the working class that produces the place and the occasion for them. Through words like "mystery," "grand deception," and "profound illusion" the passage intimates that this upper class employs a deceitful and illusionary spatial code that makes one forget the working class as the producer of the space. It even makes one think of the food as being freely given to them without any cost. As the passage proceeds, it becomes clearer that the text mockingly exposes the upper class's blindness to the production of social space, as evidenced by the image of the "musing" and "speculative" eyes that relish the "jocund visions."

In addition, the passage shows how this ideological spatial code is connected to an illusionary sense of self, human relations, and reality. The repetitive verbal plays of "eye"/I here points to the upper class's illusory sense of self as well as the relation between self and other/universe. Such imaginary views of self, social relations, and reality in general culminate in the figure of Hugh, whose selfhood is forged and secured by a prior exploitation and erasure of the lower class and an attendant illusion of the harmony between himself and the "entire universe." In short, Lady Bruton's party scene indicts the amnesia regarding the production of social space, unequal relations, and the attendant ideological construction of self and other.

Lady Bruton's luncheon party prefigures the issues of class, identity, and the production of social space that are dealt with in the opening depiction of the Clarissa's party. Contrasting sharply with the mysterious and spontaneous luncheon table at Lady Bruton's, Clarissa's party scene actively brings the servants' busy movements, perspectives, and names—Lucy, Mrs. Walker, Jenny, Mrs. Parkinson, Mrs. Barnet, and so forth—into the narrative, drawing our attention to their existence as organizers and producers. Note the following:

> Lucy came running full tilt downstairs, having just nipped in to the drawing-room to smooth a cover, to straighten a chair, to pause a moment and feel whoever came in must think how clean, how bright . . . she appraised each; heard a roar of voices; people already coming up from dinner; she must fly! The Prime Minister was coming, Agnes said. . . . Did it matter, did it matter in the least, one Prime Minister more or less? It made no difference at this hour of the night to Mrs. Walker

among the plates, saucepans. . . . All she felt was, one Prime Minister
more or less made not a scrap of difference to Mrs. Walker. . . . But it
was the salmon that bothered Mrs. Walker. . . . (165)

In a sense, the fact that it is the working-class points of view that perceive,
record, and analyze the upper class people in the above passage can be interpreted as an active effort to restore their individuality and agency. Instead of
reducing these servants to a "generic identity" (Zwerdling 96), it is the Prime
Minister's identity and his authority that are blurred through a servant's
viewpoint. In this way, the passage reverses and dismantles the spatial code of
the privileged that has obscured the working class labor in domestic space
and marginalized their perspectives on and experience of their master's
house.

SPATIALIZING FEMINISM

The patriarchal division between private/domestic and public spaces was one
of Woolf's constant preoccupations. Woolf's critical view of the gendered
division and confinement of women to domestic space had been shaped
since her early career, as illustrated by a less known short story "The Journal
of Mistress Joan Martyn" written in 1906.[2] Woolf's feminist concern with
the separation of public and private space develops into a stronger criticism
in *Three Guineas* (1938), where the writer investigates a male-centered public
world structured by militarism, fascism, patriotism, sexism, and violence.
Joan's rather passive yearning for the man's world reappears in *Three Guineas*
as a more active and critical search for a radical intervention into public
space through a critical analysis of it. However, Woolf's strong antipathy
toward the public world that she sees as embodying various 'isms' and social
and psychological evils tends to render public space rather abstract and static
in *Three Guineas*. It is in *The London Scene* that Woolf's spatial politics finds
a more sophisticated and strategic articulation. While critically observing the
current socio-economic conditions and hierarchal social relations between
different classes and genders existent in various public places, Woolf figures
public space here as a more dynamic, alterable social space through her
emphasis on its constructedness, flexibility, and heterogeneity. Offering an
alternative perspective on authoritative as well as often-neglected places in
London, the essay collection destabilizes and broadens the definitional and
physical boundaries of public space that the society has set up.

"The Journal of Mistress Joan Martyn" is comprised of two parts. It
opens with a narrative of Rosamond Merridew, a historian who tells us how

her archeological zest compelled her to leave her husband and family to pursue her professional career. In her search of old manor houses, Rosamond encounters the fifteenth-century journal of a medieval woman named Joan Martyn among the Martyn family papers. The rest of the story is composed of excerpts from the journal that conveys Joan's sense of being confined to home and yearning for the man's world.[3] Like the Brangwen women in *The Rainbow*, Joan is unhappy about the narrow orbit of the "life of a woman" living like a "flitting shadow . . . unconsidered in her father's house" (51), and her longing for the man's world frequently takes her to the window that looks out on the world outside the home (48). Leaning upon the windowpane, she dreams of journeying to the city: "my thoughts naturally dwelt upon this journey [to London], and upon the great city which perhaps I may never see, though I am for ever dreaming of it" (48). With all her longing, Joan realizes that what waits for her in the future is a conventional life as a woman. The story ends with the "last pages" of the journal where Joan anxiously muses on the end of her writing and self, in the face of her impending marriage.

In *Three Guineas* (1938) Woolf's concern with the age-old exclusion of women from the world outside domestic space reoccurs in a more critical tone, as it is aligned with other socio-political issues of the time. Written in the form of a letter to a barrister who has asked Woolf how to prevent war, *Three Guineas* advances a feminist-pacifist critique by unraveling the complex threads that interweave the patriarchal social system with capitalism, militarism, patriotism, nationalism, fascism, imperialism, war, violence, and masculinity. Instead of summarizing Woolf's points, which many critics have already articulated, I want to show that the spatial politics in the essay is integral to Woolf's feminism by investigating her critical approach to public space—the man's world.

Throughout the essay the sense of exclusion from male/public space prevails. In the following passage, for example, the narrator critically observes the separation of spaces and the attendant routinization of spatio-temporal practices, both of which reflect unequal relations between women and men. Reminiscent of Joan looking enviously over the city from the window, the narrator watches men moving around the city from a window of her own:

> We who have looked so long at the pageant in books, or from a curtained window watched educated men leaving the house at about nine-thirty to go to an office, returning to the house at about six-thirty from an office, need look passively no longer. We too can leave the house, can mount those steps, pass in and out of those doors, wear wigs and gowns, make money, and administer justice. (61)

The passage conveys a more rebellious voice than "The Journal," a difference that is probably due to the changes that have probably happened by that time—both in the advancement of women entering into the public world and in the growth of Woolf's own spatialized feminism. Woolf proposes here that women's emancipation may begin with women's breaking the routinized socio-spatial barriers and occupying the forbidden spaces.

This does not mean, however, that Woolf simply equates woman's emancipation and independence with their occupation of the man's place. Like Ursula's search for independence, which moves toward a critical intervention into public space through a revolt against the ideological limits and practices of the man's world, Woolf's feminist spatial politics involves a critical analysis of and fight with the man's world and the problems that this space stands for and activates: fascism, sexism, violence, war, and so forth.

In fact, Woolf develops a complicated politics. She distinguishes her political stance from the male barrister's on the grounds that there is a "gulf" formed by their differences in education and status, a gulf that makes her relationship with public space different. Therefore, Woolf suggests, her reaction to public space cannot help but diverge from his reaction to it. Even while she agrees with the barrister's pacifist agenda, she writes that she still cannot but hesitate to "join your society" because her acute awareness of her marginalized status in the nation as a woman makes her doubt that her influence can be effective in preventing war. At first glance, as Woolf herself states, her refusal to join the barrister's society derives from her uncertainty about her impact on the public world. But a close reading suggests that Woolf's hesitation derives from a more complex and strategic calculation. To begin with, through her recurrent emphases on their different situations, and consequently their different views about and relations with war, nation, and other public affairs, Woolf intimates that despite his dissenting voice, the barrister is still an insider of a society that has marginalized women and fostered the various evils that he himself wants to fight.[4] As Woolf argues throughout the essay, diverse social and psychological evils that pervade the current world are rooted in the very structure that has produced the male-centered society. As long as the barrister benefits from that society, then, he still—though unwittingly—can help to perpetuate and reproduce its problematic social system. In this view, consenting to "become active members of your society" could mean the loss of her difference (104) from the barrister and ultimately, her subjugation to another male cause that seeks to utilize women.[5] Indeed, from the beginning, Woolf points to the barrister's complicity with the man's world. She proposes to describe his world "as it appears to us who see it from the threshold of the private house . . . from the bridge which connects the private house with the world of public life." She continues:

> Your world, then, the world of professional, of public life, seen from this angle undoubtedly looks queer. At first sight it is enormously impressive. Within quite a small distance are crowded together St. Paul's, the Bank of England, the Mansion House, the massive if funereal battlements of the Law Courts; and on the other side, Westminster Abbey and the House of Parliament. There, we say to ourselves . . . our fathers and brothers have spent their lives. All these hundreds of years they have been mounting those steps, passing in and out of these doors . . . administering justice. It is from this world that the private house . . . has derived its creeds, its laws, its clothes and carpets, its beef and mutton. And then, as is now permissible, cautiously pushing aside the swing doors of one of these temples, we enter on tiptoe and survey the scene in greater detail. (18–19)

Going beyond a critical exposure of the gendered spatial division between private and public space and the attendant exclusion of women from the man's world, the passage takes a more radical turn, as it intimates the subversive potential of the daughters of educated men as the marginalized within the man's world, while obliquely undercutting the authority of the barrister by pointing to his fundamental implication in the male-centered society, a society that she associates throughout the essay with world-wide violence and other evils. At this point, it is important to note that Woolf does not naively presume the privilege of women's perspective and their place (the private house) as a critical place outside the social system. As Woolf herself explicitly states, the private house (and women) have directly or indirectly supported the public world. The choice between private and public realms is not a real alternative, because each "the private house" and "the public world" is "bad" (86). But then, abandoning both spaces cannot be the solution either. Like Ursula, who "threatened" the social system "at the point where [she] is included" (391), Woolf's spatial politics seeks to dismantle and remold these spaces from within.

While mindful of her own implication in the public space produced by the dominant social system, Woolf explores a possibility for critical intervention into public space by posing a disruptive spatial code. Woolf—who had learned to take advantage of her position as an outsider in the Victorian house as a critical spectator, thus opening the oppressive domestic space to resistance and change—provides us with the image of the daughters of educated men

who "enter on tiptoe and survey" the public world "in greater detail," intimating their alternative spatial perspectives that challenge dominant ones.
The strong critical strain in *Three Guineas,* however, tends to depict public
space as a rather rigid, abstract, oppressive structure associated with various
"isms" and evils. It is in *The London Scene* that Woolf provides alternative
spatial codes that destabilize the discursive and physical structure of public
space by "enter[ing] on tip toe," "surveying" and remapping various public
places whose landscape ranges from the pompous architectures of St. Paul's,
Westminster Abbey, and the House of Commons to marginalized and
anonymous places like small city churches and a graveyard.

REMODELING PUBLIC SPACE

Woolf's six essays on London were originally called *Six Articles on London
Life* and appeared as installments in *Good Housekeeping*—a magazine that
primarily addressed a North American and European bourgeois readership—
in 1931 and 1932. The essays are "The Docks of London," "Oxford Street
Tide," "Great Men's Houses," "Abbeys and Cathedrals," "'This is the House
of Commons,'" and "Portrait of a Londoner." The first five essays were published as *The London Scene* in 1975.

The essays have recently begun to draw critical attention. Susan Squier,
for example, has read the essays as Woolf's socialist-feminist social commentary. Squier argues that Woolf attempts in the essays to attain "an authentic
voice" as a woman writer living in the patriarchal city marked by the contrast
between the comfortable surface world of the upper and the middle-classes
and the underworld of the working class (*Virginia Woolf and London* 3). In
Squier's view, however, the essays fail to offer a sustained social criticism;
some essays perform subversive politics through the affirmation of the freedom and vitality of the outsider over the security of the insider, but others
frequently drown out a realist portrait and social criticism, complying with
the conservative readership of *Good Housekeeping,* as evidenced by the narrator's frequent identifications with the insider—men and the consuming
upper and the middle-classes—at the end of the essays. For Squier, it is in
later works such as *Three Guineas* and *The Years* that Woolf's social criticism
blooms more fully.

In my view, Squier's dichotomy between insider and outsider is what the
essays in fact seek to destabilize. As Pamela Caughie points out, the narrator's
shifting identification reflects Woolf's refusal to step outside the social-eco-
nomic system in order to judge it, a refusal based on her awareness of her
own implication in it. From this perspective, Caughie contends that the six

essays register Woolf's "different" attitude toward the social order, an attitude that "neither accepts nor dismisses the supporting structures of society but exaggerates their functioning so they can be noticed, and changed" (130). Largely agreeing with Caughie's reading, my discussion attempts to show how reading the essays in light of a spatial code that simultaneously reflects and challenges the dominant social system can illuminate the spatial politics of the narrator's self-positioning.

Read together, these essays deliver the multifaceted and dynamic texture of London, refusing to fix its urban space in a single term. As the titles suggest, the itinerary of the narrator covers diverse locations, from domestic, commercial, political, and religious places to the places of rest, life, and death; from docks, streets, houses, and the House of Commons to churches and graveyards. Among the essays, the first two, "The Docks of London" and "Oxford Street Tide," deserve particular attention in that they most effectively convey the dynamic ambiguity of London through conflicting spatial codes. The essays disrupt the dominant socio-spatial order by exposing hidden disparities, contradictions, and the fundamental constructedness and mutability of the city. Through these spatial codes, London emerges as a multifaceted social space that is open to perpetual remodeling.

"The Docks of London," portrays the port of London and its surrounding scenery: the ships coming from India, Russia, and South America, the sordid dwelling places of the working class people whose labor underpins imperial mercantilism, and the "hub" of the city crowded with the upper and middle-class consumer and the "stateliest buildings,"—symbols of the social system governing the process of economic production (10). The essay ends with the narrator's observation that "a change in ourselves" can change the routine of the docks (14).

Comparing the first manuscript of the essay with the published version, Squier contends that the revised version has weakened the critical commentary on imperialism, utilitarianism, and commercialism. She makes this argument on the grounds that the writer deletes more overt depictions of the painful price for the process of commercial production and keeps aesthetic distance from the filthy dwelling places of the poor. Furthermore, Squier argues that the narrator's "self-congratulation" on the power to change the dominant socioeconomic order at the end of the essay reveals the narrator's identification with the consumer middle-class, signaling Woolf's turn toward complacency (*Virginia Woolf and London* 57). In my view, however, the changes that Squire points out reflect the writer's reluctance to assume a detached, self-righteous position to evaluate the social system and the subsequent search for an alternative critical spatial code.

Critics have usually neglected the fact that the essay begins with a male poet's words, which are quoted by the anonymous narrator:

> "Whiter, O splendid ship," the poet asked as he lay on the shore and watched the great sailing ship pass away on the horizon. Perhaps, as he imagined, it was making for some port in the Pacific. (7)

The perspective of the poet (which is delivered first in a direct quotation, and then in a free indirect discourse) gives way to that of an anonymous narrator who narrates from the second passage onwards. What is notable about this shift in narrative perspective at the beginning of the essay is that it invites us to look at the voice of the anonymous narrator in relation with that of the poet and to think about the significance of their juxtaposition. Throughout the essay, the narrator mocks, reverses, and challenges the poet's perspective on the cityscape. The second passage, for example, begins with the narrator's subtle rebuke about the aesthetic distance that the poet's posture and his view on the scenery of the Docks indicate: "However romantic and free and fitful they [ships] may seem, there is scarcely a ship on the seas that does not come to anchor in the Port of London in time" (7).

Instead of "lay[ing] on" the shore and watching the scenery, the narrator walks through the place. In contrast with the poet, who dismisses the socio-political contexts of working-class labor and imperialism in romanticizing the ship as an embodiment of freedom and glory, the *flâneuse* lays bare what the dominant social system has hidden or euphemized. The essay presents the port as a conflicted and dynamic social space produced by a series of "incongruous" juxtapositions of contrasting and contradictory features (9): the "splendid" "romantic," and "free" ships coming from colonized countries versus the "dismal" prospect of "dingy, decrepit-looking" warehouses and a "forlorn" "joyless," and "sinister dwarf city of workmen's houses" (8); the sordid trash dumps at the docks versus the "stateliest buildings" of the central city (10); trees and fields—the reminiscence of the past world of nature and "pleasure" before the onset of industrialism—versus factories. The home where the ships anchor is not a snug haven but the "most dismal" and "joyless" landscape filled with dingy warehouses and workingmen's houses.

In the narrator's eyes, the seemingly glorious ships are in fact no better than passive agents that serve the huge system of the imperial home/nation. Once they are anchored, the narrator notes, "a curious change takes place." She continues:

They have no longer the proper perspective of sea and sky behind them, and no longer the proper space in which to stretch their limbs. They lie captive, like soaring and winged creatures who have got themselves caught by the leg and lie tethered on dry land. (8)

As the essay proceeds, we come to see that it is not only ships but the entire place and its inhabitants that are "caught" by the dictation of "the authority of the city" (10). For the narrator, the city is "the knot, the clue, the hub of all those scattered miles of skeleton desolation and ant-like activity. Here growls and grumbles that rough city song that has called the ships from the sea and brought them to lie captive beneath its warehouses" (10). This observation is followed by the following passage:

> Barrels, sacks, crates are being picked up out of the hold and swung regularly on shore. Rhythmically, dexterously, with an order that has some aesthetic delight in it, barrel is laid by barrel, case by case, cask by cask . . . in endless array down the isles and arcades of the immense low-ceiled, entirely plain and unornamented warehouses. . . . And not only is each package of this vast and varied merchandise picked up and set down accurately, but each is weighed and opened, sampled and recorded, and again stitched up and laid in its place . . . by a very few men in shirt-sleeves. . . ." (11)

In a sense, the above passage points obliquely to the worker's slavery, which is already foreshadowed by the recurrent image of the ship "tethered" and "captive" to the social system. The prevailing passive mood in the above passage performs the ways in which the domination of utilitarianism, commercialism, and industrialism over this place entails the obscuration of the laboring human body. Indeed, in the following passage, the narrator states how "the temper of the Docks is severely utilitarian." Everything at this place is "tested for" their "mercantile value" (11) and measured in terms of the "needs of commerce" (14). In the passage cited above, utility and purpose come before individual human beings; it is only after a long lists of objects that "a very few men" appear. With the text having intimated the ceaseless labor lying behind the seemingly delightful façade, what the narrator calls "aesthetic delight" gains an ambiguous connotation. Pointing back to the poet's romantic perspective, the above passage suggests that aesthetic delight is contingent upon an emotional, social, and physical distance from the labor. In other words, the passage suggests how a sense of aesthetic delight at the sight of this place is in fact "caught" by, and thus complicit with the dominant social system in its blindness to and romanticization of human labor.

Certainly, the narrator of the essay is a middle-class person who is self-conscious about the class barriers that lie between the working-class and herself (and the middle- class consumer to whom she addresses in the essay): "If we turn and go past the anchored ships towards London, we see surely the most dismal prospect in the world" (8). The inevitable boundary that the pronoun "we" sets up between the middle and working classes is always in danger of turning the working class whom "we" observe—however sympathetically—into an object of observation. Or, it is easy to accuse the middle-class gaze directed at the other of complacency or aesthetic distance. At first glance, the narrator who feels "aesthetic delight" in the ways in which ant-like workers "rhythmically, dexterously, with an order" handle the spoils of the colonized land disclose her ideological limitations, despite her effort to distance herself from the poet's aesthetic perspective on the place. From this perspective, following Squier, we may argue that the critical edge the narrator displayed at first is dulled.

Of course, it is hard to tell in the passage cited above whether the narrator self-consciously exposes the ideological limits of her sense of delight at the Docks. One might argue that she unwittingly reveals the ideological limits that she shares with the poet. However, a close reading of another passage where the narrator brings up the "element of beauty" helps us to view the narrator's remark about "aesthetic delight" from a different perspective. In the midst of her depiction of utilitarianism and commercialism, the narrator states:

> [E]very commodity in the world has been examined and graded according to its use and value. Trade is ingenious and indefatigable beyond the bounds of imagination. . . . And the aptness of everything to its purpose, the forethought and readiness which have provided for every process, come, as if by the back door, to provide that element of beauty which nobody in the Docks has ever given half a second of thought to. The warehouse is perfectly fit to be a warehouse; the crane to be a crane. Hence beauty begins to steal in. The cranes dip and swing, and there is rhythm in their regularity. The warehouse walls are open wide to admit sacks and barrels; but through them one sees all the roofs of London . . . the unconscious, vigorous movements of men lifting and unloading. (13)

The passage is about how the sense of beauty—to which no workers in the Docks "has ever given half a second of thought"—"steals in" to the psyche of the middle-class consumer, the onlooker at the place of labor and commercialism. The passage points to the ways in which the ideological spatial code erases workers' bodily and psychological existence through the image of "indefatigable" commerce. Instead of the "dingy, decrepit-looking warehouses," this spatial code celebrates its fitness to its function: "The warehouse is perfectly fit to be a warehouse" (12). To put it differently, the narrator confronts the middle-class with the ideological limits of their own discourse by constantly pointing to the discrepancy between a critical spatial code and an ideological, aestheticized, romanticized one. In this way, the narrator warns us that the seemingly innocent amazement and delight at the urban scenery is in fact constructed through the ideological blurring of working people's labor and poverty. It is simply a by-product of the social system; "Use produces beauty as a by-product," she notes (13).

From this perspective, we can read the narrator's remark about change at the end of the essay differently as well. She writes that "the only thing, one comes to feel, that can change the routine of the docks is a change in ourselves"(14). The impulse to change the routine, I think, is inherently incompatible with the sense of complacency, given the fact that the word "complacency" connotes the state of satisfaction and stasis, and thus, that it can be associated with the desire to relish the benefits of the social system as it is. Furthermore, considering that the routine of the docks the narrator portrays is characterized by incongruous juxtapositions that point to the exploitation of the working class labor, their poverty, and the unequal distribution of wealth throughout the urban area, the call for change sounds more critical than complacent and conservative. The narrator continues, "[i]t is we—our tastes, our fashions, our needs—that make the cranes dip and swing, that call the ships from the sea" (14). Reading this passage as an expression of self-congratulation on the power of the middle-class consumer, Squier contends that it signals the narrator's (Woolf's) turn toward a conservative position. Unlike Squier, I argue that this passage points once again to the ideological limits of middle-class psychology by intimating the affinity between the middle-class's power to "call the ships from the sea" and the tyrannical city whose constant "growl and grumble" "call the ships from the sea and brought them to lie captive beneath its warehouses" (10). Through the image of the consumer, the narrator suggests how the middle-class has helped to make the city that is the "hub of all those scattered miles of skeleton desolation and ant-like activity" (10). In other words, the narrator reminds middle-class readers of their contribution to the unequal distributions of labor, wealth, and quality of life, while avoiding the assumption of a self-righteous voice of admonition. At the same time, through her appeal to middle-class power to change, the narrator calls for a collective effort to change the "routine of the docks," and so to contribute to making a less exploitive and unjust society. In this way, Woolf differentiates the middle-class from the city—a metonymy of the dictatorial abstract social system—in terms of agency.

In short, the essay shatters mindless middle-class self-complacency embedded in the everyday experience of and perspective on the urban area by exposing its complicity with the oppressive social system. Challenging the ideological blindness embedded in conventional spatial codes (such as the male poet's or that of the complacent middle-class), the narrator offers another spatial code that relocates the docks and the surrounding urban area in a material socio-economic context, a code that unveils, not erases, the daily toil of the workers, their inferior living conditions, and the larger socio-economic system as well. Instead of assuming a self-righteous critical position, Woolf exposes both the ideological limits and subversive potential through the narrative perspective that she at once shares and criticizes.[6] In this way, the docks and the surrounding area emerge as a contradictory and heterogeneous social space, the meaning of which varies—from freedom, leisure, and beauty to poverty and toil—according to social standings. Urban space is subjugated to a larger social system, and yet it is alterable.

The next essay, "Oxford Street Tide," develops a more powerful spatial politics by exploring the conflicting spatial codes that render Oxford Street dynamic, flexible, and mutable. The essay begins with the "city change" that the narrator encounters as she navigates through Oxford Street, leaving behind the "crudity" and "enormity" of the docks (16). As in "The Docks" to some extent, the essay achieves its critical force through a narrative strategy that echoes and subverts the dominant spatial code, thus reflecting the narrator's simultaneous implication in and resistance to the social system. For example, the narrator's enthusiasm at the affluence and excitement of the urban spectacle is somewhat akin to the perspective of Hugh Whitbread who has a little job at Court, dallying in front of shops in Oxford Street, a figure heavily satirized in *Mrs. Dalloway*. As the essay proceeds, however, we come to see a profound difference behind the surface affinity between these two figures. In contrast with Hugh, the narrator of the essay does not fall into naïve complacency and superficiality. Hugh—who "do[es] not go deeply," "brush[ing] surfaces," "afloat on the cream of English society" (155)—is blind and deaf to the suffering and inequalities present in the urban space in contrast to the narrator, who is attentive to them. She writes of the many tragedies of the urban inhabitants that permeate the "gaudy" street—divorces, suicides, anxiety, poverty that forces a woman to steal, and the travails of sellers who live from hand to mouth, shrinking from the surveillance of the police. In this way, the

narrator highlights the "careless[ness]" and "remorseless[ness]" of the city
where "life is a struggle" (22), instead of enjoying the place as a mere spectacle. At this point, the contrast between the docks and Oxford Street suggested at the beginning collapses. Both places embody "the pressure of
making a living" (21).

On one level, considering the social criticism that Woolf's predecessors
like Charles Dickens achieve through their penetrating portraits of the
underside of urban life, the narrator's record of the "thousand voices" of agonized urban inhabitants from various social standings in the essay is not
unique (21). On another level, however, as in "The Docks of London," the
essay is notable in that it carefully advances the politics of spatial code by pit-
ting the middle-class narrative voice against another middle-class, but more
conservative one. Noting the "city change," the narrator says: "Oxford Street,
it goes without saying, is not London's most distinguished thoroughfare.
Moralist have been known to point the finger of scorn at those who buy
there, and they have the support of the dandies" (16). As the essay proceeds,
it becomes clear that the narrator makes a self-conscious effort to distance
her spatial code from that of a male moralist—"a man with a balance in the
bank" (21). The presence of the male moralist here obliquely reveals the narrator's self-consciousness about the ideological limits that she might share
with him as a woman from a privileged class; like the moralist himself, the
narrator muses on the cityscape, walking through the street. But the narrator
differentiates herself from the moralist in terms of financial status, while subtly building a connection between herself and the urban poor. Having dissociated herself from the moralist, the narrator draws on his vocabulary only to
transform its conservative impetus into a subversive one. Unlike the narrator,
the moralists "point the finger of scorn" at everything that is "flimsy." The
narrator continues: "For such thinness, such papery and powdery brick
reflect, they [the moralists] say, the levity, the ostentation, the haste and irre-
sponsibility of our age" (19). While the moralist who values solidity and stability indicts the city of levity and mutability, the narrator tells us that she is
fascinated by the very consistent shifts, flimsiness, and transitoriness of a
modern commercial center, because she detects the subversive possibility for
change in the flimsy façade of the city (21). For her, Oxford Street has been
built by shattering the "illusion of permanence" that the old builders, their
patrons, and the nobility of England held on to (20). In this sense, the narrator intimates, Oxford Street disrupts the conservative impulse to privilege
architectural durability that is embedded in the moralist's spatial code, a code
that inherits the legacy of a more rigid hierarchal society. "The charm of
modern London," the narrator continues," is that it is not built to last; it is

built to pass. . . . We do not build for our descendants . . . but for ourselves and our own needs. We knock down and rebuild as we expect to be knocked down and rebuilt. It is an impulse that makes for creation and fertility. . . . The mere thought of age, of solidity, of lasting for ever is abhorrent to Oxford Street" (19–20). To reiterate, the narrator dismantles the spatial code of the male moralist by exposing its ideological limits, while turning the very vocabulary that she appropriates from him to a subversive impetus that resists the status quo.

Together with celebrating the changeability of the city, the narrator portrays London as a more inclusive and variegated space produced by people from various social standings and backgrounds than in "The Docks." In a sense, the city in "The Docks" was somewhat statically divided—oppressive to the lower class and beneficiary to the privileged—and the "we" is the middle-class reader. But here the city is a more flexible place that hails differences and challenges. Furthermore, the narrator's evocation of "we" as builders of the ever-changing city adds a new dimension of meaning to the city dweller. Rather than simply depicting the less privileged as passive victims, Woolf restores the suffering, afflicted, and oppressed who appeared at the beginning to the status of producers of London. Or, to put it more precisely, the narrator seeks to bridge different classes by attributing the collective potential to remold the city to a more inclusive and hybrid urban population.

My interpretation is confirmed by the connection that the narrator makes between different classes through the two images—an umbrella point and a workman's pick—that function as the metaphors for subversive force to unsettle the urban socio-spatial order. Note the following:

> [I]t cannot be denied that these Oxford Street palaces are rather flimsy abodes—perhaps grounds rather than dwelling places. One is conscious that one is walking on a strip of wood laid upon steel girders, and that the outer wall, for all its florid stone ornamentation, is only thick enough to withstand the force of the wind. A vigorous prod with an umbrella point might well inflict irreparable damage upon the fabric. . . . [A]ny day of the week one may see Oxford Street vanishing at the tap of a workman's pick as he stands perilously balanced on a dusty pinnacle knocking down walls and façades as lightly as if they were made of yellow cardboard and sugar icing. (19)

As I suggested above, the essay's stress on the changeability and ephemerality of urban space fights the illusion of the city's stability that is cultivated by dominant ideologies. The passage suggests that much subversive mutability derives from critical urban inhabitants from both the (upper) middle and working classes—who are at once builders and destroyers of the city. The curious association of the image of the umbrella—a synecdoche of the upper and the middle-class—with destructive force rather than with power or authority reveals Woolf's awareness of the subversive potential that her own writing carries. Like the "vigorous prod with an umbrella point," her pen "inflict[s] irreparable damage" upon the fabric of the city through the relentless exposure of the ideologically obscured underside of urban space. The image of the umbrella leads to a more powerful image of a "workman's pick" that literally and symbolically demolishes the urban structure, while blurring the distinction between the classes through their shared subversive power.

Through these devices, Oxford Street in the essay surfaces as a multifaceted place for struggle and conflicts, as well as excitement. While critically unveiling the inequalities and hardships of the urban dwellers interwoven with the affluent and gaudy façade of the street, the essay goes beyond the mere reproduction of the dominant social order by consistently pointing to the "perishable" structure of the city (22).

In "Oxford Street Tide" the narrator states that "it is vain to try to come to a conclusion in Oxford Street" (22). Together with "The Docks of London," "Oxford Street Tide" refuses to subsume the complex texture of various urban places to a single authoritative spatial code. By juxtaposing different spatial codes the essays show that our perception and experience of space is not neutral but always cultural and ideological. The essays constantly draw our attention to the oppressive social system that shapes urban space by highlighting the experiences of the marginalized. Yet instead of rendering London as a purely oppressive structure, the essays feature it as a flexible and dynamic space, an open site for different discourses and practices. In these ways, these essays offer a vision of alternative public space—an ambiguous and flexible place pregnant with infinite ambiguities, conflicts, and change, at once oppressive and liberating.

* * *

Lawrence's and Woolf's critical approaches to the conventional ways of structuring, conceptualizing, and representing private and public spaces are integral to their class and gender politics and social criticism. Challenging the dominant spatial codes that contribute to maintaining the status quo by obscuring unequal power relations between different genders and classes that exist in both private and public spaces, Lawrence and Woolf demonstrate that every space is produced by and reifies social relations, exploitations, and domination. Far from rendering private and public spaces as a purely oppressive determinant of human life, however, Lawrence and Woolf figure private and public spaces as social space—a heterogeneous and dynamic socio-cultural arena filled with conflicts, tensions, and resistances, a multifaceted space that individuals perceive, interpret, and use differently according to their social standings and individual experiences. In other words, Lawrence and Woolf shatter the conceptual and actual ground of private and public spaces by uncovering their constructedness, thus, suggesting that however oppressive these spaces may seem they have been always challenged and disrupted from within the social system. As Lefebvre suggests, the production of social space and that of spatial codes are deeply interconnected and mutually constitutive. In this way, Lawrence's and Woolf's representation of public and private spaces as social space, together with their employment of subversive spatial codes, ushers us into a new way of conceptualizing, producing, and envisioning human geography.

Remolding Home and Nation

Part Two Introduction

In the previous section, we have seen how Lawrence and Woolf expose the ideological implications embedded in the Victorian picture of domestic space as being maternal, asocial, harmonious, and permanent. In this section, I investigate the ways in which Lawrence and Woolf challenge other key components of the Victorian idea of home: the emphasis on protection, enclosure, and safety, components that sustain another domestic space as well, the nation.

As Malcolm Andrews suggests in his discussion about Charles Dickens' complex portrayal of England, the idea of home in the Victorian era can be characterized as "all that is enclosed and sheltered" by "walls" (2). In *Dickens and the Concept of Home,* Frances Armstrong also characterizes the Victorian concept of home in terms of "shelter," physical and psychological "walls," "a sense of "comfort," and "protection" (3). According to Armstrong, the sense of rapid change and unpredictability that prevailed in the Victorian era fuelled an impulse in the contemporary English to create the fantasy of home as a kind of substitute for religious faith (16). Armstrong argues that the Victorian English sought to build a psychological and physical home that promised enclosure and eternity through the equation of heaven and home based on "the Biblical image of the house of many mansions" (15).

In a number of instances we witness the Victorian English imagining home and nation in similar terms—such as enclosure and protection. In "On Queen's Garden," for example, John Ruskin regards both home and nation primarily as places where various virtues like order, comfort, and love are realized, and thus, are precious territories to defend. He writes:

> Now the man's work for his own home is, as has been said, to secure its maintenance, progress, and defence; the woman's to secure its order, comfort, and loveliness. Expand both these functions. The man's duty

as a member of the commonwealth, is to assist in the maintenance, in the advance, in the defence of the state. The woman's duty, as a member of the commonwealth, is to assist in the ordering, in the comforting, and in the beautiful adornment of the state. (*Sesame and Lilies* 136)

Dickens also depicts the Victorian ideal of home as a place of "comfort, cleanliness, and decency," which serves as a basis for the Victorian national identity and stability (Andrews 6).

The cultural tropes such as the single-family house, the English country house, or an island further illustrate the preoccupation with privacy and enclosure that bound the idea of home and nation during the Victorian period. According to Sharon Marcus, the architectural debates between 1840 and 1880 that privileged the single-family house in England over apartments in France often privileged the concept of a superior English national identity which secures privacy and enclosure. The country house is another example that demonstrates the home/nation analogy. According to Raymond Williams, from about 1880—the period that saw the birth of Lawrence and Woolf—there was "a marked development of the idea of England as "home," and the English country house was one of the central metonymies for the nation (*The Country and the City* 281). Another cultural trope that bound home and nation is that of an island. As Armstrong notes, the image of an island in Dickens' early novels evokes both home and nation. As Dickens' depiction of the islands in *A Child's History of England,* Ruskin's frequent references to "our little island," and a recent scholar, T. A. Jenkins' definition of Britain as first and foremost "an island nation" suggest, the idea of an island has long been central to English national identity (Andrews xv, xvi; Jenkins *Britain* 4). Although each of these tropes has different connotations, they are similar in that all of them fit well into the Victorian valorization of protection, enclosure, and safety. The country house met the need for "the isolated alien settlement" and a sense of "belonging" (Williams 281), and the idea of an island similarly evoked a sense of isolation as well as a sense of exclusive community.

As other studies have discussed, and part of my discussion in the previous chapter demonstrates, the ideological implications of the Victorian ideal of home and nation are multiple. For example, the Victorian cult of domesticity that underscored domestic virtues like "cleanliness" and "decency"— virtues that sustained the national identity as well—also functioned to maintain the patriarchal social order. The Victorian ideology of home oppressed women by imposing tremendous burdens of responsibility and duties as the center of home and a bearer of the national identity (Andrews

6). From another angle, the alignment of home and nation during the Victorian era can be seen as an effort to reintegrate the nation that was undergoing swift and dynamic social and religious changes and increasing inequities of wealth and social unrest. My focus in this section is on the ideological implications embedded in the emphasis on enclosure and safety that prevailed in the discourse of home and nation, ideological implications that Lawrence and Woolf rigorously investigate and criticize.

The stress on the need to enclose and protect the sacred home goes hand in hand with the view of the world outside the home as dangerous, vicious, and hostile. Indeed, for Ruskin, one of the primary responsibilities of the husband is to make sure that "the outer life" does not penetrate the home (qtd. in Armstrong 15). Once "the hostile society of the outer world" enters, Ruskin states, "it ceases to be home; it is then only a part of that outer world" (Armstrong 15). In a similar vein, the image of the island as a metaphor for a home in Dickens also reveals an impulse to secure isolation in the face of the possible invasion from without.

Lawrence Stone's recent article about the "stately homes of England" from the years between 1500 and 1990 offers a useful entry point to think about the emphasis on walls and enclosure from a different perspective. Stone's study shows how the increasing call for privacy as a central value of home in the nineteenth century was materialized by the English country house through the erection of walls within and outside the home, walls that segregated different classes and genders within the home, as well as achieved privacy for all members of the household from the world outside. To put it differently, Stone's study suggests that the seemingly neutral or even "positive" "moral and psychological" attributes like "intimacy," "security" or "privacy" associated with the word "home" are in fact ideological (227). Indeed, changes in the architectural features of the English house between 1500 and 1900 testify to the connection between the demand for privacy and socio-spatial "segregation" as well as "discrimination" based on class, race, and gender (235). According to Stone, the country house as English family home also entails the hierarchal division between inside and outside, between "the superior moral virtues of a country life"(the home), on the one hand, and the essentially degrading city life (the public world), on the other (231). In a similar vein, Marcus' study of the architectural debates during the Victorian era demonstrates that the emphasis on privacy and enclosure reflects the Victorian (upper) middle-class aversion to socio-geographical mingling with people with lower social standings. According to Marcus, the debates also illustrate how the English family-house functions as a signifier for the Victorian national identity that the English wanted to propagate in reference to other inferior nations.

From this perspective, the emphasis on enclosure, protection, safety, hygiene, and morality that permeates both the architectural manifestation and the discourse of home and nation becomes ideologically suspicious. As Stone points out, the search for privacy and enclosure always involves the question of who is excluding whom and leads the inhabitants to erect barriers that physically and morally distinguish the inside(r) from the outside(r). As T. A. Jenkins suggests in his introduction to *Britain: A Short Story*, the geographical condition of Britain as an island nation gave the British an "acute perception of the boundaries between themselves and others," a perception that complied with the attempt to define the national identity in reference to other nations and peoples and supported imperial expansion as well (4).

The aim of this section is to explore the ways in which Lawrence and Woolf expose ideological implications or power relations embedded in the ideal of home and nation. Or, to borrow Michel Dillon's words, I examine how these writers excavate those instances where the discourse of home functions as the "progenitor" of a "discourse of danger" (*Politics of Security* 16). Indeed, Dillon's observations concerning the "politics of security" illuminated the ideological implications embedded in the Victorian middle-class preoccupation with safety, enclosure, and the possibility of the invasion from the outside during a period when the nation saw an increasing monopolization of wealth by the middle-class and rapid imperial expansion.

Lawrence's and Woolf's critical investigation of the preoccupation with enclosure and safety touches on the fundamental questions that Dillon raises in his recent book *Politics of Security*. Words like safety and protection, which I address in reference to the ideology of home and nation, are not exactly identifiable with what Dillon calls "security." For Dillon, security signifies the entire scheme of "continental thought" that he seeks to deconstruct, a scheme that has consolidated brutal networks of "power-knowledge" in Western civilization and "discourses of Modernity" (16). To elaborate, the word "security" in Dillon is a kind of signifier invested with "a plurality of meanings," a signifier which finds its expression as "the principle, ground or *arche*." Security is concerned with securing the "very ground of what the political itself is," and in this respect, it is what metaphysics pursues (13). Like Derrida's *différance*, security is neither a concept to be analyzed, nor "a noun that names something" (16). Instead, it is "a principle of formation" whose "terminal paradox" "subverts its own predicate of security" (15).

Despite surface differences, there are interesting affinities between Dillon's observations and Lawrence's and Woolf's critical explorations of the ideology of home and the nation. To elaborate on this point, I will briefly discuss Dillon's deconstructive reading of Leibniz's observations. In a passage quoted by Dillon, Leibniz writes: "If one builds a house in a sandy place, one must continue digging until one meets solid rock or firm foundations. . . . In the same way, if one is to establish the elements of human knowledge some fixed point is required, *on which we can safely rest and from which we can set out without fear* (emphasis in original, 13). For Dillon, this passage suggests the fact that there is no such a thing as an *a priori* ground for Western metaphysics. Western metaphysics is always already something that has been constituted by the "need for the familiar," the need that arises out of the *instinct of fear*" (emphasis in original, 17). For Dillon, the passage is an example of how the politics of security "bears its own deconstruction within itself" (22). According to Dillon, the impulse that lies behind the urge to secure security, or behind the need for knowledge, is the "will to uncover under everything strange, unusual, and questionable, something that no longer disturbs us," and this insatiable enterprise of power-knowledge has specified what it is to be "the political," "what it is to be human," what it is to be the "ideal community," or, what "makes us the 'we' of the 'West'" (17, 13, 19). Dillon's project to "make security questionable" therefore involves "the exposure of the processes of valuation," exposure that alerts us to "what is being devalued as well" (32). In sum, deconstructing the politics of security helps us to confront the following questions: "what does a representation of danger make of 'us' and of those who are not 'us'?" "How does the specification of threat and its discourse of danger determine the 'who,' the 'we,' and the 'what' that is said on the one hand to be endangered, and on the other to be doing the endangering?" "[F]rom whence does the anger in (d)anger arise?" In addition, Dillon asks, "What is lost and forgotten, and who or what pays the inevitable price, for the way that 'we' are thus habited in fear?" (35).

A close look at the ways in which Lawrence and Woolf investigate and challenge the ideology of home and nation conveys a political significance that is similar to that involved in Dillon's deconstructive approach to Leibniz. Although Dillon does not draw direct attention to the significance of the house, which Leibniz uses as a metaphor for human knowledge, his observations concerning "security" as the (absent) ground of Western metaphysics are suggestive for addressing the idea of home. If there is a close affinity between a house and knowledge, it is not so much because both are to be firmly grounded in a secure spot. Instead, the affinity between the two comes from the fact that both of them always involve the process of representing danger and the Other as a way of speaking about and securing safety and the Self, a process of exclusion and denigration inseparable from that of inclusion and valorization. Like Dillon who is concerned with "how security is spoken about, and who or what does the speaking" (15), Lawrence and Woolf explore how the ideal of home and nation is spoken about, and who or what does the speaking.

Anticipating Gilles Deleuze and Félix Guattari's statement that "home does not preexist," but the building of home always "involves an activity of selection, elimination and extraction" (*A Thousand Plateaus* 311), Lawrence and Woolf expose the impulse to domesticate or expel those outside the home/nation. They also anticipate Dillon in their awareness that this exclusionary homemaking impulse is tied up with the politics of identity and difference, politics that privilege the insider and his/her exclusionary community—home—over the outsider. Woolf and Lawrence question the very process of valuation and devaluation embedded in the discourse about home, exposing how the obsessive call for securing the safe home is in effect indicative of an anxiety about and fear of the dominator. Lawrence and Woolf disrupt "the house" built on the process of domesticating, denigrating, or "extirpating the 'foreign, strange, uncanny, [and] outlandish'" (Nietzsche, *The Gay Science* 109; qtd. in Dillon 35) by disclosing the "inescapable violence and the dogmatic imperatives" sequestered within such a seemingly innocent discourse of home and nation (Dillon 33).

Jacque Derrida's reflection on the status of "Marx" and/or Marxist social goals in the wake of the collapse of communism is relevant to my discussion here. The immediate context in which Derrida's book *Specters of Marx* is located may appear distant from the concern of my study. However, Derrida's observations concerning "Marx—*das Unheimliche*" that are propelled by the author's questions about the "nature of responsibility" as a Western scholar in the face of the emerging new international order–are especially suggestive of the politics of Lawrence's and Woolf's critique of the ideology of home and the nation (174; Magnus and Cullenberg, "Introduction" x). Let me briefly discuss his reflection on the German idiom *Es spukt*. As a way of explaining the status of Marx as a specter that haunts this era, Derrida notes how "we" are filled with "anxiety and the desire to exclude the stranger" (*das Heimliche-Unheimliche*) who haunts us (172). He continues, "one confuses what is *heimliche-unheimliche* . . . with the terrible or the frightful" (173). For Derrida, such a confusion, or, in Dillon's words, such a discourse of danger, is the very (absent) ground on which the entire imperial scheme has been founded and/or searched, a scheme that has formed the "we," our "ideal community," or, "home." The construction of the fearful image of the Other in turn has worked to justify the cause of subjugating, domesticating, or expelling the "stranger," since "fear is not good for the serenity of research and the analytic distinction of concepts" (173). Derrida continues: "Marx remains an immigrant *chez nous*" (174). Here, it is no accident that Derrida evokes the idea of home, or the house with the French phrase that means "at our house," "home," or "room." The issue of the self and the Other is integral to building a home. He continues:

> He [Marx—*das Unheimliche*] belongs to a time of disjunction, to that "time out of joint" in which is inaugurated, laboriously, painfully, tragically, a new thinking of borders, a new experience of the house, the home, and the economy. . . . One should not rush to make of the clandestine immigrant an illegal alien or what always risks coming down to the same thing, to domesticate him. To neutralize him through naturalization. To assimilate him so as to stop frightening oneself (making oneself fear) with him. He is not part of the family, but one should not send him back, once again, him too, to the border. (174)

In works of Lawrence and Woolf we frequently witness the haunting Other who knocks on the door of the house. But this does not mean that these writers alert us to the existence of the fearful Other outside the home, for, doing so is no better than simply reproducing the imperial drive that sustained the production of the ideology of superior home, self, and nation. Instead, the focus in these writers falls on insiders' fear of and anxieties about outsiders and the problematic ways in which insiders seek to assimilate, naturalize, domesticate, or expel the strange Other. Lawrence and Woolf expose how the rhetoric of defending the safety of the home is tied up with the aversion to socio-spatial mingling with the Other, as well as with the formation of the superior self that is inseparable from the process of Othering. Through these means, these writers destabilize the home and the nation from within and seek to envision a less exclusionary and more open structure for self, home, nation, and ultimately for human relationships.

In Chapter Three, I investigate the ways in which Lawrence exposes ideological implications embedded in the Victorian idea of home and its mirror image of the nation. In essays like "On Coming Home," "Germans and English," and "Returning to Bestwood," Lawrence unveils the Victorian middle-class egotism, the sense of superiority, the aversion to contact with others, and imperialism that lie beneath the desire to secure a safely enclosed home and nation. A short story "England, My England" demonstrates that the ideal of a safe home serves to maintain and justify tyrannical domination and suggests that the territories of both the Victorian home and the imperial nation are sustained by violent exclusion of any unconventional or disturbing others. In his novella *The Virgin and the Gipsy,* the critical exposure of ideological implications underpinning the construction of the psychological and physical home, self, and nation leads to a more subversive vision of the destruction of the Victorian household. Through the protagonist who crosses over the threshold of the house for the forbidden meeting with a gipsy man, the story exposes the ways in which the Victorian fantasy of home is sustained by the stigmatization of the Other. The story culminates in the image of the rectory house being demolished by water at the end, an image that Lawrence self-consciously associated with a politics of literature. *Kangaroo* explores the ways in which the conventional idea of home can serve as a basis for a problematic view of self, Other, and human community in general. Through the protagonist's at times contradictory, at times subversive, musings on home, self, and the dark god, the novel destabilizes the ideology of home and nation from within and moves toward a better vision of home and nation.

In Chapter Four, I examine the political significance of the ways in which Woolf deals with the idea of home and nation. In her short story "The Journal of Mistress Joan Martyn," Woolf shows how the discourse of home that underscores safety and enclosure can function to domesticate, stigmatize, or expel less privileged people who are outside the territory of home and the nation. By analyzing the image of the English country house, the waves, and the characters' soliloquies on their self, home, and nation in *The Waves,* I argue that the novel deconstructs the imperial home and nation. In my reading of *The Years,* I show the ways in which the novel problematizes the Victorian middle-class aversion to socio-spatial mingling with marginalized urban popularity by investigating the Pargiter family's diverse reactions to the changing architecture of home from the single-family house to flats and rented rooms in urban areas in London. Although the novel conveys the deep anxiety of the middle-class family in the face of the increasing need to live in proximity with the Other, I argue that the novel offers us a glimpse of an optimistic vision of an alternative home and nation by illuminating the political significance of Sara's and Maggie's choices of dwelling places.

Chapter Three

A number of Lawrence's protagonists are repelled by home and at times leave it. Paul Morel decides to leave home at the end of *Sons and Lovers*. Rupert Birkin in *Women in Love* tells Gerald: "each couple in its own little house, watching its own little interests, and stewing in its own little privacy—it's the most repulsive thing on earth. . . . One should avoid this *home* instinct. It's not an instinct, it's a habit of cowardliness. One should never have a *home*" (352). Near the end of *Kangaroo*, Richard Lovatt Somers declares, "I won't delude myself with the fallacy of home" (333).

Why do these characters repudiate the very idea of home, and at times leave their home and family? Reading much of Lawrence's fiction as a reflection of the author's own personal experiences, a number of critics have interpreted the male protagonists' repulsion against home in Lawrence's works in terms of Oedipal drama, Lawrence's own resentment of female domination at home, or his effort to escape from the suffocating mother.[1] F. R. Leavis, for example, sees Somers' revulsion against home in relation to Lawrence's relationship with women. In Leavis' view, Somers' wish to go "beyond women" and the attendant craving for male/political/impersonal activity are deeply connected to the disastrous relationship the writer had with his mother and wife.[2] Ironically, while Leavis' aim was to highlight the degree of self-knowledge and complex dimension in Somers' dilemma, some feminist scholars have found the very impulse to escape from home in Lawrence highly problematic. They often indict Lawrence's male protagonists' wish or decision to leave home as an expression of the writer's own misogyny bound up with his urge toward patriarchal leadership, arguing that what Lawrence ultimately seeks in the name of independence and freedom is men's emancipation from women's will-to-power.[3]

To some extent, these views rightly point out problems that Lawrence confronted and struggled with in his life and work. There is certainly the almost ubiquitous presence of the suffocating mother at home in *Sons and Lovers* and part of the protagonist's agonized relationship with the mother seems to reflect the writer's own intolerance of female domination in the home and of the male psyche. Some of Lawrence's essays (like "Matriarchy" that I briefly discussed in Chapter One) are apt examples that reveal Lawrence's ideological limits as a male writer who inherits the Victorian ideology of home as a female zone.

However, the significance of home in Lawrence cannot be restricted to merely a feminine space where a suffocating mother wields power over her son. It is not merely male protagonists who leave home. There are also a number of female protagonists who find home suffocating. These include a young wife in "The Woman Who Rode Away," Ursula in *The Rainbow*, or Yvette and her mother in *The Virgin and the Gipsy*, all of whom find the domestic milieu stifling and wish to or actually do escape from home and family. They revolt not only against devouring mothers, but also against domineering fathers or husbands. At times, a male character, such as Egbert in "England, My England," leaves home not because of his mother or wife but because of his father-in-law, a picture of paternal godhead.

Lawrence and his characters express a sense of suffocation in home, hometown, or home country for various reasons. As we have seen in the previous chapter, Mrs. Morel's and Miriam's sense of confinement in *Sons and Lovers* registers women's frustration with the narrow orbit of domestic life. Paul's feeling of being smothered is inseparable from his mother's choking affection, but, at the same time, it reveals Paul's painful awareness of the social limits and class barriers that he encountered as an aspiring artist born into a working class family in mining country. Several of his essays written in the 1920s—"On Coming Home," "Germans and English," and "Return to Bestwood"—invite us to look at the theme of the claustrophobic home in Lawrence from another angle: the critique of the ideology of home and nation.

REVISITING HOME/NATION

In an essay, "On Coming Home"—written when he returned to England from Mexico in 1923 and published posthumously—Lawrence expresses a deep sense of suffocation and confinement in England, instead of the feeling of coziness or comfort that the word "home" usually evokes. He records the claustrophobic atmosphere hovering over the "deathly sense of stillness"(*Phoenix II* 251) and "shut-in-edness" of England (253). As the essay proceeds, it becomes clear that Lawrence's wish to escape from the suffocating home comes from his intolerance of English selfhood, home, and nation, all of which are built upon the impulse to exclude, stigmatize, or subjugate others. The essay constantly evokes only to attack the Victorian ideal of home and nation. The ideas of safety, privacy, and enclosure—central to the Victorian home—in the essay are not virtuous but problematic.[4] For Lawrence, "the feeling of intolerable shut-in-edness" is comparable to the feeling that one might have when "shut in inside box after box of repeated and intensified shut-in-edness" (253). Lawrence proceeds to point out the profound sense of "fear," impotence, and "subdued malice" lurking beneath the façade of self-sufficient, "complacen[t]," and "superior" selfhood (254). Lawrence suggests that this sense of fear and malice is a kind of signifier that points to unjust stigmatization or exclusion of the less privileged, a signifier that undermines the very belief in the superiority of the insider by revealing that this superiority is not inherent but constructed through the "imagination of men," that is, through the fictive construction of the superior self and inferior Other (254)

Given that the middle-class myth of the superior self contributed to shaping the proud Victorian national identity—while suppressing the context of violence and domination through the emphasis on morality and superiority—it is no accident that the essay's challenge to the egotistic fantasy of the self entwined with the Victorian ideology of home in the essay disrupts the imperial nation and national identity as well. Discovering the anxiety of the "Englishmen at home" that curiously corresponds to the "bitterness" of Englishman abroad on the brink of "England's downfall," Lawrence suggests that the anxiety that pervades the psyche of the English in the face of the demise of the British Empire points to the fundamental affinity between class and imperial hegemonies in its construction of the imperial house. After exposing the anxiety to secure one's safety by building "safety boxes"— anxiety that is rather typical for the psyche of the dominator facing his downfall and the attendant possible revenge of the oppressed, as Frank Füredi suggests[5]—Lawrence goes on to observe the British imperial disease that has been contaminating the entire nation: the impulse not to make contact with or even recognize Others except to dominate them while fabricating the image of the superior self safely ensconced in the home. Note in the following the ways in which Lawrence once again brings up the home-nation connection through the cultural tropes of the gentry-house and the island, not so much to underscore the English home as a moral basis for the nation as to criticize the egotistic aversion to socio-spatial mingling with the Other and the latent imperial drive. Here again the ideas of safety and seclusion are interwoven with the claim of superiority that seeks to justify domination. He writes:

> England seems to me the one really soft spot, the rotten spot in the
> empire. . . . And here you get an island no bigger than a back garden,
> chock-full of people who never realize there is anything outside their
> back garden, pretending to direct the destinies of the world. It is
> pathetic and ridiculous. And the "superiority" is bathetic to lunacy.
> These poor "gentry," all that is left to them is to blame the Americans.
> . . . One could shout with laughter at the figures inside these endless
> safety boxes. (255–56)

In "Germans and English" written in 1927 Lawrence again criticizes
the conventional ideology of home and nation. Inspired by the image of
young German tourists in Florence, Lawrence attempts to examine the
nature of the English in comparison with that of the Germans. Cautioning
against privileging the German over the English, Lawrence muses on how
the German search for the "pure Ideal"—shared by other Western countries—has supported militarism and industrialism. This does not mean, for
Lawrence, of course, that the English are without defect. Interestingly, to
criticize the nature of the English, Lawrence again picks up symbolic and literal geographies—the houses and the island. He contends that both the
"endless little private houses of England" and the "imperial nation" are built
through the English cultural identity as "an islander" that has cultivated
"fatal individualism" and the fierce wish to "preserv[e]" "privacy" (248).
Lawrence suggests that English individualism and preoccupation with privacy are problematic in that they express the cultural impulse to avoid any
"living contact" with the Other, while exposing the fundamental affinity
between the desire to an exclusionary "private little house" and the imperial
nation (248).

In a similar vein, in another autobiographical piece written in 1926,
"Return to Bestwood," Lawrence critically portrays the impregnable walls
and closed doors of the house as a material indicator of the inhabitants' egoism and the desire to avoid "living contact" with the marginalized and to
expel them from the privileged territory of home/nation. Returning to the
"native district" "in the brink of class war" (265), Lawrence feels
"depress[ed]" because of the rigid class barrier and the loss of the working
class vitality (265). As the crisis in the British Empire provokes anxiety and
the impulse in the imperial subject to set up more protective walls around
the domestic border, as we have seen in "On Coming Home," the class war
makes the oppressive social system the more prominent. In this time of "the
great coal strike," Lawrence notes, "[t]here are policemen everywhere" (258).
Recalling those days when his mother always pushed him and his sister to

"get on," Lawrence turns toward his sister's "lovely house" with a garden among the "hideous rows of miners' dwellings," the house that points to both her social success and her capitulation to the middle-class desire to erect an impregnable wall against the working class (261). Lawrence's critical approach to the image of the house as a metonym for hierarchal society—a society whose stress on privacy and isolation obscures the exploitation, stigmatization, or exclusion of the Other—finds another expression through the image of Hardwick Hall, a house built for Elizabeth, Dowager Countess of Shrewsbury, in 1597. Finding that this great house is "shut," Lawrence writes, "of course! The strike! They are afraid of vandalism" (262). Through this passing remark, I think, Lawrence intimates that this great house can be seen as an indicator of the psyche of the dominant who define the struggle of the less privileged for a better life ("strike") as simply a criminal attack on their property ("vandalism").[6]

In these respects, it is no exaggeration to say that a considerable part of Lawrence's sense of suffocation and the wish to leave home and nation arises from his intolerance of the psychological and physical barrier between inside(r) and outside(r) and the attendant domination and exclusion that precludes sound human relationships and social changes. "Everything muffled, or muted, and no sharp contact, no sharp reaction anywhere," Lawrence laments in "On Coming Home" (251). In "Germans and English" he again detects the antipathy to contact with the Other in the architecture of the English home and nation. His critical view of the conventional home/nation has Lawrence seek new ones. In "Return to Bestwood" Lawrence envisions an alternative home built by a counter-cultural impulse to meet with the suppressed, dominated, or expelled Other. Asserting "I don't want to own a house," Lawrence offers a new definition of home built through the "struggl[e] against fixations": "it is they[miners] who are, in some peculiar way, 'home' to me" (264). The vision of a new home sounds a bit vague here, and yet we can see that it valorizes openness and changeability instead of enclosure and stability. Indeed, as we shall see, an alternative home in Lawrence's works is not surrounded by impregnable walls or borders. It is an open and mutable structure that invites contacts. Lawrence writes, "What is alive, and open, and active, is good. All that makes for inertia, lifelessness, dreariness, is bad. . . . What we should live for is life and the beauty of aliveness, imagination, awareness, and contact (265–66).

IMPERIALISM AND THE DISCOURSE OF HOME

A short story, "England, My England," composed about 1915, shows that Lawrence associated his critical view of home with that of the nation from his early career. Borrowing the title from the well-known poem, "England, My England," by the Victorian poet, critic, and editor William Ernest Henley, the story engages in an interesting dialogue with the Victorian legacy of the idea of the nation and its sustaining trope and unit, home.[7]

First appearing in *A Book of Verses* (1888), Henley's "England, My England" established the poet's fame (though short-lived) and his appeal to a wide range of contemporary readers. Beginning with an affectionate address to England—"What have I done for you,/ England, my England?/ What is there I would not do, England, my own"–the poem celebrates England's imperial "master-work" and declares patriotic willingness to sacrifice oneself to the nation: "Take and break us: we are yours, /England, my own!/. . . . Death is death; but we shall die/ to the Song of your bugles blown" (140).[8]

Why did Lawrence evoke this patriotic poem filled with imperial fervor in his story about a man who, after a paradisal early-married life, becomes a wanderer and eventually dies in battle during World War I? Despite a considerable amount of critical attention, the story has often received somewhat cursory or simplistic interpretations. Critics have interpreted the story in light of the defeat of the old cultural values (Egbert) at the hands of industrialization and commercialization (Winnie's father, a London businessman) (Leavis 334) or the tension between "two qualitatively different life modes"(Thornton 43). Despite varying degrees of sympathy or criticism toward Egbert, these views generally assume that the protagonist is fundamentally inadequate or even suicidal and nihilistic in contrast with Winnie's father.[9] While it is not difficult to notice the contrast between Egbert and his father-in-law, Godfrey Marshall, the underlying significance of Lawrence's creation of Egbert, who is by nature opposed to "the whole convention of the domestic home" (325), has not received substantial attention.

The story is Lawrence's complex exploration of power, domination, and resistance centered in the idea of home and nation. The story begins with an Edenic domestic setting where the newly married couple, Egbert and Winnie, enjoy their life. As time proceeds, however, Egbert's refusal to work for money and an accident that leaves his daughter crippled put their life under the financial and paternal power of Winnie's father, Marshall. Egbert is gradually estranged from home, which by now is under the rein of Winnie's father. Winnie's father puts pressure on Egbert to join the army to earn money, and the story ends with his death in the war.

At first glance, Egbert's inadequacy seems obvious in contrast with his father-in-law's reliable and benevolent "parental godhead" or "fatherhood" (314). However, a close reading enables us to look at Lawrence's exploration of the danger of patriarchal power couched in the name of home and family, an examination that invites us to rethink Egbert as a misfit in the conventional home. At the core of the effective and protective father figure, Lawrence intimates, lies the impulse for maintaining a safe stronghold of home, which serves as the base for the whole society as well. As "a pillar of society" (312), Winnie's father would "not let the world intrude far into his home" (305). As the story goes on, it becomes clear that the protective power is no better than "dominion over the souls of his children" (314). This domestic milieu is problematic, Lawrence suggests, for it aims to maintain the status quo by bringing up a docile and dependent subject who is deprived of the very desire for independence and freedom by the lure of a safe home. Winnie, for example, has grown up to be a woman who is unable to seek "feminine independence." Instead, she "would hunger, hunger all her life for the warmth and shelter of true male strength" (315).

In a sense, Marshall is the figure who embodies the connection between the ideology of home, the patriarchal system, and imperial nationalism that endorses violent warfare for the cause of the safe home/nation. It is no accident that Lawrence likens Marshall to the "pillar of the society"—the phrase that he used in "Germans and English" to metaphorically designate the self-centered English man who has built both the "private house" and the "imperial nation" (248). Marshall's authority secured in the name of protection and stability of home becomes problematic in the story, as it turns out to be an exclusionary power that would expel any member who is not subservient to the benefit of home and its extended territory of nation. The alliance between father and daughter, who insist on living up to the conventional idea of home, gradually alienates Egbert. Marshall's advice for Egbert to enlist in the army finally leads to the latter's death on the battlefield. In this way, ironically reversing Henley's patriotic willingness to die for the nation, the story shows how the deceitful cause of homeland security—the hiding of imperial interests—literally kills Egbert.

In addition, the story points to the danger that lies not outside but inside the home(land). Those critics who read the story in terms of Lawrence's critique of nihilism or incompetence have interpreted Egbert's death in the war as a natural outcome of his inherent nihilism, his inadequacy, or a suicidal impulse that has him passively accept Marshall's advice in the first place. But in my view, Egbert's death has already taken place even before he goes to war, not literally, but symbolically. To put it differently, his death on the battlefield is a reenactment of his prior death in the home at the hand of Marshall, who represents the ideology of home in his attempt to expel any unconventional or dissident member who does not fit in the cultural code of home. Indeed, throughout the story Egbert appears as a figure who squarely opposes the ethic of home and nation; he is likened to wandering Ishmael (325), and, more explicitly, the narrator points out his dispositional opposition to "the whole convention of the domestic home" (325).

Given the connection between the ideology of home and nation in Marshall, it is no wonder that Egbert's rebellion against "the whole convention of the domestic home" is tied up with his aversion to war, imperialism, and nationalism: "when the war broke out his whole instinct was against it: against war. . . . He had no conception of Imperial England, and Rule Britannia was just a joke to him. . . . No, he had no desire to defy Germany and to exalt England. . . . A man was good or bad according to his nature, not according to his nationality. . . . There was nothing national about crime" (326). In Egbert's mind, there is no fundamental difference between the "English non-military idea of liberty and the 'conquest of peace,'" and "German military aggression" (327).[10]

"England, My England" is a critical study of the idea of home and its mirror image of the nation. Ironically echoing the voice of a patriotic persona in Henley's poem, Lawrence unveils the dangerous impulse lying behind the idea of nation and home—the impulse that seeks to raise docile subjects and expel any unconventional or disturbing ones out of the territory. The story points to how the conventional discourse of home centered on the ideas of safety and protection serves to conceal domination and violence both at home and in the nation.

DEMOLISHING HOME/NATION: *THE VIRGIN AND THE GIPSY*

The critique of the ideology of home and nation finds more radical expression with the vision of the collapse of the Victorian house in the novella *The Virgin and the Gipsy*. Written in 1925 and published posthumously, the story is about Yvette who longs to be freed from the stifling confines of her middle-class family. In her search for freedom she meets a gipsy, and the story ends with the spiritual (and sexual) consummation between Yvette and the gipsy set against the collapse of the rectory by a flood.

Throughout the story Lawrence evokes the conventional picture of home to unveil its ideological implication. The depiction of the elopement of Yvette's mother from the house at the beginning exemplifies the ways in which the story reverses the conventional discourse of home through irony. When Yvette's mother disappeared, the narrator comments: "the glamour was gone. . . . The danger of instability . . . was also gone, there was now a complete stability, in which one could perish safely" (8). Here we witness that the ideas of safety, stability, and enclosure central to the Victorian ideology of home are not rendered as beneficial but as "stifling" and even fatal (14). The ambiguous narrative perspective illustrates the ways in which the oppressive power of the dominant discourse of home is at work even in the omniscient narrator's psyche. The subversive voice that would see the mother's escape from the home as a "glarmour[ous]" action is immediately followed by a conservative one that defines the mother's elopement as "danger" that threatens the stability of home. The narrative ambiguity becomes more disturbing in the following phrase; the restoration of the "stable" home through the disappearance of Yvette's mother turns out to be nothing better than a grave—in which "one could perish safely." Through these remarks, the distinction between safety and danger, and between home and grave, becomes unstable.

Having begun with this disruptive allusion to the idea of home, the story proceeds to expose ideological implications staged in the middle-class Victorian household: Saywell House. As its name intimates, the Saywell House serves as a symbolic and material arena where any disturbing language or behavior that goes against the conventional idea of home and family is suppressed. Granny rules the house; she is a figure of middle-class conventionality and will-to-power who sees her home and family as "her own extended ego" (9):

> Naturally she covered it [the family] with her power. And her sons and daughters, being weak and disintegrated, naturally were loyal. Outside the family, what was there for them but danger and insult and ignominy?. . . . So now, caution! Caution and loyalty, fronting the world! Let there be as much hate and friction *inside* the family, as you like. To the outer world, a stubborn fence of unison. (9)

The description of the Saywell home is telling, for it suggests that the assumption about the danger outside the home serves as a basis for Granny's power. It also notes that the idea of home is sustained by smoothing out inner conflicts and by imposing an illusive unified identity on individual members. The "fence of unison" is not a representation of reality but a deceitful illusion that supports Granny's rule over the home.

The image of the Granny who dictates the rectory that reifies Victorian middle-class domestic norms and ethics suggests an analogy to Queen Victoria, who died at eighty-one years of age after sixty-three year reign under which the British Empire doubled in size and constructed its proud national identity, "Victorian England." This analogy is one of the indicators of the connection between the home and the imperial nation that the novella makes.[11]

As in the essays of the 1920s that we have seen before, the novella lays bare the domination and oppression operative in the cultural fantasies of both home and nation. To take an example, when the "six rebels"—Yvette and her friends— look down at the town at the top of the hill, what they see is the "roof of England, stony and arid as any roof" (22), evoking the current discourse that would conceive of England through the image of a house. The image of the house reminds us of "implacable" "stony," and "relentless" Granny who represents "the static inertia" of "unsavoury power" (18). Reversing the Victorian discourse, the home is connected to the nation not through positive values of comfort and safety but through relentless power and restriction.

The challenge in the novella to the cultural myth of home/nation involves an exposure of domestication, discrimination, or exclusion of the less privileged in the name of the safely secluded home. As we have seen, Granny's description of the world through free indirect discourse outside the home as being filled with "danger, insult and ignominy" illustrates the ways in which she consolidates her power by creating a wall between the safe inside and the dangerous outside, a border that helps her exaggerate or fabricate the danger outside while concealing danger and oppression inside.[12]

One of the most docile and loyal subjects, the rector, Granny's son, articulates more explicitly how the construction of the Victorian house and the middle-class self-image is founded on the process of Othering and aversion to contact with the marginalized. For example, when the rector—who is "afraid of the unconventional" (68)—finds out about his daughter Yvette's acquaintance with the gipsy, he immediately prohibits any further meeting with the "dark" gipsy, associating him with promiscuity, moral depravity, madness, and disease while revealing his "fear" of contamination from outside. The rector threatens Yvette that if she continues seeing the gipsy— whom he believes to be a picture of "depravity" (68)—he will send her to a criminal-lunacy asylum because he "cannot have them [his mother and sisters] contaminated"(70).

Challenging the psychological and physical wall that Granny and the rector erect around the house, the novella continuously brings up only to disrupt and reverse the conventional idiom of home. Yvette's perspective on the rectory, for example, mocks the middle-class ideal of home characterized by cleanliness and comfort. For her, the rectory is surrounded by the "dank air of that middle-class, degenerated comfort which has ceased to be comfortable and has turned stuffy, unclean" (11). In Yvette's eyes, it is not the rectory but the gipsy caravan—whose lack of fixity and supposed filth go against the conventional ideal of home—that is clean: "She loathed these houses with their indoor sanitation and their bathrooms. . . . The whole stagnant, sewerage sort of life, where sewerage is never mentioned, but where it seems to smell from . . . Granny to the servants. . . . If gipsies had no bathrooms, at least they had no sewerage. There was fresh air. In the rectory there was *never* fresh air" (34). Yvette's wish to "live in a camp, in a caravan, and never set foot in a house" gets deeper to the extent that she feel[s] "intensely that that [the gipsy camp] was home for her" (78).

Yvette's antipathy to the Victorian home and the hypocritical self-image of the middle-class grows into a rebellious crossing over the wall to seek forbidden relationships with people who are to be kept away from the house. Transgressing the socio-cultural and geographical boundaries, she seeks love across classes and reshapes her selfhood, wishing "she were a gipsy" (33). Yvette is fascinated by the gipsy man "of a race that exists only to be harrying the outskirts of our society," the man who shows in his manner the "half-sneering challenge of the outcast" (26) and "ever-unyielding outsidedness" (74). Her contact with the gipsy culminates in the moment of consummation in her attic room in the midst of the collapse of the rectory by flood.

The destruction of the Saywell House and its mistress, Granny, by water at the end epitomizes the subversive force of the novella to dismantle the dominant ideology of home. Architectural discourse that pervaded throughout the nineteenth century further confirms my point. To illustrate the emphasis on impenetrability and self-containment of the house in nineteenth-century architectural discourse, Sharon Marcus echoes a historian's observation: "openings in the walls are not in the least desirable and can only be considered necessary evils" (94). Before examining the ending scene of the novella, which squarely challenges this architectural discourse, it is interesting to note that the image of the collapsing house is crucial to the political project that Lawrence attempts to perform through an aesthetic achievement. About two years before the composition of *The Virgin and the Gipsy*, Lawrence writes in an essay, "Surgery for the Novel—Or a Bomb," about the needed future of the novel:

> It is got to have the courage to tackle new propositions without using abstractions; it's got to present us with new, really new feeling, a whole new line of emotion, which will get us out of the old emotional rut. Instead of sniveling about what is and has been, or inventing new sensations in the old line, it's got to break a way through, like a hole in a wall. And the public will scream and say it's a sacrilege: because, of course, when you've been jammed for a long time in a tight corner, you get really used to its stuffiness and its tightness, till you find it absolutely stinkingly cosy; and then, of course you're horrified when you see a new glaring hole in what was your cosy wall. (*Phoenix* 520)

Here again note Lawrence's use of an architectural language that immediately evokes the image of home—where the confining and stifling wall ("stuffiness" and "tightness") feels illusively "cosy" (to the conventional insider). The task of the novel, Lawrence believes, is to initiate a profound restructuring of the cultural production of psychological, discursive, and physical domestic space. Aware of the subversive aspects of disrupting the cozy and inviolable wall of the house—as evidenced by his anticipation of the outraged response from the contemporary who will "scream and say it's a sacrilege"–Lawrence deliberately performs the rebellious task in the novella. As if mocking the discourse of his precedents that regarded "openings in the wall" as "evil," the novella as it comes to a close is replete with subversive images such as the "awesome gap in the house" (81), "the gaping mouths of rooms," and the rector's "torn-open study" (85), all of which powerfully dramatize the demolition of the Victorian home and nation by the devouring flood.

This demolition of the home, one might add, brings new understanding of the Other, an understanding that heralds a better human relationship. The waters that strip both Yvette and the gipsy enable the former to see the vulnerable man "beneath the fantasy figure" (Cushman 165), as evidenced by the revelation of the gipsy's name, "Joe Boswell" (90) at the end. The revelation of the gipsy's rather mundane name is important because it suggests that the ultimate relationship of Yvette with the man is made possible through her encounter with his individual self; for, as far as the gipsy man remains purely enigmatic for Yvette, her relationship with the man is in danger of reinscribing, instead of blurring, the barrier between self/inside and Other/outside. As a matter of fact, much of the powerful image of the gipsy who "rob[s] her [Yvette] of her will" grows out of Yvette's imagination, pointing to her sexuality, but more importantly, intimating her potential complicity with the construction of the middle-class self through the mystification of the Other—a process that is an obverse side of the rector's stigmatization of the gipsy.[13] The destruction of the Saywell house, the story suggests, is not complete without the demolition of the illusionary wall between self/inside(r) and Other/outside(r).

"I WON'T DELUDE MYSELF WITH THE FALLACY OF HOME": TOWARD AN ALTERNATIVE HOME/NATION IN *KANGAROO*

Written during Lawrence's brief sojourn with his wife in Australia on the way to America in 1922, *Kangaroo* is a story about an English writer, Richard Lovatt Somers, and his German wife, Harriett's, experience of the political and physical landscape of the Australian continent. The novel begins with the couple's arrival in Australia from India to which they had traveled to escape from the worn-out and restricting culture of Europe. The rest of the story shows Somers' temporary interest in the political scene that revolves around the conflict between the Socialists and the Diggers, his gradual disillusionment with politics, and the couple's final departure for America.

On the basis of biographical research, many critics have suggested that the real theme of the story is not politics but Lawrence's desire to escape from the problems in his relationships with his mother and his wife. Judith Ruderman argues that the novel deals with the issue of "independence from the mother that informs Lawrence's other works, especially those of his leadership period" (105). According to Ruderman, the novel is "so nakedly a story of Lawrence and Frieda" that the writer could not directly attack and destroy Harriett (109). Instead, it is to the Australian leader, Benjamin Cooley, nicknamed Kangaroo, that Somers/Lawrence was able to attach every aspect of the devouring mother. Ruderman argues that Somers' rejection of Kangaroo at the end marks his final break with the maternal string. Reading the novel through the multiple threads of the writer's marital problems, his relations with political society, and his misanthropy, Julian Moynahan argues that Somers' eventual detachment from political activity registers no better than a "state of moral bankruptcy" that makes Somers "one of those revolutionary simpletons" (106).

Although these readings provide useful personal, psychological, and social backgrounds of the novel, they fail to capture the politics that the novel performs through its critical investigation of the ideology of home and nation. Ruderman touches on the issues of home and home country but much of her argument seems to be built on the assumption that the home/nation is always equal to the devouring mother, reducing the novel to an expression of a man torn by the agonizing love/hate relationship with the mother, and neglecting broader socio-cultural contexts to which the novel responds. Moynahan's reading is yet more problematic. According to Moynahan, Somers' temporary interest in political activity is basically motivated by his wish to make a place for himself and thus to assert his "masculinity" by "getting out of the house and into some active role in public life" (104). Moynahan's interpretation of Somers' psychology is exactly what Lawrence observes in "Matriarchy," as we have seen in previous chapter. The problem here is that Moynahan's reading is in danger of reducing the complex meaning of the novel to one of Lawrence's most problematic gendered statements. Furthermore, Moynahan's indictment of Somers' final withdrawal from public life as a form of moral bankruptcy leaves out the political significance of Somers' decision and reveals the critic's own consent to the gendered division between private/feminine and public/masculine.

As we have seen, the home in Lawrence is not always identifiable with the mother. Lawrence's critical investigation of home involves a broader social criticism of various forms of domination, oppression, and exclusion. *Kangaroo* can be read as another example of Lawrence's critical investigation of the ideology of home and nation, an investigation that leads to a vision of alternative visions of home/nation and human relationships.

The issue of home keeps returning throughout the novel. Central characters like Somers, Harriett, and Benjamin Cooley imagine or speak about home differently, revealing different ideological limits or critical potentials. The marital conflicts between Somers and Harriett frequently revolve around the issue of home. Somers' momentary fascination with and eventual repudiation of Cooley has much to do with the latter's vision of home/nation, a vision that Somers once shared but finally turns away from. Somers constantly mulls over and interrogates the idea of home. In *Kangaroo* we witness Somers' initially contradictory idea of home move toward a better vision of home, a vision that provides a corrective to corrupt human relationships.

In the imaginary dialogue between Somers and Harriett in Chapter IX, titled "Harriett and Lovatt at Sea in Marriage," Somers' view of marriage and his gendered belief in leadership are bound up with his conventional concept of home. After the omniscient narrator's rather schematic account of what marriage can be, the dialogue between Somers and Harriett aboard a ship named "Harriett and Lovatt" begins. To Harriett, who advocates comradeship in marriage, Lovatt replies, "Never." He adds, "I will be lord and master but ah, such a wonderful lord and master that it will be your bliss to belong to me" (172). As the conversation proceeds, it become clear that at the center of Lovatt's request for Harriett's submission to his nearly apotheosized leadership lies the patriarchal view of home as nest, a nest from which the male lord/Phoenix rises (173). In its identification of home with woman this view denies woman's individuality, as evidenced by Lovatt's statement that, "you are the nest" (173). Feminist critics have often found this dialogue to be one of the most disturbing parts of the novel. Hilary Simpson, for example, indicts the scene for Somers' absurdity and inconsistencies that she believes are Lawrence's own. Lawrence's works like *Fantasia of the Unconscious*, written in 1921, certainly suggest that Lovatt mouths much of Lawrence's own view on marriage during that time. And yet, the assumption that Lovatt's defective thoughts are Lawrence's own is in danger of entirely leaving out the writer's critical self-analysis or questioning, as well as the textual dynamics that go beyond the author's intention.

The free indirect discourse that oscillates between Lovatt's and Harriett's perspectives helps us hear Harriett's critical stance towards Lovatt, suggesting

Lawrence's awareness of ideological problems, or at least his knowledge of the psychological ground of Lovatt's obsession with masculine authority. As Harriett points out, Lovatt's comparison of her with a nest reveals his megalomaniac masculinist belief in his authority, authority that is dependent upon a prior erasure and enslavement of her. "I don't exist," Harriett retorts (173), and the following free indirect discourse further delivers criticism of Lovatt: "Obstinate and devilish as he was, he wanted to . . . seat himself in glory on the ashes, like a resurrected *Phoenix,* with an imaginary crown on his head. And she was to be a comfortable nest for his impertinence. In short, he was to be the lord and master, and she the humble slave" (173). Besides, Lovatt's buried wish to counterbalance his "uxorious interest in Harriett" (Moynahan 102), or his dependence on Harriett in the first place, is exactly what Harriett detects in his claim for masculinity: "He had nothing but her, absolutely. And that was why, presumably, he wanted to establish this ascendancy over her, assume this arrogance" (175). Harriett further exposes the fact that Lovatt's claim of authority and male fulfillment is sustained by the patriarchal concept of home as a nest, an ideology that prescribes woman's place and her instrumental role:

> She could *not* stand these World-Saviours. And she, she must be safely there, as a nest for him, when he came home with his feathers pecked. That was it. . . . [H]e would turn her into a nest, and sit on her and overlook her, like the one and only *Phoenix* in the desert of the world, gurgling hymns of salvation. (175)

The imaginary dialogue reaches an "impasse" (175), suggesting that neither Lovatt nor Harriett has gained a better understanding of home, marriage, or human relationship. But the fact that the novel, however momentarily, stages Somers' married life with Harriett as a journey on the sea, rather than in the conventional arena of a home as a fixed abode, can be interpreted as an optimistic indicator of changes their married life will undergo, as well as of an alternative home the couple will build.

Benjamin Cooley, an Australian lawyer and political leader, more explicitly endorses the patriarchal ideology of home than Somers. Critics have often seen this figure of a "benevolent tyrant" (200)—who bases his national movement on the notion of a "new aristocracy" (184)—as mouthing Lawrence's own leadership theory and fascist tendency. Less observed is the fact that this would-be fascistic dictator attests to the dangerous association between the establishment of dictatorship and the conventional idea of home. Attempting to persuade Somers to join his political group, the Diggers, Cooley says to Somers:

> Because man builds himself in to his old house of life, builds his own blood into the roads he lays down, and to break from the old way, and to change his house of life, is almost like tearing him to pieces. . . . Man needs a quiet, gentle father who uses his authority in the name of living life, and who is absolutely stern against anti-life. . . . I offer my mind and my will, for the battle against every obstacle to respond to the voice of life, and to shelter mankind from the madness and the evil of anti-life. (112–13)

This remark shows that Cooley bases his power on the patriarchal idea of home. He sees himself as a builder and owner of the house, the house which is first identified with his own self, and then, with the territory that he protects and dominates. In addition, Cooley's picture of home is based on a hierarchal relation between inside(r) and outside (r). It creates an illusion of the unitary and normative interior against the exterior world of "anti-life." Like Winnie's father in "England, My England"—who sees his home and family as his property that he has to protect—Cooley draws on the patriarchal concept of home to legitimize his authority to fight and expel the "anti-life," authority which in fact is constructed by his own definition of "life." Throughout the novel, however, there are many instances that suggest that Cooley's power might bring about incarceration rather than emancipation, violence rather than safety, or dictatorship rather than protection. Indeed, as if anticipating Michel Foucault's account that the complicity of medical and architectural practices with dominant power has contributed to the historical process of denigrating, segregating, or criminalizing the sick, less intelligent, mad, or poor others, we are told that Cooley's fight against the "anti-life" is supported by "doctors and architects" as well as by the diggers, the returned soldiers (156).[14]

Indeed, throughout the novel sinister intimations of violence and ruthless domination disturb the vision of home that Cooley proudly claims to protect as a father.

Note, for example, the scene where Somers meets Cooley for the first time:

> "You have come to a homely country," said Kangaroo, without the ghost of a smile. "Certainly to a very hospitable one."
> "We rarely lock our doors," said Kangaroo.

"Or anything else," said Jack. "Though of course we may slay you in
the scullery if you say a word against us." (108)

The remark of Jack Calcott, one of the followers of Cooley, here discloses
violence lurking beneath the image of home, shattering Cooley's contention that this home is safe enough not to lock doors and hospitable to
other people. Harriett certainly senses the threat that Cooley and the
home/nation that he represents poses to her.[15] Later, when Jack explains to
Somers why he likes the fatherly Cooley, his language further exposes dangerous aspects of the ideology of home—home that is aggressively
defended through ruthless exclusion of the Other. After saying to Somers
that "I don't want to be kissing and hugging a lot of foreign labour tripe:
niggers and what the hell. I'd rather have the British Empire ten thousand
times over," Jack adds: "That's why I like Kangaroo. . . . We shall be just
cosy and Australian, with a boss like a fat father who gets up first in the
morning, and locks up at night before you go to bed" (187). Contrary to
Cooley's previous remark that there is hardly any need to lock the house,
Jack suggests that Cooley is the father who "locks" the door. In addition,
Cooley is the father who keeps strange bedfellows like "a crowd of niggers
and Dagoes" or foreign laborers out of the house by locking up securely at
night. "I know Kangaroo well enough to know," Jack continues, "he's not
mixing his family in. He'll keep Australia close and cosy" (187). Jack's
remarks show that the sense of being safe and cozy at home comes from a
prior eradication or subjugation of any disturbing Other. They also show
how the idea of a cozy and safe home functions to consolidate Kangaroo's
dictatorship within and outside the home. In addition, they also point to
the dangerous liaison between the exclusionary impulse that builds the
home and racism, nationalism, and imperialism.

Up to a certain point, Somers shares Jack's fascination with Cooley.
Part of Somers' initial fascination with Cooley springs from Somers' attraction to the latter's claim for power, the claim that Cooley makes look rather
natural and even legitimate through a shrewd maneuvering of the patriarchal
concept of home. In a sense, Somers' assertion of his mastership that he
advances along with the image of the nest in "Harriett and Lovatt at Sea in
Marriage" chapter can be seen as an effort to test out Cooley's theory. But
Somers fails to convince Harriett of his superiority and mastership, primarily
because of the problematic assumptions (from Harriett's perspective) that lie
behind the image of the nest, the idea upon which he seeks to found his
claim of superiority and domination, as Cooley does. Thus, the imaginary
dialogue conveys multiple significances. While revealing Somers' deplorable

affinity or sympathy with Cooley, it also shows Somers confronting the fundamental problem that he shares with Cooley: the concept of home that
entails subjugation or negation of the Other. It is doubtful that Somers gains
a clear understanding about this. But it is nevertheless significant that in the
chapter the patriarchal concept of home becomes a source of contestation,
thus functioning to destabilize instead of supporting the claim of mastership
and power. Or, to put it differently, the chapter intimates a fundamental
dilemma that Somers, the novel, and/or the writer faces and grapples with:
the impulse to search for masculine mastership (founded on the ideology of
home) that goes hand in hand with the critical view of the ideology of home.
As I shall show, Somers frequently articulates sentiments that go against the
conventional discourse of home. Given the connection between the drive for
masculine dictatorship and the conventional idea of home, Somers' anti-
home sentiment is to some extent an indicator of his contradiction. But at
the same time, it grants him subversive potential, enabling the novel to
destabilize the drive for masculine authority and dictatorship from within.
Notably, Somers' growing distance from Cooley goes hand in hand with his
increasingly explicit attack on the conventional idea of home. In this respect,
the novel invites us to look at Somers in line with characters like Egbert or
Yvette, who detect various dangers lurking right beneath the deceitful façade
of a safe home and who end up rebelling against the ideology of home.

Somers' musings on dark gods is another example that shows the ways
in which the novel challenges the ideology of home. Chapter XV opens with
a "metafictional aside" (Daly xx), where the narrator warns the reader about
the lack of plot in the novel. Here we see Somers pondering over "gods":

> The lord thy God is the invisible stranger at the gate in the night,
> knocking. He is the mysterious life-suggestion, tapping for admission.
> And the wondrous Victorian Age managed to fasten the door so tight,
> that really, there *was* no outside, it was all in. . . . The great dark God
> outside the gate is all these gods. You open the gate, and sometimes in
> rushes Thor and gives you a bang on the head with a hammer. . . .
> When they come through the gate they are personified. But outside the
> gate it is one dark God, the Unknown. And the Unknown is a terribly
> jealous God, and vengeful. . . . That is why we dare not open now. . . .
> Who knocks? (285)

Many critics have explored the significance of Lawrence's dark god. Some critics have interpreted it in terms of Lawrence's fascination or preoccupation with
primitivism, libidinal sexuality, or some unknown (mystical, cosmological, or

religious) existential dimensions. A lot of critics have found Lawrence's dark god ideologically and politically problematic, aligning it with his advocacy of "blood consciousness" and his call for an elite class of dictatorial leaders.[16] Feminist critics detected in the image of dark gods Lawrence's craving for ascendancy over the mother-wife.[17]

The focus on the issue of home, however, helps us to approach the above passage from a new perspective. To return to "On Coming Home," Lawrence suggests that the sense of fear and anxiety found in the dweller of the "safety boxes"—who imagines himself as being "superior"—originates from unjust exclusion of the Other. From this perspective, the above passage can be read as an allusion to the psychological state of the insider who has eradicated or expelled less privileged people to build a cozy and safe house. To put it another way, the passage can be read as a critical comment on the Victorian cult of home that "fasten[s]" its door "tight"—the ideology of home that Cooley inherits and reappropriates as a basis for his dictatorship. Anticipating Lawrence's critique of those "who never realize there is anything outside their back garden" in "On Coming Home," the above passage mocks the "wondrous Victorian age" that constructed the illusion of an all-inclusive inside by means of a willful neglect or failure to recognize the outside. Because the creation of such a safely enclosed interior world is founded on the violent exclusion of the Other, however, the home always remains as an illusion. It never brings a genuine sense of safety and self-containment. Those outside keep returning through the very psyche of the insider, haunting the wall of the house, as the fearful, vengeful Other.

The passage suggests what happens when the father fastens the door to keep the strange Other out of the house. To apply Füredi's observation concerning the Western subject's fear of the vengeful Other—fear which proves or arises out of the unjust exploitation or subjugation—the fear of the insider in the above passage who "dare[s] not open" the door can be seen as a penalty that s/he has to pay for the act of eradication or exclusion. At the same time, the passage demonstrates how the construction of home has been tied up with that of the insider's self-image, a construction that is inseparable from the process of Othering. As we have seen, Yvette's rebellious crossing over the wall of the house in search of contact with the Other culminates in her encounter with the demystified gipsy man, Joe Boswell, in *The Virgin and the Gipsy*. Similarly, the above passage proposes that a better human relationship can begin by shattering the psychological as well as the physical wall between inside(r) and outside(r). It is only by opening the gate, the passage suggests, that the fearful God "[is] personified." "But outside the gate it is one dark God, the Unknown."

Ruderman associates dark and violent gods with Somers/Lawrence's desire for "ascendancy over the mother-wife" (108). In this view, the dark god is the Master that Somers/Lawrence wants to be, or identifies himself with, in his fantasy. For Ruderman, therefore, the vengeful god is hardly distinguishable from Somers seething with "destructive urges" toward the suffocating wife/mother (108). Up to a certain point, Ruderman's interpretation holds. Indeed, when the dark god first appears at the end of the "Harriett and Lovatt" chapter, it is not difficult to see Somers' desire as the dark "Master" who seeks to establish his kingship by dethroning the devouring mother: "Richard who was so strong on kingship must open the doors of his soul and let in a dark Lord and Master for himself, the dark god he had sensed outside the door" (176). But throughout the novel, the significance of the dark god becomes complicated as much as that of the home does. As I have demonstrated, the novel addresses the idea of home in light of one of the central metaphors and practices that have perpetuated various forms of subjugation, domination, and exclusion. Along with the association of the home with psychological, geographical, and socio-political phenomena, the dark god becomes increasingly aligned with those marginalized who have been unfairly expelled, stigmatized, or dominated in the process of building the home: the female, racial, foreign, and colonial Other, those who Cooley has kept out of the home.[18] It is no wonder therefore that in Chapter XIII, titled "'Revenge!' Timotheus Cries," the vengeful gods with whom Somers identifies himself refer to "just everybody, except those that have got hold of the money or the power" (264), including the colonial Other—the Irish and the Indians (262). As Somers' following musing suggests, the dark God includes the female Other as well: "I must admit that only the dark God in her [Harriett] fighting with my white idealism has got me so clear: and that only the dark God in her answering the dark God in me has got my soul heavy and fecund with a new sort of infant" (263).

The disruption of the ideology of home in the novel finds an interesting expression as its critical force is leveled at the cultural myth of the nation as an island as well. Around the middle of the novel, we find a chapter, "Volcanic Evidence." The chapter begins with an ominous atmosphere that intimates an impending eruption. We are told that since Somers "had come to the end of his own tether" he is just about to "be savagely tugging at the end of [his] rope, or to wander at random tether-less" (149). Critics have associated the recurrent image of volcanic eruption in the novel with Lawrence's misanthropy (Moynahan) or his destructive urge toward the suffocating mother (Ruderman). Read closely, however, Somers' fury is directed neither at the entire human being nor at the mother/wife: "He tried to write, that being his job. But usually, nowadays, when he tapped his unconscious, he found himself in a seethe of steady fury, general rage. He didn't hate anybody in particular, nor even any class or body of men. He loathed politicians" (163).

In my view, the chapter enacts Somers' subversive rage poured against the ideology of home and nation through an interesting textual device: insertion of a news article about volcanoes. Somers "no longer believe[s] in great events" or political activity but this does not mean, as Moynahan suggests, his entire detachment from socio-political concerns (161). Anticipating "Surgery for the Novel, Or a Bomb" and *The Virgin and the Gipsy* where Lawrence bridges aesthetics and politics by exploding the home, Somers expresses his subversive force when he imagines himself as a "human bomb" in charge of "explod[ing] and mak[ing] breaches in the walls that shut life in" (165). Somers' imagination of himself as a bomb is followed by an article he reads about the volcanoes of Australia excerpted from an old Sydney Daily Telegraph. Under the subtitles, "Earthquakes. Is Australia Safe? Sleeping Volcanoes," "Volcanic Evidence," and "Islands that Vanished," the article reports the existence of latent volcanoes surrounding the continent of Australia. The article disrupts the cultural myth of the island—the notion of safety, isolation, and insularity—by exposing geographical uncertainties as well as historicizing the birth of the island and its fundamental relatedness with other geographical locations. "Australia . . . which appears to be the most immune country" can be put in danger by latent "volcanic action," we are told (165). The article ends by pointing to the "tremendous chasm" and "vacancy" within and outside the island and the fundamental relatedness of the island of Australia: "[T]he present continent of Australia is only a portion of the original and . . . in some remote period it extended hundreds or thousands of miles to the eastward, including Lord Howe . . . possibly New Caledonia" (168). Inserted into the middle of this novel that is deeply concerned with the idea of home, the article destabilizes the whole ground of the imagined territory of home and nation.

As a matter of fact, throughout the novel Somers constantly confronts and grapples with the idea of home. He does not put forward any systematic theory of home, nor does his understanding of home show a neat progress. He reveals occasionally problematic or contradictory concepts of home. And yet, we can see his gradual awakening to a better understanding of home at the end, the possibility of which has partly been adumbrated throughout the novel. Note for example the distinct responses of Somers and Harriett to their house—a camp, but actually built quite similarly to an English family house (81)—in Australia, *Coo-ee*. Harriett's view of the house remains within

conventional idioms of home, as evidenced by her sense of being inside, suf-
ficient, and self-complacent as well as by her association of the camp with
stability, safety, and enclosure: "she had for the moment a home, where she
felt for the moment as rooted, as central as the tree of life itself. She wasn't a
bit of flotsam. . . . [W]here she camped with Lovatt Somers was now the
world's center to her, and that was enough" 101). But Somers' perspective
delivers a quite different feeling:

> the sea was shut out but still calling outside the house. . . . [T]hank
> God, he felt cold and fresh and detached, not cosy and domestic. He
> was so thankful not to be feeling cosy and "homely." The room felt as
> penetrable to the outside influence as if it were a sea-shell lying on the
> beach, cool with the freshness and insistence of the sea, not a snug, cosy
> box to be secured inside. (147)

For Somers also, home is the place where a certain sense of seclusion and
comfort is clearly felt and experienced, as the phrase, "the sea was shut
out," suggests. However, being at home does not bring an entire breach
with "the calling outside the house." Instead, home is an open place consistently interrupted by the "knocking" at the door, or "calling outside,"
rather than being an isolated island. Or, it is an island connected to the sea.
It has a "penetrable" structure, blurring borders between inside and outside, center and periphery. Somers' feeling is a telling presentiment of his
final disagreement with Kangaroo and his decision to leave Australia. More
importantly, it heralds Somers' new understandings of home, himself, and
Harriett.

Somers envisions an alternative home through a critical revision of the
conventional language of home. Echoing Kangaroo's use of the trope of the
house, Somers muses on the human mind in architectural terms: [t]he mind is
busy in a house of its own"(296). The house/mind, here, however, is no longer
an exclusive territory to rule over, territorialize, and fence in. Instead, the
house/mind turns to "the universe" which recognizes the existence of the outside: "There is always something outside our universe"(296). This is also an
interesting prelude to the writer's mockery of the English fantasy of home and
the nation in "On Coming Home" that I have quoted before: "here you get an
island no bigger than a back garden, chock-full of people who never realize
there is anything outside their back garden." As evidenced by the following
passage, the door of the house for Somers serves as a threshold, rather than a
barrier, where the effort to communicate and cohabit with the outsider takes
place. This vision does not, of course, arise out of a naïve optimism that

believes in the possibility of crossing over boundaries once and for all. Instead, it recognizes unfathomable gaps between inside and outside:

> There is always something outside our universe. And it is always at the doors of the innermost, sentient soul. And there is throb-throb, throb-throb-throb, throb-throb . . . homely universe. . . . But all the righteousness and goodness in all the world won't answer the throb, or interpret the faint, but painful thresh of the message. There is no morse-code. There never will be. Every new message more or less supersedes the current code. Nowadays, when we feel the throb, vaguely, we cry: "More love, more peace, more charity, more freedom, more self-sacrifice." Which makes matters all the worse, because the new throb interpreted mechanically according to the old code breeds madness and insanity. . . . The neurasthenia comes from the inattention to the suggestion, or from a false interpretation. . . . Alas, there is no morse-code. And there never will be. It needs a new term of speech invented each time. A whole new concept of the universe gradually born, shedding the old concept. (296–97)

The task of building new homes, Lawrence intimates, should involve an attempt to break away from the mechanical encoding and misinterpretation of the language of the Other. It needs "a new term of speech."

In the penultimate chapter, "Kangaroo is Killed," Somers at last confronts squarely the question "what was home?"—the question that has haunted him throughout the novel.

> Home again. But what was home? The fish has the vast ocean for home. And man has timelessness and nowhere. "I won't delude myself with the fallacy of home" he said to himself. . . . Back to Harriett, to tea. Harriett? Another bird like himself. (333)

As Somers' questions aptly epitomizes, *Kangaroo* is a novel that seeks an alternative vision of home and human relationship through critical exploration of "the fallacy of home." As the image of the "vast ocean" suggests, the newly envisioned home is not surrounded by any dividing wall. The new home is not an island but an ocean that by nature goes against enclosure, exclusion, or fixation. As a fallible hero, Somers once again momentarily falls into a conventional association of home with daily routine and wife: "Back to Harriett, to tea." But then his train of thought is suddenly interrupted by a question, "Harriett?"—a question that marks the moment of Somers' self-criticism. His musing proceeds, and at this time, Harriett is no longer a nest but "another bird like himself"—a bird which comes and goes like himself, building, demolishing, and rebuilding new homes, continuously traveling.

The novel ends with Somers and Harriett's departure from Australia for America in search of a new home. For all the strange power of the Australian landscape, what Somers has encountered is the age-old idea of home and nation, the idea that he mistakenly believed to have left behind in England and Europe. Somers' rejection of Cooley and Australia marks his break with the ideology of home and nation that the old continent bequeathed to Cooley, the ideology that has built a patriarchal, imperial, nationalist home/nation, part of which Somers himself shared.[19] It is no wonder that Somers bids farewell not only to Australia but also to his imperial nation, as well. On the ship, Somers says to himself: "farewell Australia, farewell Britain, and the great Empire" (358).

Chapter Four

Like Lawrence, Woolf is keenly aware of the ideological implications embedded in the cultural association of home and nation. In *Three Guineas,* for example, Woolf shows how militaristic patriotism and injustices towards those marginalized on the basis of gender, class, or nationality, are buttressed by a nationalist fiction of England as "the home of Liberty." Thus, her famous interrogation of male patriotism from a feminist perspective stems from her critical response to the contemporary rhetoric of home and nation. Wondering, "What then . . . [of] 'patriotism' which leads you to go to war?" Woolf quotes Lord Hewart, the Lord Chief Justice of England:

> Englishmen are proud of England. . . . Liberty has made her abode in England. England is the home of democratic institutions. . . . It is true that in our midst there are many enemies of liberty—some of them, perhaps, in rather unexpected quarters. But we are standing firm. It has been said that an Englishman's Home is his Castle. The home of Liberty is in England. And it is a castle indeed—a castle that will be defended to the last. . . . Yes, we are greatly blessed, we Englishmen. (9)

"But," Woolf asks,

> the educated man's sister—what does "patriotism" mean to her? Has she the same reasons for being proud of England, for loving England, for defending England?. . . . History and biography when questioned would seem to show that her position in the home of freedom has been different from her brother's. (9)

In Woolf's works, we see that her awareness of a different position in the home often enables her to have a critical perspective about the home and its mirror image of the nation. Critically exposing the impulse to marginalize, stigmatize, or expel those less privileged in the Victorian ideal of home and nation, Woolf envisions a less exclusionary home and nation through her subversive imagination that "overflow[s] boundaries" (*Three Guineas* 218).

AN UNCANNY STORY: "THE JOURNAL OF MISTRESS JOAN MARTYN"

A short story by Woolf, "The Journal of Mistress Joan Martyn"(1906), demonstrates that she explored the issue of home in relation to that of the nation from early on in her career. As I have discussed in the previous chapter, the story has been usually read in light of Woolf's feminist concern with women's confinement at home. Less observed is the fact that the theme of the narrow orbit of women's life in the story is combined with an interrogation of the idea of home and nation. Set against the period of a civil war in the medieval age, Joan's journal takes up directly the issue of the dangerous outside(r) threatening to intrude and shatter the home/nation with an emphasis on the idea of safety and enclosure. It begins as follows:

> The state of the times, which my mother tells me, is less safe and less happy than when she was a girl, makes it necessary for us to keep much within our own lands. After dark indeed . . . we have to be safe behind the hall Gates; my mother goes out as soon as the dark makes her embroidery too dim to see, with the great keys on her arm. "Is everybody within doors?" she cries. . . . Then she draws the Gates close, clamps them with the lock, and the whole world is barred away from us. (45)

As we shall see, by choosing a period of national crisis when distinctions between insider and outsider, safety and danger, protector and rebel, and judge and criminal emerge as crucial issues, Woolf demonstrates how the construction of home and nation is entwined with stigmatization, exploitation, or exclusion of those less privileged.

From the first, the national demand for quelling or expelling disturbing rebels is juxtaposed with and then replaced by the domestic need to keep the poor, wandering Other at bay. For example, when Joan listens to her mother's conversation with the priest about the civil war, the bloody deeds in the battlefield immediately evoke in her mind robbers outside the home: "So the talk makes me, and Jeremy [her little brother] too, tremble and think that every rattle of the big door, is the battering ram of some wandering highwayman" (47). As the narrative goes on, instead of a story of civil war, fearful rebels, thieves, or murderers, it turns into a story of poor people without home as well as of the colonized without nation, all of whom the insider believes to be vicious and dangerous, and thus, to be domesticated, subjugated, or expelled. Despite the prohibition on going outside (especially for women) in this period of danger, Joan constantly longs to go outside the home, and eventually she takes an opportunity to join her brother and a steward, Anthony, on a trip to a neighboring country. During her venture into the exterior world Joan experiences several incidents that reveal problematic assumptions or impulses embedded in the rhetoric of the safe home and nation. On their way to a cottage, the company encounters a "strange man . . . with the look of one who knows not which way to take"(52). Joan's journal proceeds to illustrate how the poor strange man without fixed abode is immediately criminalized. Anthony tells her that this man "is prowling out of bounds in search of food. He had robbed or murdered, or perchance he was only a debtor," and her little brother, Jeremy, even fancies that he saw "blood on his hands" (52). Suppressing the tale of poverty, at the sight of the loiterer, Anthony and Jeremy establish themselves as protectors and legitimize in advance possible violence in the cause of defense. Joan writes, "Anthony held my hand firmly," and "Jeremy would like to defend us all with his bow and arrows" (52).

For Woolf, such a fabrication of the image of the poor Other is problematic as it works to conceal a prior exploitation and to justify violence in the name of defense. Note the critical undertone that surrounds Joan's description of the tension-charged encounter between Anthony, the steward, and the poor cottager whom the Martyn family exploits:

> There was but a rotten log on which a woman sat, nursing a baby. She looked at us, not with fright, but with distrust and dislike written clear in her eyes; and she clasped her child more closely. Anthony spoke to her as he would have spoken to some animal who had strong claws and a wicked eye: he stood over her, and his great boot seemed ready to crush her. (53)

The discrepancy between Joan's view of the woman and that of Anthony—that Joan presumes on the basis of his attitude to her—intimates Joan's critical distance from Anthony's belief in the poor woman's wickedness and dangerousness. Where Joan reads the look of "distrust and dislike" in the woman, Anthony speaks to the woman as if she were a ferocious animal. What the passage emphasizes is the potential violence of Anthony against the woman—rather than the latter's against the former—reversing the story of the danger outside, which the narrator has been continuously told in her house. Anthony's remark that follows the encounter further substantiates the connection between the will-to-dominate and the construction of the image of the Other as vicious, uncivilized, and dangerous: "These are the people we must rule, and tread under foot, and scourge them to do the only work they are fitted to do; as they will tear us to pieces with their fang" (53). Taken together with Joan's description of the woman and Anthony's attitude toward her, Anthony's remark instigates our suspicion about his vindication of violent domination, instead of confirming the woman's vice. After all, it is Anthony who is frightened and violent, not the woman, and in this respect the story points to the anxiety of oppressors and their consequent overreaction against the oppressed.

The above episodes set the stage for the critique of the contemporary ideology of home and nation. Throughout the story, Woolf shows that the territories of both the home and the imperial nation are built by aggressively defended physical and psychological boundaries and unequal power relations between a safe and cultivated inside/home (that is to dominate) and a dangerous, wild outside (that is to be tamed, conquered, or extirpated). Woolf explores ideological implications embedded in the current discourses that often yoke together home and nation through the image of a sequestered, enclosed, and self-contained terrain. For example, in the middle of Joan's journal we encounter a story of a nation-building concerned with the issue of home. As Joan's marriage date approaches, her mother starts teaching a "theory of ownership" to her daughter (59). In order to be "the Ruler of a small island," the mother urges her to be keenly aware of "how one is . . . set in the midst of turbulent waters; how one must plant it and cultivate it; and drive roads through it, and fence it securely from the tides; and one day perhaps the waters will abate and this plot of ground will be ready to make part of a new world" (60). As her mother's speech proceeds, "a small island," which originally referred to the domestic space that the narrator is supposed to take care of after her marriage, curiously turns into a metaphor for the whole country. "Such is her [my mother's] dream of what the future may bring to England," Joan writes, "and it has been the hope of her life to order her own province in such a way that it may make one firm spot of ground to tread on at any rate. She bids me hope that I may live to see the whole of England thus solidly established"(60).

At this point, the house becomes a microcosm of a larger community, the nation. As property that should be preserved by setting up fences against the threatening waves, both home and nation try to exclude or tame any disturbing figures—whether they be instigators (in the context of the civil war), poor people with no fixed habitats, or possibly women who desire to be outside of the domestic sphere. The image of an island is especially telling, for it illustrates Woolf's interrogation of the ideological bearings of the cultural myth of England as an island that imagines its domestic space as enclosed, compacted, cultivated, and superior.

Although Joan transcribes her mother's conventional analogy of home and nation with respect, her journal is saturated with a subtle sense of doubt, pointing to her subversive potential. She writes: "But I confess that deeply though I honour my mother and respect her words, I cannot accept their wisdom without a sigh." She continues: "when I imagine such a picture, painted before me, I cannot think it pleasant to look upon" (60). Joan is not able to articulate what exactly makes her mother's picture of home and nation unpleasant, or what her own alternative picture would be. And yet, she knows that she yearns for something else: "what it is that I want, I cannot tell, although I crave for it, and in some secret way, expect it" (60). As the journal proceeds, we come to see that Joan's alternative picture that she "secret[ly]" craves includes a vision that discloses her subversive yearning to have contact with others. She writes, "often, and oftener as time goes by, I find myself suddenly halting in my walk, as though I were stopped by a strange new look upon the surface of the land which I know so well. It hints at something; but it is gone before I know what it means. It is as though a new smile crept out of a well known face; it half frightens you, and yet it beckons"(60).

How should we read this somewhat enigmatic experience of confronting the look of the land, new but familiar, frightening but friendly at the same time? Derrida's observations regarding "the indefiniteness of the '*es spukt*" read together with Dillon's discussion on the politics of security, I think, provides us with a possible clue for reading the passage. Roughly speaking, one of the tasks that Derrida and Dillon's deconstructive discourses seek to perform is to help us to look at those instances where western metaphysics deconstructs itself from within. To apply a Derridian project, I would argue that the above-cited passage from Joan's journal deconstructs the ideology of home—and the related construction of the self/inside based on the hierarchal barrier between self/inside and Other/outside. Like Lawrence's encounter with the dark god who delivers undecipherable messages, or the meeting of the self with the "unnameable," "undecidable," and "*heimliche-unheimliche*" haunting stranger in Derrida (172), Joan's encounter with the simultaneously familiar and strange, hostile and friendly look of the land destabilizes the very ground of self/home/nation by questioning the seemingly self-evident barriers between self/inside/familiar/virtuous and Other/outside/strange/degenerate. Instead of simply reversing the image of the Other or granting the Other a subversive force (namely, reinforcing fictive walls that perpetuate domination and discrimination, thus being recaught in the vicious circle of the ideology of home), the passage deconstructs the ideology of home instilled in Joan's psyche by pointing to both her "anxiety and the desire to exclude" and the desire "to invite" "the stranger" (Derrida 172). That is to say, Joan's encounter with the Other shows that the homemaking ideology is at once operative and dismantled by the indefinite image of the Other—who is familiar, hospitable, strange, and hostile all at the same time—the image that refuses to be fixed by any imperial gaze, constantly pointing to the ungroundedness and constructedness of self/home/nation. In a sense, reenacting Joan's previous encounters with people outside the home—the experiences that reverse rather than confirm what she has been told about them—Joan's curious meeting with the undecipherable look of the land gives us a glimpse of a new horizon of relationships with the Other.

Joan's journal in the short story explores the ideology of home and nation. It demonstrates how the ideal of a safe home can function in maintaining the dominant social order by erecting physical and psychological barriers between inside(r) and outside(r). Joan's meeting with poor, wandering people during her journey outside the home points to the discrepancy between what she discovers in these people and what her family has described about them, exposing the problematic process of excluding, criminalizing, or domesticating less privileged people involved in the discourse of home. Through Joan's conversation with her mother, who draws upon the metaphor of an island to teach her daughter how to build and maintain the home and the nation, the story demonstrates how the ideology of home serves as a basis for building and legitimizing the imperial nation. Going beyond exposing ideological implications embedded in the discourse of home and nation, the story suggests a possibility for a better vision of home and human relationships through Joan's writing that is filled with doubts and interrogations that deconstruct the wall between safe/virtuous/inside(r) and dangerous/vicious/outside(r).

DEMOLISHING THE IMPERIAL HOME/ NATION: *THE WAVES*

Woolf's critical exploration of the ideology of home and nation finds a more explicit attack on British imperialism in *The Waves* (1931). Woolf scholars have increasingly drawn their attention to the political implications of the novel in reference to British imperialism.[1] My aim here is to demonstrate that the critique of the ideology of home in the novel is integral to the attack on British imperialism by analyzing the ways in which the tropes of home/nation, such as the country house and the island, and the characters' discourses of home/nation at once expose and disrupt ideological implications embedded in the process of building the imperial home/nation.

Composed of nine interludes alternating with nine episodes, the novel presents six characters speaking in monologue from childhood to old age. As if the wish of Joan's mother, Mrs. Martyn in "The Journal" has been fulfilled, the novel begins with an interlude in which appears a miniature of the nation, the English country house and a garden on a shore. Far from conveying an image of a cozy Edenic haven, however, the portrait of the country house becomes loaded with violence and anxiety. The garden turns out to be a place of violence and decay, anticipating Percival's violent domination of the colonized in India in the fourth episode. Note the use of language that evokes and disrupts the imperial discourse about the colonized (land and people). Searching deep down the "dark" avenues into the "unlit world," one of the birds in the garden "beautifully darting, accurately alighting, spiked the soft, monstrous body of the defenceless worm, pecked again and yet again, and left it to fester" (74). The garden is filled with "decayed" flowers, "rotten" fruits, and dead bodies of worms (75). In this horrid picture of a garden the distinction between the "beautiful" bird and the "monstrous" worm becomes blurred. The passage goes on to reverse the imperial discourse by rendering the bird "savage" (75).

The colonial subtext becomes more explicit by the end of the third interlude through the racialized image of the waves on the shore:

> The wind rose. The waves drummed on the shore, like turbaned warriors, like turbaned men with poisoned assegais who, whirling their arms on high, advance upon the feeding flock, the white sheep. (75)

In a sense, the image of the threatening waves—that has already appeared in the imagination of Joan's mother as the "turbulent" "tides" to be "fence[d]" off to "secur[e]" the small island of home/nation—points to the sense of anxiety surrounding the imperial house. To borrow Füredi's observations again, the above passage can be read as a reflection of the white western elite's fear and anxiety in the face of the rapid decline of their hegemony.[2] Indeed, as Sonita Sarker points out, Woolf was aware of the contemporary "anxiety about white racial decline and fears of the encroaching hordes from Asia and Africa" and warnings about "imminent racial wars" or "racial revenge" (3). It is no wonder that the songs of the birds in the garden are ridded with "fear"

(73). Like Lawrence's vengeful dark God, the fearful image of turbaned warriors with assegais is an indicator of the anxiety of those who consciously or unconsciously colluded in the act of suppression or domination.[3] The cry of the Turks that haunts Rhoda later is another pointer to the anxiety of the imperial subject. At the reunion dinner, Rhoda says, "We hear a drumming on the roofs of a fasting city when the Turks are hungry and uncertain tempered. We hear them crying with sharp, stag-like larks, 'Open, Open'" (230). In these ways, the third interlude disrupts the conventional pictures of home and nation by connecting them not through decency, morality, and comfort, but through decay, anxiety, and violence.

The country house in the interludes reappears as a setting against which the six characters' childhoods are depicted in the first episode. As time passes those six characters disperse to distinct geographical locations, and yet the country house as a crucial icon of the English home and nation binds these characters together. In the novel the characters—who share the memory of a childhood revolving around the country house—in one way or another express a collective fantasy about the colonized. For example, in the forth episode where the characters gather together at a farewell party for Percival—who is leaving for India—they imagine the nation by employing the Victorian discourse of home, discourse that revolves around the ideas of inside, outside, enclosure, and walls. Neville, for example, relishes a sense of safety by "being walled in here" while "India lies outside." For Rhoda, the colonized territory is "part of our proud and splendid province." In her fantasy, the entire world—"forests and far countries on the other side of the world . . . seas and jungles; the howlings of jackals. . . ."—is enclosed within the "globe whose walls are made of Percival"(145). Neville, Susan, and Jenny also enumerate things that are within the wall, revealing the imperial psyche that imagines the whole world to be their own. Bernard's monologue epitomizes this imperial spirit: "what is outside?. . . . We are creators. . . . We . . . stride . . . into a world that our own force can subjugate and make part of the illumined and everlasting road" (146). As the novel proceeds, the embodiment of the British Empire, Percival finds a sudden death by falling from a horse. In the sixth episode we see the characters struggling to survive in the aftermath of his death, and here again we encounter an instance that attests to the connection between the ideologies of home and imperialism. Susan, now a mother of a baby, speaks: "Sleep, I say, and feel within me uprush some wilder, darker violence, so that I would fell down with one blow any intruder, any snatcher, who should break into this room and wake the sleeper" (172). Susan's soliloquy reveals a violent and exclusionary drive lying beneath her seemingly natural maternal instinct to protect the baby and the home. The "warm shelter" that Susan defends is in effect the home that raises an inheritor of Percival, the imperial soldier. The home is the place to which Susan's son will return from India "bringing [her] trophies" (172).

Going further than exposing the imperial drive lurking beneath the discourse of home, the novel dismantles the imperial discourse of home/nation from within, first through the disruption of the cultural fantasy of the self and the Other, and, second, through the characters' contradictions, self-consciousness, or self-questioning. In the forth interlude, for example, we encounter a shift in the connotation of the waves. Whereas the waves in the previous interlude were rather explicitly associated with the racial Other threatening the "white sheep," here they are aligned with the imperial soldiers, destabilizing the previous association of the racial, colonized Other with danger, invasion, and threat. The waves are likened to "the lances and assegais" not of turbaned warriors but of the "riders" of "horses" (108), and the image of Percival who dominates in India, "rid[ing] a flea-bitten mare" and using "violent language," further confirms the connection between the waves and imperial power (136). The description of the waves goes on to align imperialism with ruthless, mechanical, and masculine force: they "swept the beach . . . [and] drew in and out with the energy, the muscularity of an engine which sweeps its force out and in again" (108).

As we have seen, the characters mouth imperial sentiment in their employment of the discourse of home. This does not mean, however, that the novel reduces them to an unredeemable homogeneous group of the imperial subject.[4] Although they are implicated to varying degrees in the imperialist discourse, they contradict or challenge dominant ideologies. For example, in comparison with Louis, who frequently employs typical imperial discourse, Rhoda reveals an awareness of her own complicity in the imperial project, an awareness that brings her a more acute sense of anxiety than others (as evidenced by the fact that she is the only one who keeps being haunted by the colonized Other) and keeps her from blindly replicating imperial language. Speaking their feelings for Percival in India, Rhoda speaks to Louis about her imaginary hearing of the "dancing and drumming of naked men with assegais." To this, Louis responds by drawing upon imperial language that defines the nature of the colonized as being violent and uncivilized: "They are savage; they are ruthless. They dance in a circle . . . over their painted faces, over the leopard skins and the bleeding limbs which they have torn from the living body" (140), suppressing the context of brutal imperial invasion. Instead of subscribing to Louis's discourse, Rhoda draws Louis's attention to the fact that they are "conspirators" facing impending death as the British Empire comes to an end: "Louis, we are aware of downfalling, we forebode decay. The shadow slants. We who are conspirators . . . note how the purple flame flows downwards" (141). As Rhoda foresaw, Percival, the symbol of the British empire, dies and the rest of the interludes portrays the gradual demise of the empire through the emblem of the imperial nation—the sun and the "island" both sinking (182, 236).

Bernard's soliloquy employs more complex and contradictory discourses than those of others, at times revealing articulate imperial ideology and at times demonstrating subversive potential, especially in his rebellion against the conventional idea of home. Where Rhoda is reluctant to submit to Louis's domination, Bernard questions it: "How then, I asked, would Louis roof us all in? How would he confine us, make us one, with his red ink, with his very fine nib?" (282). Bernard's comparison of Louis to a house is significant because, I think, it once again signifies a critical redecoding of the cultural icon of the house—not as a place of virtue and comfort that is a microcosm of the nation, but as a place of confinement and domination that mirrors and sustains the Empire. In the last episode Bernard speaks to an anonymous and invisible companion about his self-positioning in the past as an inheritor of the culture and power that Percival represented: "I was the inheritor; I, the continuer; I, the person miraculously appointed to carry it on" (253–54). Bernard's recollection of the past self as an imperial subject curiously leads to his visit to a house—"the dry, uncompromising, inhabited house, the place with all its traditions, its objects, its accumulations of rubbish, and treasures displayed upon tables" (255). In the house—as a metonymy for the imperial nation as well as a literal location—people talk about "what is to be done about India, Ireland or Morocco?" (255). And here Bernard employs the imperial/Victorian discourse of home, discourse that contrasts home (associated with virtuous features like safety, order, or reason) with the outer world (filled with danger, noise, or violence). He speaks: "Outside the undifferentiated forces roar; inside we are very private, every explicit, have a sense indeed, that it is here, in this little room, that we make whatever day of the week it may be" (255). Capable of self-questioning, however, Bernard shows a critical awareness of problematic beliefs in historical progress and militarism that sustain imperialism: "But it is a mistake, this extreme precision, this orderly and military progress; a convenience, a lie," he says (255). More importantly, he proceeds to imagine a new vision of home, human relationships, or life in general, referring back to the "walls of this globe" "made of Percival" within which every character felt proud and safe in the previous episode. Far from securing enclosure, it is hardly visible. It does not divide the inside from the outside. He speaks, "The crystal, the globe of life as one calls it, far from being hard and cold to the touch, has walls of thinnest air" (256). And finally, like Birkin or Somers in Lawrence, Bernard voices a strong wish to demolish the conventional home: "Was there no sword, nothing with which to batter down these walls, this protection, this begetting of children and living behind curtains?" (265), epitomizing the subversive impulse that propels Woolf's writing of the novel, the impulse to destruct the protective/aggressive and inclusive/exclusionary wall of the imperial home and nation.

TOWARD AN ALTERNATIVE HOME/NATION IN *THE YEARS*

As I briefly mentioned in the introduction to this section, the period from approximately 1840 to 1880 saw the prevalence of the single-family house in the metropolis of England. As architectural studies have illuminated, the preponderance of the family house around that time is a notable indicator of the contemporary British ideology of domestic space.[5] The single-family house was a material embodiment of the ideal of home as a self-enclosed private terrain, an ideal that was tied up with the (upper) middle-class impulse to maintain physical and psychological distance from less privileged people. At the same time, contemporary architectural discourses testify to the fact that this form of residence served as a powerful symbol of national identity that would distinguish England from other countries. Some articles that appeared in *The Builder*—England's leading architectural periodical at that time—for example, pointed out the risks of standardization and social and spatial blending that they found in the popularity of the apartment in France. Privileging architectural individuation over French apartments, they claimed the superiority of the English urban residence that secures the division between the genders within the family as well as the upper- and middle-class's distance from the less privileged urban populace, often associated with filth, disease, moral deviation, or sexual looseness.[6] Other architects made pleas (though not successfully) for the apartment building, claiming that the apartment provides privacy and separateness as much as the single-family house does. Despite their different evaluations of the apartment, these debates reveal the ideological implications that underpin the valorization of the single-family house, and testify to the connection between the construction of home and that of class and national identity as well. At the same time, the architectural debates attest to the cultural anxiety that began to surface in the face of the increasing need to live in the proximity to the rapidly growing urban populous, whom the British elite often stigmatized in terms of their economic or class standings, race, or nationality.[7] Along with the growing socio-geographical mobility since the Victorian era onwards, the

Victorian ideal of home and home country became less and less sustainable, and, accordingly, so did the self-image of the privileged, their home, and their nation as superior.

The story of three generations of a middle-class family, the Pargiters, in *The Years* (1937) provides a glimpse of an alternative vision of home and nation set against the decline of the single-family house from 1880 to 1937. Stressing Woolf's original plan to deal with the "sexual lives of women" (*Diary* 4: 6), many critics have read *The Years* in light of the writer's feminist concern with or participation in the contemporary intellectual attack on the Victorian family system that she found repressive to women's psychological and physical lives.[8] Other critics have emphasized the issue of time evoked by the novel's title.[9] Hardly any critic has drawn her/his attention to the fact that one of the working titles of the novel was "Other People's Houses" (*Diary* 4: 335). This title is telling, for it reveals that Woolf was concerned with space as much as with time, and it invites us to look at the novel's concern with other people's (not merely women's) lives and houses.

The Years explores the shifting sense of home and national identity from 1880 to 1937, a socio-geographical and psychological phenomenon that has much to do with the decline of single family houses and the increasing predominance of flats and rented rooms as a new form of home. Set in the late Victorian era, the novel begins with the Pargiter home in Abercorn Terrace—to which all the daughters are confined and from which they dream of escape. About a decade later, however, we come to see that the daughters of the Pargiter family have just started leaving their father's house. Delia, for example, has left Abercorn Terrace to pursue her sexual and political life. The musings of Eleanor, the eldest daughter, on life in the immigrant neighborhood of London where Delia lives, describe the changing urban landscape that surrounds Delia's new home: "The houses were let out in offices, to societies, to people whose names were pinned up on the door-posts. The whole neighbourhood seemed to her foreign and sinister. . . . Rooms were let out to single gentlemen only. There were cards in them which said 'Furnished Apartments' or 'Bed and Breakfast.' She guessed at the life that went on behind those thick yellow curtains" (114–15). In the 1910 section we see Delia's cousins, Maggie and Sara Pargiter, living in a shabby flat after leaving their family house. The scene where Rose, Delia's youngest sister, visits this dwelling place, shows that the days of "a large family living in a large house" have almost gone (168). The next chapter, set in 1911, further shows the socio-spatial change around that time. The death of the father Abel Pargiter finally emancipates Eleanor from the house. Coming home from Greece and Spain, she feels "no attachment at the moment any where" and seeks a new place to live (195). More significantly, Abel's death marks the demise of the family house and the emerging demand for flats. Eleanor tries to sell Abercorn Terrace but it would not sell easily. "The agent wants me to cut it up into flats" (206), she says to her sister-in-law, Celia. Two years later Abercorn Terrace is still for sale. Viewing Abercorn Terrace as an embodiment of "an abominable system"—"the family life"—Margin thinks, "No wonder the house would not let" (222). The novel ends with Delia's party for the family reunion that takes place in rented rooms.

These allusions to housing reflect the architectural change between the late Victorian era and 1930s; as the Victorian age came to an end, English urban society saw the increasing demand for flats or rented rooms instead of for single-family houses. We may infer that, given the (upper) middle- class aversion to socio-spatial mixing as illustrated by the architectural debates over apartments during the mid-nineteenth century, the increasing preva-lence of flats or rented rooms as a new home might have something to do with social and cultural, as well as psychological changes during that time.

My point here is not, of course, to simplify the significance of living in flats and lodgings by interpreting it as a liberating and subversive movement toward a less exclusionary, less repressive home and nation. Not all members of the Pargiter family welcome their new homes in flats and rented rooms. Many of the Pargiter daughters leave the fathers' house not in order to live close to urban neighbors, most of whom were the marginalized poor, but to seek emancipation and independence. A lack of money forces them to seek cheap rooms in poor urban districts, those places that have been socially taboo. In the novel, most of the Pargiter daughters are averse to, complaining of, or at least uneasy about the geographical proximity with those poor or foreign Others. To put it differently, their feminism is frequently accompa-nied by anxiety that points to class or nationalist ideology inculcated by mid-dle-class education. In this respect, the novel shows the possible complicity of middle-class women with the patriarchal system that causes jingoistic nationalism, fascism, Nazism, hierarchy, and war, an issue that Woolf expounds in *Three Guineas*. In the novel, however, characters like Sara or Maggie invite us to look at their feminist choice of a dwelling place in slums as an active political choice that heralds a less inclusive and discriminating home and nation.

In *The Years*, members of the Pargiter family prefer, are forced, or choose to live in different dwelling places for diverse reasons, expectations, or complaints, revealing distinct ideological limits or possibilities. The novel opens with the depiction of Colonel Abel Pargiter on his way to his mistress Mira's boarding house, located in a poor and dingy district. From the first, the novel demonstrates the middle-class man's bias against poor inhabitants, with whom he associates filth, disease, and lack of morality. In the Colonel's eyes, even children living in these dingy habitats seem to be "sordid, mean," and "furtive"(7). He finally meets Mira, but she is "untidy," and her dog appears to be infected by eczema (7). Instead of merely depicting the Colonel's reaction to this less privileged area and its inhabitants, the novel uses irony to disrupts and mock his bias. For instance, it is the Colonel himself who is "furtive" in the sense that he is the most concerned about being observed, keeping his affair with Mira secret until death. Furthermore, his aversion to filth is mocked by the recurrent image of "a dark stain" on his armchair (18; 213).

Abel's youngest daughter Rose has traumatic encounter with an exhibitionist at the pillar box. That is an example of the complex ways in which Woolf interweaves her feminist concerns with female confinement at home and repression of female sexuality, her own traumatic experience of sexual abuse at home, and the issues of the class and nationalist ideologies implicated in the Victorian home. One evening, Rose, aged ten, asks her brother Martin to accompany her to Lamley's, a toy store, but they argue, and she goes out alone. On her way to the shop and again on her way back to home, Rose encounters and is terrified by a sexual deviant who exposes himself to her. This traumatic experience haunts her through nightmares of the man's invasion of the house but she cannot talk about it with anyone. Woolf scholars have uncovered multiple layers of meaning in this exhibitionist episode. As critics like Laura Moss Gottlieb and Susan Squier have noted, the episode demonstrates the social and geographic restrictions on women in the later Victorian period. The incident with the sexually perverted man is a kind of social penalty that Rose pays for her violation of the injunction on women never to go outside the home alone. Critics such as David Eberly, Roger Poole, and Margot Gayle Backus have analyzed the episode in relation to Woolf's own need both to excavate and to bury her childhood incest trauma that she was forced not to speak about within the Victorian home. [10]

From another angle, Woolf's careful displacement of the danger of the molestation of young girls by men within the home onto a poor man in the street functions as an apt device to explore the class bias and imperialism underlying the cultural myth of home in the context of a feminine fear of being in public spaces alone.

> Now the adventure has begun, Rose said to herself as she stole on tiptoes to the night nursery. Now she must provide herself with ammunition and provisions; she must steal Nurse's latchkey; but where was it?

Every night it was hidden in a new place for fear of burglars. . . . She turned the latch of the front door with extreme gentleness, and closed it with scarcely a click behind her. Until she was round the corner she crouched close to the wall so that nobody could see her. When she reached the corner under the laburnum tree she stood erect. "I am Par-giter of Pargiter's Horse," she said, flourishing her hand, "riding to the rescue!" She was riding by night on a desperate mission to a besieged garrison, she told herself. She had a secret message—she clenched her fist on her purse—to deliver to the General in person. All their lives depended upon it. The British flag was still flying on the central tower—Lamley's shop was the central tower. . . . All their lives depended upon her riding to them through the enemy's country. Here she was galloping across the desert. She began to trot. . . . the pavement stretched before her broad and dark. Then there was the crossing; and then there was Lamley's shop on the little island of shops opposite. She had only to cross the desert, to ford the river, and she was safe. . . . As she ran past the pillar-box the figure of a man suddenly emerged under the gas lamp. "The Enemy!" Rose cried to herself. "The enemy! Bang!" she cried, pulling the trigger of her pistol and looking him full in the face as she passed him. It was a horrid face; white, peeled, pock-marked; he leered at her. He put out his arm as if to stop her. He almost caught her. She dashed past him. The game was over. She was herself again, a little girl who had disobeyed her sister, in her house shoes, flying for safety to Lamley's shop. (26–28)

As in "The Journal of Mistress Joan Martyn," the passage points to the ways in which poor people outside the home—burglar and the man at the pillar-box—are connected with the colonized outside the nation through the image of an enemy who threatens home and nation. Rose's search for the latchkey located in the Victorian household links her feminine fear to the middle-class's anxiety to secure its property, anxiety that might partly derive from its awareness of the unjust exploitation of poor lower-class Others as well as from actual danger.[11] Rose's fantasy of being on her way to rescue people for the cause of the "British flag" introduces patriotism and imperialism into the scene as well. The world outside the home is likened to the desert, the enemy's country, a dangerous space that threatens the imagined territory of the nation. Rose imagines herself as a soldier passing through the desert toward the "safe" Lamley's shop located on an "island." This use of the English cultural trope of the nation intimates the connection between the Victorian ideology of home and imperial nation. Curiously reenacting the reaction to people in the poor district displayed by Rose's father, Abel, the former colonial officer, the episode points out how the construction of the middle-class self/home and the imperial self/home are founded on the construction of the Other/outside as dangerous and inferior, a construction that justifies violence by the former against the latter in the name of protection and safety. In short, the episode complicates the feminist issues of the powerlessness of women in the face of the male sexual assault and the ideology of separate space by bringing up the issues of the class and imperial ideologies tied up with the ideology of home. Woolf's ambivalent treatment of Rose further confirms her critical insight into the potential violence of the cultural fantasy of the middle-class self, home, and nation. Rose grows to be a militant suffragette and goes to prison for throwing a brick through a window. For the confirmed pacifist like Woolf, Rose's violence and militarism are problematic in their alliance with the masculine power structure that sustains the patriarchal and imperial English nation.[12]

Throughout the novel, characters reveal various responses to the changing landscape of home. To some extent, their choices of or preferences for specific dwelling places are indicative of different ideological limits or possibilities. For example, one of the most conventional figures in the novel, Milly, who is compared to the "trap of the family," lives in a country house that gives her a sense of stasis and an illusion of permanency as well as secures the conventional distance from people with lower social standings (374). The servant Crosby's strong attachment to Abercorn Terrace and her antipathy toward flats are tied up with her prejudice against other marginalized people, indicating that the hypocritical obsession with cleanliness and morality and the class bias Abel illustrates has been instilled in this domestic worker's psyche as well. As the Pargiter family leaves Abercorn Terrace, Crosby also moves to a "single room" at a top floor of a flat (216). Instead of enjoying any benefits brought by the spatial change from the dark and dank basement at Abercorn Terrace to the new dwelling place,[13] she misses the traditional family house. For her, only Abercorn Terrace is "home" and she "[does] not like flats" (216, 221). Ironically mimicking the middle-class bias against lower-class people, she grumbles that her flat is located on Richmond Street which "a common sort of people liv[e] in" (219). Her antipathy to social blending is revealed again later through her biased view of a foreign neighbor she now serves. Extremely angry at the "dirty Belgian," she thinks resentfully, "I've been used to work for gentlefolk, not for dirty foreigners" (302, 304). Crosby gathers all the relicts from the family house and attempts to recuperate the home centered on a picture of Martin in his military dress (218). This can be read as another incident that points to the connection between the Victorian ideology of home and the imperial nation. That is to say, Crosby's negative response to the new form of home once again discloses the prejudices against poor, lower-class, or alien people and the impulse not to make contact with these people that underpins the Victorian ideal of home and English nationhood.

Unlike most other Pargiter family members, Sara and Maggie, the daughters of Abel's brother Digby and Eugénie, show somewhat different responses to the new architecture of home and the attendant socio-spatial blending. After their parents died and their family-house on Browne Street was sold, Sara and Maggie move to a run-down apartment in a slum area, Hyams Place. During her visit to this place, Rose is annoyed by the "swarm of sound, the rush of traffic, the shouts of the hawkers, the single cries and the general cries"(163) constantly coming into the room. To Rose's question, "don't you find it rather noisy?" (165), Sara answers affirmatively, but goes on to stress the convenience of the location. Later, in the 1917 section, we see Maggie living in "one of the obscure little streets under the shadow of the Abbey" with her husband Renny, a French expatriate (179). When Eleanor visits Maggie and Renny's home, they dine in a basement with no servant in sight (282). In the "Present Day" section we come to know that Sara is now living alone in a shabby lodging-house room located in a "dirty," "sordid," and "low-down street" near the Prison Tower (311). Echoing Rose's slight tone of rebuke, North, on his visit to Sara, asks "why d'you always choose slums?" (314) and is bothered by the noise from children's screams, a trombone player on the street, and the voice of a woman practicing her scales (315).

To some extent, those shabby rooms point to the genteel poverty that middle-class women seeking independence had to fight. But their dire economic condition is not the only factor in Sara and Maggie's choices for their dwelling places. As the complaints of their cousin Rose or nephew North about the location of their abode intimate, Maggie and Sara probably could have found a better place to live. Their choice of home is indicative of their being less hampered by class or imperial ideology, and with them Woolf gives us a glimpse of a positive vision of home and nation in the future. Woolf herself was keenly aware of the politics of the location of home. After her father's death, the Stephen children decided to move from Kensington to Gordon Square, Bloomsbury. For the purpose of my study, one of the most significant aspects of Bloomsbury is that it was an area of "shabby-genteel poverty"—as Thomas Burke puts it in *Living in Bloomsbury* (qtd. in Snaith 256). Virginia reveals her awareness of the bad reputation of that area: "Jack [Hills] . . . showed us the neighbourhood which he thinks bad and says we should never get anybody to come and see us, or to dine (*The Letters of Virginia Woolf* 1:

120). Despite their knowledge of the bad reputation of that place, Vanessa and Virginia decided to live there, and part of the sense of liberation that Virginia felt in her new home (*Diary* 1: 86), I believe, comes from a vision of a more open human relationship.[14]

Although Woolf did not live in shabby flats, the above incident suggests that she was aware of the political significance that the location of home has. As Jean Moorcroft Wilson suggests, when Woolf has Sara live in lodgings near Waterloo station—which is socially taboo for her class—she means to show how little Sara cares for conventional norms or social niceties (Wilson 13). More telling indications of the political significance that Woolf attached to the location of Sara's home can be found in *Three Guineas*. At one point Woolf expresses her hope that women will build their rooms in "the new house, the poor house, the house that stands in a narrow street where omnibuses pass and the street hawkers cry their wares" (83). Thus, in *The Years* Woolf has Sara and Maggie move out of the family house into an inexpensive room at Hyams Place, where Rose is annoyed by the "swarm of sound, the rush of traffic, the shouts of the hawkers, the single cries and the general cries," and later again, Sara moves into another "cheap-lodging-house" where North's attempt to speak with Sara is constantly interrupted by "the voice of the singer" and the "screaming" children in the street (314).

Through such spatial and discursive practices, the novel criticizes traditional ideologies of home and delivers glimpses of an alternative home and human relationships. Woolf's own reflection on these characters is especially telling in this respect. Disapproving of Stephen Spender's complaint about her negative treatment of all characters in the novel, Woolf, in her letter to Spender on April 30, 1937, writes that although she depicted most characters as being "crippled in one way or another . . . [that she] meant Maggie and Sara to be outside that particular prison" (*Letters* 6: 122). Sara and Maggie emerge as pioneers who escape from the prison of the single-family house to seek an alternative home—the thin walls of which bring their lives into close contact with the marginalized.

Indeed, Sara's and Maggie's choices of dwelling places are not ill considered. Their housing decisions point to their ability or willingness to live in propinquity with other people in a less exclusionary, repressive, and isolated home. This capability, in some sense, has been developed by distinct spatial experiences they had in childhood. Sara and Maggie have been brought up in domestic surroundings quite different from those of Abercorn Terrace. Contrary to the tidy, quiet, and orderly rooms in Abercorn Terrace, the house of Digby and his wife Eugénie is characterized by its openness and naturalness. In the eyes of Colonel Pargiter, who is accustomed to neatness and orderliness,

Eugénie's house is untidy and noisy: "Here the door opened and as he went upstairs he thought he hears, from somewhere in the background, a shout of laughter"(118). The "untidy" drawing room where the piano and windows are open remains an enduring image in the memory of anther visitor, Martin, who, like his father, had deep affection for Eugénie. "I liked her [Eugénie]," Martin says to Eleanor, "I liked going there." In his mind's eye, "he saw the untidy room; the piano open, the window open . . . and his aunt coming forward with her arms open" (152). Another episode is suggestive of the openness and generosity that Eugénie's house embodies. Just before the scene in which Abel Pargiter arrives at Eugénie's house, an Italian housemaid in a basement talks with an Italian manservant about a hat that Eugénie gave her "to atone for the mess in the drawing-room" (117). In contrast with Eugénie's attitude toward the Italian servants, as illustrated by this scene, Abel does not like to be served by these "Italian dagoes"(118). His bias against foreigners is clear. As daughters of Eugénie, Sara and Maggie learned not to be restricted by cultural imperatives but to come to terms with living with the less privileged and the foreign. The legacy of their mother's character and her distinctive spatial practices in the home enable Maggie and Sara to live in contact with other classes and types of people. It is no accident that Sara is a close friend of a homosexual foreigner, Nicholas, and Maggie is married to a French expatriate, Renny.

In contrast to Eugénie's house, where the servants' laughter could be heard and the drawing room was left untidy, order is maintained at Abercorn Terrace by means of relentless exploitation of servants' labor. In contrast with Eugénie's house—where the housemaid dances, the manservant reads a paper, and the servant is rewarded for her labor—, the rooms of Abercorn Terrace are filled with "all the solid objects that Crosby dusted and polished every day" (117, 35). Every family member in Abercorn Terrace is ordered to follow conventional norms and decorum, performing culturally imposed roles (13). Here there can be no communication between servants and masters. Crosby never talks back but only "grin[s]" (152). Here Abel's daughters live with the suffocating patriarchal father who does not tolerate noise, untidiness, and unconventional gender roles. Abercorn Terrace serves as an embodiment of the middle-class preoccupation with hygiene and order combined with its prejudice against poor, lower-class, and foreign Others, prejudice that has sustained the fantasy of the superior self and home. In Abercorn Terrace "everything seemed to take such an intolerable time" (10) and "the world outside seemed thickly and entirely cut off" (20). In Delia's mind, her mother's sick room characterized by its "cleanliness, quiet and order" (22) is an "an obstacle, a prevention, an impediment to all life" (22). As these phrases suggest, Woolf, like Lawrence, detects inertia and the desire for the status quo and enclosure that secures the distance from the Other in the physical and psychological structure of the Victorian ideal of home and nation.

Sara and Maggie are the only characters who are self-conscious about the middle-class antipathy to living in close contact with the poor urban populace. The scene in which Sara and Maggie talk about their home is telling in that both the text and the conversation are concerned with how the privileged class easily imagines the poor as morally degraded and sexually perverted. Sara has just come back home from a meeting (most likely a suffragette meeting that she attended at Rose's invitation):

> There was a sound of brawling in the street outside. . . . "Another row?" Maggie murmured, sticking her needle in the stuff. Sara got up and went to the window. A crowd had gathered outside the public-house. A man was being thrown out. There he came, staggering. . . . Sara stood for a moment at the window watching them. The she turned; her face in the mixed light looked cadaverous and worn, as if she were no longer a girl, but an old woman worn out by a life of childbirth, debauchery, and crime. (188–89)

The description of Sara's face plays out the association of poverty, female suffering, promiscuity, and crime. The immediately following dialogue between Sara and Maggie shows their awareness of the cultural meaning attached to their dwelling place and its inhabitants. "'In time to come,' Sara says to her sister, 'people, looking into this room—this cave, this little antre, scooped out of mud and dung, will hold their fingers to their noses'—she held her fingers to her nose—'and say, Pah! They stink!'" (189). Maggie agrees with Sara: "It was true. . . . They [Sara and herself] were nasty little creatures, driven by uncontrollable lusts" (189). Here, Sara and Maggie mock the way in which people of their class associate dwellers in poor districts with filth and excessive sexuality, revealing their awareness of the social disapproval of their choice of dwelling place. Indeed, Sara's frequent echoing or imitation of the words of others, loaded with derision,[15] confirms that she deliberately foregrounds the class bias against poor urban Other which upholds the construction of the middle-class self-image and home.

As Sara predicted, when her nephew North visits her shabby room, he "mak[es] noise like 'Pah!'"(340), expressing his loathing of social and spatial mingling with the marginalized. North tries to read to Sara "The Garden" by Andrew Marvell, a poem which celebrates solitude, but his reading is violated by the sound in the opposite room of "the Jew having a bath" (339). When Sara tells him that she shares the bath with the Jew who leaves grease and hair in the tub, North feel[s] "a shiver run through him" and "physically sick" (340). Critics have often read the episode in terms of an anti-Semitism that Sara shares with North,[16] but a close look at the conversation shows that it is North's deeply felt antipathy, not Sara's, that surfaces. Here, Sara seems to have already known what North's response would likely be and deliberately instigated his disgust that reveals his aversion to living together with poor urban neighbors. Sara admits her own initial disgust at the shared bath with the Jew, but then she begins to mock the contemporary urban discourse so as to subtly (not forcefully) awaken North to problematic ideologies embedded in this discourse, ideologies from which neither North nor Sara is exempt.[17] On the day when she first confronted her own anti-Semitism, Sara recalls:

> I came back into the sitting-room and breakfast was waiting. Fried eggs and a bit of toast. Lydia with her blouse torn and her hair down. The unemployed singing hymns under the window. And I said to myself— She flung her hand out, "Polluted city, unbelieving city, city of dead fish and worn-out frying-pans."(340)

In the above passage, Sara deliberately foregrounds the middle-class gaze directed at servants and the entire urban landscape. She mocks the middle-class discourse that associates the lower class with untidiness and possibly with moral and sexual looseness (through the image of Lydia). Sara goes on to echo the contemporary elitist urban discourse that associates the urban space (and by implication, the urban populace) with pollution, filth, distrust, and odor while suppressing the exploitation of lower-class labor and trivializing the issue of financial hardship through the image of the unemployed singing. Through this, Sara conveys a criticism of North's egotistic impulse to evade the agony and suffering of other people by building an impregnable wall of solitude.

The political significance of Sara's dwelling places are a kind of prelude to Delia's family reunion party at the end of the novel, a party which gives us a glimpse of an alternative home and nation, a space for coexistence with different people with different social standings, value systems, and perspectives. Delia's party conveys the vision of a new domestic space where "all sorts of people" gather, "do[ing] away the absurd conventions of English life" (398). Here, "there [are] nobles and commoners; people dressed and people not dressed; people drinking out of mugs," homosexuals, the colonized like an "Indian in a pink turban," and foreigners (354).

The episode of the caretaker's children singing in front of the party guests epitomizes the novel's concern with the ideological limits and possibilities of the middle-class in the face of the changing landscape of home that put their lives in close contact with the marginalized. At this symbolic moment of encounter with the working class children, we encounter Delia's perspective on the children delivered in free indirect discourse:

> The children took the slices and stared at them with a curious fixed stare as if they were fierce. But perhaps they were frightened, because she [Delia] had brought them up from the basement into the drawing-room. (428–29)

Reminiscent of Joan Martyn's curious encounter with the look of the land that is simultaneously hostile and friendly, the contradictory image of the children—"fierce" or "frightened"—points to both the "indefiniteness" of the uncanny Other. It also points to the arbitrary construction of the image of the outsider, a construction that projects the insider's anxiety and fear grounded in his or her unjust exploitation, subjugation, or exclusion, while blurring the distinction between who is frightful and who is frightened. As the children start singing, most of the family members find their "unintelligible" song "hideous," revealing their class prejudice as well as the latent resentment toward the invasion of the working class Other into their drawing room (430). But there are others who show more positive responses to their song. Turning to Maggie, Eleanor says "Beautiful?" To this, Maggie replies, "Extraordinarily" (431).

Given the fact that Eleanor's constant yearning for a better world—"another life"—to be realized in the "here and now" (428) and Maggie's capacity to live in close contact with less privileged people, it is no wonder that they show a more open understanding of the incomprehensible language of the working-class children, while they are cautious against translating it into the middle-class language.[18] In this sense, Eleanor and Maggie's responses deliver Woolf's argument for living together with other people, not with fear, anxiety, reluctance, or disgust, but with joy and understanding.[19]

Set in London from the late Victorian era to the 1930s, *The Years* critically shows how the Victorian middle-class home and its imperial nation have been built by the impulse to keep the lower-class, colonial, racial, and poor Other at bay. Through different reactions of Pargiter family members to the changing architecture of home from the single-family house to flats and boarding rooms, the novel demonstrates the ideological limits of and possibilities for the family. Although most of members of the Pargiter family reveal their ideological limits through their aversion to the socio-spatial mingling with the urban populace, characters like Maggie and Sara—"who do[es] not believe in force" and always cries "No idols" as did Woolf herself—heralds a dawning of a less exclusionary home, a vision that seeks to "to form" "new combinations" of people (232, 425, 296).

* * *

As we have seen, Lawrence and Woolf detect the problematic impulses to domesticate, stigmatize, or exclude less privileged people in the Victorian discourse of home, a discourse which revolves around the ideas of protection, safety, and enclosure. Their critical understandings of the conventional idea of home enable them to interrogate the metonymic association between home and nation. They illuminate how the nation, conceived through the trope of home, conceals domination for the cause of an organic whole, stability, and identity within the nation on the one hand, and imperial invasion abroad on the other hand. Thus, in their works, Lawrence and Woolf frequently draw on the home/nation connection not so much to reinstate the dominant ideologies as to expose patriarchal, class, gender, nationalist, or imperial ideologies operative in both the ideal of home and its mirror image of the nation.

At the core of Lawrence's and Woolf's critical investigations of the ideology of home and nation lies their desire to reestablish relationships with Others, who have been forgotten, suppressed, excluded, or denigrated as inferior or enemies, along with the construction of psychological and physical walls between inside and outside, home and away from home. However, instead of providing a naïve optimism for the new relationship with the Other—one that dreams of demolishing the age-old wall once and for all— Lawrence and Woolf seek to destabilize the wall of the house from within by bringing to the surface the anxiety and fear of the Other that sits uneasily beneath the insider's psyche, thus pointing to the prior acts of repression or suppression of the Other.

Part Three

Utopic Spaces Here and Now

Part Three Introduction

The literary scene where Lawrence and Woolf produced their works saw the appearance of various literary trends, including discourses of utopia. In addition to their immediate predecessor William Morris, contemporary writers such as H.G. Wells wrote influential works of and about utopia. Lawrence and Woolf, both diligent readers, certainly knew utopian works such as Morris' well-known socialist utopian fantasy, *News from Nowhere* (1890), or Wells's *A Modern Utopia* (1905), as evidenced by their mentions of them in novels, diaries, essays, and letters.

This does not mean, however, that Lawrence and Woolf advanced systematic theories or thoughts about utopia or utopian writing. Although Lawrence and Woolf did not locate their works in a direct relation to the traditional genre of utopia or utopian thinking, their acute sensitivity to the injustice, inequalities, and violence of their era compelled them to persistently envision and present a better world. To varying degrees, both writers at times expressed their yearning for a better world in traditional idioms of utopia, with their political possibilities and limitations. But in a greater number of instances, their remarks and literary works mark their shared impulse to break with traditional utopian visions and seek alternative ones. First of all, these writers' antipathy toward dogmatic prescriptions about the way the world ought to be that were rather typical of conventional utopian writings and thinking compelled them to seek less authoritative discourses about utopia. Furthermore, their understanding of space as a socio-cultural, historical, and discursive territory that was open to reinterpretation, restructuration, and reformulation, as we have seen in the previous chapters, enabled them to locate utopia in an ever-changing, dynamic space of everyday life, rather than in a remote, static, ideal space. Finally, their endorsement of diversity, dynamics, and process as important factors for the formation of the self and social change, helped them to shape their own alternative utopias, which emerge as open-ended processes in a dynamic chronotope of the here and now. In these respects, the visions of alternative utopias in Lawrence and Woolf anticipate recent scholars' attempts to redefine utopia and their arguments for a politics of utopian space that is anchored in everyday life.

Both as a model of an ideal society and as a literary genre, utopia has constituted a significant frame for thoughts, desires, political activities, and literary practices for centuries. As Ruth Levitas notes, utopia is fundamentally about "how we would live and what kind of a world we would live in if we could do just that" (1). As such, more than an image of an ideal life, utopia becomes "a claim about what it could and should be," thus constituting an important past of human culture and history (1). But my study does not aim to engage in a detailed examination of the concept of utopia and its philosophical, social, or political functions. Thus, my brief discussion about the theme of utopia in the following will be limited to looking at aspects of some recent theorists' views of utopia that are relevant to illuminating Lawrence's and Woolf's critiques of the ideological limits embedded in conventional visions of utopia, and so the political implications of their alternative utopian visions.

Ever since Thomas More coined the term "utopia" in his book *Utopia* (1516) by collapsing two Greek words—*eu-topia,* the good place, and *ou-topia,* no-place/nowhere–the term "utopia" has been a conceptual and ideological battleground.[1] It was not until the 1960s, however, that utopia emerged as an object of academic inquiry. Since then, an increasing number of scholars have mounted attacks on utopianism on the ground that it is fundamentally totalitarian or reactionary. Utopia, they contend, proposes authoritative and dogmatic prescriptions for a perfect society. It also reveals the desire for stasis, homogeneity, conformity, and harmony, and the fear of change and diversity.[2] It is at times associated with escapist impulses, the inability or refusal to engage with actual social life, or with a psychologically regressive desire to return to the womb. The adjective form, "utopian," is even more derogatory than the noun. It often connotes impractical idealism or elusive and impossible dreaming.

Since Fredric Engels' rejection of utopian socialism endorsed by early socialists, Marxists have often been opposed to utopianism. For them, utopianism is "static, devoid of temporal progression, and therefore reactionary" (Knight 13) in its construction of "blueprint of a future society that is incapable of realization" (Levitas 35). Interestingly, the charge of utopianism has also been leveled at Marxism on similar grounds. The downfall of the various Marxisms (especially Stalinism), Hegelianisms, and historicisms has contributed to a broad rejection of utopianism in socialist/communist tradition over the past two decades.

Pointing out a profound affinity between Marxism/Leninism—which claims to have discovered the deterministic laws of history—and utopian thinking, scholars have indicted both for determinism and totalitarianism. They argue that the visions of a perfect society in utopianism and Marxism preclude any sense of time or history. Subject to a grand narrative of History, these visions reduce the future to a predetermined set of events, thus denying genuine human agency. Applying these ideological implications to literary studies, some critics have contended that utopian fictions replace open human temporality with determinism through the insidious effects of literary closure that provides the blueprint of a perfected society.[3]

But there have also been influential Marxist/socialist-oriented thinkers such as Karl Mannheim, Ernst Bloch, David Harvey, and Fredric Jameson, who have attempted to integrate utopianism and socialist tradition in a more productive way.[4] Furthermore, a number of scholars have attempted to redefine or broaden the very notion of utopia from various perspectives. Levitas, for example, defines utopia as the "expression of the desire for a better way of being" (*The Concept of Utopia* 8), refusing to limit utopia to a socialist project or literary genre. In Levitas' view, such a broad definition of utopia is useful and necessary since the form, function, and content of utopia have changed over time.[5] Through a new understanding of utopia Levitas proposes to recuperate the critical force of utopia that relativizes the present and stirs the human will to move toward a better world.

Recent interdisciplinary concerns with social space, time, social being, and social relations have also contributed to reconceptualizing utopia, as shown by Louis Marin's semiotic approach to utopia as "spatial play" or neo-Marxist geographer David Harvey's "spatiotemporal utopianism." Lefebvre's spatial theory also contains his idea of utopia or utopian spaces and moments, and Certeau's semiotic analysis of the city space and narrative plays with the idea of utopia. From another perspective, Michel Foucault deals with the relation between utopia, heterotopia, and space, in his lecture presented in 1967 to a small group of architects in Paris, "Of Other Spaces."

Of course, in these approaches, neither the notion of space nor that of utopia refers to the same thing. Where Marin's main concern with space is textual, Harvey's is material. Foucault's interest in space seems to shift from a discursive realm to an actual one. When it comes to the notion of utopia, Marin's concept of utopia develops primarily from his analysis of the traditional literary genre. In his groundbreaking utopian study, *Utopics: A Spatial Play*, Marin analyzes More's *Utopia* as a primary source to approach utopia in terms of a "textual product" (54) or "discursive even[t]"(41).[6] Harvey's call for a spatiotemporal utopianism derives from his rejection of both "utopianism of temporal process" and "utopianism of spatial form," which he relates to endless fluidity and totalitarianism respectively.[7] Harvey then offers a "dialectical" "spatiotemporal utopianism" that is cognizant both of the need for provisional order and stability and of the imperative to remain open to change (196). Lefebvre's understanding of utopia grows out of his view of the ambiguous, contradictory city space. Challenging one of the great temptations produced by the Enlightenment conceptualization of space as a static construct or a reified thing, Lefebvre contends that space should be viewed as a contradictory and conflicted process. The production of utopia in the urban space, that is, the production of an alternative space, Lefebvre argues, is made possible by the very ambiguity of the city space—simultaneously regulative and liberating—an ambiguity that makes the city an open-ended process wherein political intervention can always take place (Wegner, *Imaginary Communities* 13). For Lefebvre, this alternative space of utopia signifies the end of the state's dominance over space as well as of private property.[8]

Unlike other theorists, Foucault uses the term, utopia, in a negative way. In his preface to *The Order of Things* (1966), he introduces the term "heterotopia" in opposition to utopia, suggesting that each operates in distinctive linguistic spaces. For Foucault, utopia is an "unreal" place that "afford[s] consolation" by presenting "a fantastic, untroubled region" (xviii). In contrast with utopia, "heterotopia" is associated with the incongruous multiplicity of language. They "secretly undermine language" because "they make it impossible to name this *and* that." They "destroy 'syntax' in advance." They are "disturbing," "other" cultural spaces of our civilization (xviii), a place where our thoughts of contradictory or different things arise.[9] While utopias permit fables and discourse, heterotopias "desiccate speech, stop words in their tracks, contest the very possibility of grammar at its source" (xviii). In a later piece, "Of Other Spaces," Foucault again opposes utopia and heterotopia, not in terms of their discursive aspects, but in terms of their actuality. Here, Foucault privileges heterotopia over utopia on the grounds that whereas utopia is a fundamentally unreal place in that it is an inverted or perfected imaginary form of existing world, heterotopias exist in "real" places such as boarding schools, prisons, mental hospitals, or museums. In contrast with utopias, Foucault suggests, heterotopias can thus function as counter-sites that reflect, negotiate with, and disrupt the dominant social order through their very actual implication within the structure of society.

Given the diversity of connotations, assumptions, and emphases surrounding the concepts of utopia and space, it is not an easy task to bring these theoretical perspectives together. Furthermore, the various assumptions about history, human agency, and temporality that underpin these positions make the task the more difficult, contradictory, or even problematic, as it may entail selective and reductive readings of these theories. Despite my awareness of these problems, I attempt to find a productive way of integrating these various perspectives on space and utopia in a way that illuminates visions of alternative utopias in the works of Lawrence and Woolf.

First of all, these theories have some affinities. In one way or another, they reveal a certain consensus about space and history. Instead of restricting history to the evolution of time, they include space as a crucial factor in the process of human life and history. Far from being an empty background, space, in this view, is historical, human, and cultural, and is open to competing conceptualizations and claims to ownership, as well as to different uses and practices. The new understanding of space and time has triggered a new perspective on utopia. Instead of confining utopia to ideological limits such as a totalitarian tendency or desire for stasis and homogeneity, this new perspective attempts to redefine or broaden the concept of utopia so that it may regain its critical and subversive potential. In these views—with an exception of Foucault—utopia no longer designates a preexisting model, something fixed, perfected, and remote from actual life, or its literary representation.[10] The alternative view of utopia involves thinking differently about the prefix 'ou-.' In utopian studies, the idea of no-place embedded in 'utopia' has seldom drawn attention and when it has, it has been usually given negative connotations of unreality, impossibility, or pure imagination, all of which imply a fundamental dissociation with actual life. In Certeau's view, however, it is the very idea of nowhere and absence that gives utopia a unique politics. Setting up a remarkable parallel between walking in the city and narrative, Certeau likens both to the act of travel, an activity that marks a process of "lack[ing] a place," or "the indefinite process of being absent" (102). For Certeau, walking through the city "makes the city itself an immense social experience" of a space "haunted by a nowhere" (102). And it is this incessant creation of vacuum, the "dreamed-of-place" of "nowhere" (103) that enables us to react against a totalizing urban life.

In a similar vein, Marin brings up the relation between narrative, travel, and utopia/ou-topia. Echoing Certeau, Marin states, "[a]ll narrative is a travel narrative," and "all travel consists in going from a place to a no-place, a route to u-topia" ("Frontiers of Utopia" 414). For Marin, "[a]ny travel" is "a moment and a space of vacancy, an unencumbered space that suspends continuous time and the ordering of loci"(415), and utopia is operating at "the horizon of a voyage (travel)" (411). From its birth, the Greek term did "not mean a place that does not exist" (411). Utopia points to a "gap," "in-between space without place" (57), namely, an "Other World" (47).

Reconceiving the idea of nowhere in a positive and productive way, these views redefine utopia in terms of a creation of "otherness" within current society. For Certeau utopian space—at once textual and actual—produces "anti-text" or "possibilities of moving into other landscapes" (107). Likewise, in Marin's view, utopia designates "*another* referent, the 'other' of any place" (411). Interestingly, his alternative term has curious similarities with the new definitions of utopia. Foucault's use of the term, "heterotopia" also reveals a certain sensitivity to the connotation of the prefix, "ou-." As the title, "Of Other Spaces" ("Des espaces autres") directly intimates, Foucault's concept of heterotopia is concerned with the otherness of these spaces, spaces that are at once implicated within and resistant to the dominant spatial order. In this way, while Foucault refuses to use the term "utopia," his concept of heterotopia is not entirely differently from the redefined utopia that other theorists have founded on their fresh understanding of "ou-."

The idea of otherness in utopia is notable in that it grounds utopia in the realm of everyday space and practices. It is at this point that we come to see that the concept of social space is crucial to a new definition of utopia, and vice versa. As I noted before, one of the crucial elements of Lefebvre's utopia is the profound ambiguity of social space—which to a certain degree corresponds to Foucault's heterotopia implicated in and resistant to power—and the consequent on-going production of alternative spaces, of room for contestation, negotiation, and intervention within the very structure. For Certeau, the production of utopian space likewise takes place not so much on the horizon of pure transcendence as of a "lacunae"(107) generated by the ambiguity of the city space—at once manipulative and emancipating. Directly echoing Lefebvre, Certeau's utopia surfaces as "a new representational space" (70): permeable, writerly, ever-restructuring/restructured. Appropriating Foucault's notion of heterotopia as a form of utopia, Kevin Hetherington states that "modernity" should be seen as "expressing a series of utopics which aimed at ordering society through spatial arrangements that are more ambiguous, different or ambivalent in character than is sometimes assumed"(x). Obliquely echoing Marin, Hetherington locates heterotopia in an "in-between space," a space that fights with the ideological force to eradicate "social ambivalence," a space that is consistently reinscribed, reflecting, and challenging our ordinary *topoi* (ix,x). To put it differently, the "otherness" of Foucault's heterotopia is "not due to their transcendence in relation to ordinary space and spaces, but to the way in which they interact with everyday space by challenging it, reversing it, at once contesting and con-firming it," (Wallenstein par. 3), as in Certeau's or Marin's other spaces of utopia.

From the discussion so far, we come to see another common tendency: to see utopia as a "perpetual process"(Marin "Frontiers of Utopia" 411) rather than a completed total system of stasis that operates in a remote time/space from the present one. Although using different terms, Hethering-ton's observations also carry a similar bearing. For him, heterotopias are "spaces of alternate ordering," a "process rather than a thing (viii, ix). Once defined in light of process, utopia is aligned with counter-hegemonic force. As Lefebvre has suggested, the politics of social space—which involves the production of alternative space of utopia—works to "organize a bit of the social world in a way different to that which surrounds them" (Hetherington viii). As an on-going process, utopia challenges the ideological reification of spatial arrangements and dismantles the lure of stability. As Rob Shields points out, Lefebvre's utopia "makes us think critically about the status quo" by exposing the "difference between the potential and the already exist-ing"(101).

The issue of time is integral to the new conceptualization of utopia and utopian space. Lefebvre's observations about the relation between time and space and his theory of moments are illuminating in this respect.[11] According to Lefebvre, the ideological notion of space as an abstract thing is linked to our conception of time as well; it has "relegate[d] time to an abstraction of its own" (*The Production of Space* 393). For Lefebvre, when space and time are conceived as being abstract, they function as a "tool of power" (391). In Lefebvre's view, then, a new conception and experience of space is tied up with a new conception and experience of time, time that "comes back into its own as privacy, inner life, subjectivity" (393).

Briefly speaking, Lefebvre's moments are instants that bring passing but decisive sensations that are somehow "revelatory of the totality of possi-bilities contained in daily existence," as exemplified from monumental revo-lutionary fervor in history to daily sensations of surprise, delight, or horror (Harvey, "Afterword" 429). At once ephemeral and "timeless" (Shields 59), such moments point to an instance of sudden rupture and of eruption that enables a radical recognition of possibilities. They bring about a sudden insight into something beyond the routinized everyday life and the monot-ony of the taken-for-granted (Shields 58). This revelatory temporal experi-ence is profoundly spatial. For Lefebvre, for example, the ambiguity of the city is related to the ambiguity of our temporal experience as well; in the city we undergo diversified and contradictory time—mechanical, abstract on the one hand, and interior, different, individual, on the other. In this sense, the city can be an apt site for these subversive moments to occur (Shields 101).

Lefebvre's theory of moments reflects his effort to recuperate the private and individual temporal experience that resists the domination of mechanical and abstract time and space. And yet, this does not mean that such an experience of time is confined to an entirely isolated interior subjective realm. While acknowledging the inviolable subjective experience of time—experience that challenges the ideological concept and experience of an abstract and mechanical process of time—the moments do not negate the dimension of actual social life. Through the moments, Lefebvre suggests, one awakens to the awareness of his/her self as "becoming," and feels oneself "all together," and "in touch" with other beings and things (Shields 111, 100). To put it differently, these moments carry a rigorous interrogation of the surface of the continuum of everyday life. The revealing moments implicate a larger scale of social revolutions, for they go hand in hand with the destruction of the socially imposed selfhood social relations, the ideological view of stable space and time, and the new formation of a more fluid, open, and inclusive vision of society.

Lefebvre's theory of moments invites us to think utopia not merely in spatial terms but also in temporal ones as well. It is no accident, I believe, that Marin's utopia touches on both temporal and spatial dimensions. Utopia, he writes, is "a moment and a space of vacancy" that "suspends continuous time and the ordering of loci." And again, "*[t]he utopian moment and space of the travel*," he writes, "consists in opening up, in [the] ideological circle, a *nowhere*, a place without place, a moment out of time" (415). To apply M. M. Bakhtin, this utopia operates in a "generative," "pregnant," or a "birthing time"(206), time that locates a better world neither in the mechanical logic of historical progress nor in an unreal fantasy but in the dialectics between the real and the imaginative, and present and future.[12]

As suggested by the above discussion, I do not use the term, utopia in a traditional sense—an ideal society or its literary presentation that follows certain generic conventions. Although utopia in my study retains the original sense of a better world—embedded in the prefix "eu-"—it locates such a world not in a static, homogeneous, and remote time and space but in a dynamic, ever-changing, lived one time and space by reconceptualizing the other prefix, "ou-." Recent spatial theories have suggested that the view of space as a mere product—as either a neutral socio-cultural background or a reification of power—is ideological in that it works to serve interests of dominant power that seeks to repress the process of producing alternative spaces—spaces of opposing practices, of different formulation of selfhood and social relations—by prescribing these subversive "other" spaces as being non-existent, invisible, and unreal. Rethinking the idea of "nowhere" therefore involves recuperating the possibility and existence of "other" spaces that have been negated throughout history. In short, I mean by utopia in this section an alternative space whose production is taking place through a radical reformulation of time, space, and social being.

Chapter Five argues that although Lawrence was at times attached to traditional utopian thinking and trapped in its ideological limits, his writings register a constant search for his own vision of alternative utopia. My discussion starts by exploring the contradictions and ideological limits embedded in Lawrence's idea of utopian society, Rananim, through a reading of Lawrence's letters. Going on to a short story, "The Man Who Loved Islands," and an essay-fiction, "A Dream of Life," I demonstrate that these writings criticize static views of self, time, and space embedded in conventional visions of utopia, visions that he himself had shared. Examining essays like "Democracy," "Morality and the Novel," and his writings on apocalypse, I contend that Lawrence's aversion to closure, homogeneity, and stasis, drove him to seek his own vision of a utopian "living space" that emerges through the "insurgent Now." Through a reading of *The Rainbow* and *Women in Love*, I demonstrate that although these novels were composed while Lawrence was preoccupied with the idea of Rananim, their visions of a dynamic utopia that emerges through revelatory moments of reconceptualizing the self and its fundamental connection with other beings and things indicate that his vision of alternative utopias had been already shaped early in his career.

Chapter Six examines alternative utopian visions in Woolf's writings. I begin by discussing Woolf's essays such as "Memories of a Working Women's Guild," and *Three Guineas,* which show that there were instances when Woolf turned toward conventional utopian visions, especially during the thirties when she was more directly involved with political activities and writing. Through a close reading of *Mrs. Dalloway,* however, I contend that Woolf presents a vision of alternative utopia both through Clarissa's epiphanic moments, which engage in a critical dialogue with other socialist or escapist utopian impulses, and through her depiction of London as a heterogeneous, ambiguous, and dynamic social space, a depiction which challenges the contemporary urbanist utopianism. By investigating Woolf's notion of "moments of being," her essay, "The Moment: Summer's Night," and *Between the Acts,* I argue that all of these works reveal notable affinities between Woolf's vision of utopia and that of Lawrence; as in Lawrence, I

argue, Woolf's penchant for change and flexibility of selfhood, social relations, and human life enabled her to envision subversive utopias that emerge
from the generative chronotope of the "here and now." In these ways, I
demonstrate that both Lawrence's and Woolf's eruptive moments engage
with everyday life, rather than retreating from it.

Chapter Five

As a writer suffering from a sense of being isolated from his native land where his works were banned, ridiculed, and at times furiously denounced, as well as from despair at the deteriorating world due to industrialism, mercantilism, the Great War, and so forth, Lawrence expressed a complex desire to escape from and change the existing world and envision a better one through his lifelong travels and literary imagination. Although Lawrence did not use the term utopia, his diaries, letters, essays, and fictions reveal his preoccupation with an ideal world, from his dream of an ideal society, Rananim, through his vision of ideal relationships founded on star-equilibrium, to his fascination with primitive societies.

Lawrence's preoccupation with an ideal world has drawn some critical attention. Some critics have viewed Lawrence's utopia or utopian thinking in terms of a fundamental disengagement with the actual social world. For them, Lawrence's dream of paradise simply led to an abandonment of social life, a retreat into an asocial realm of the psyche, or a nostalgia for the past, all of which intimate the writer's inability or refusal to come to terms with the actual social world.[1] Others—especially feminist scholars—problematize the very model Lawrence sets forth as an ideal world—the male-centered, hierarchical society.

It is my argument that while Lawrence exposes some ideological limitations embedded in traditional utopianism, the above views give us only a partial picture of Lawrence's utopia. For Lawrence, utopia was a highly complicated subject that he frequently addressed, problematized, and attempted to refigure, rather than a mere expression of desire to escape from the present world. Utopia in Lawrence was composed of complex and ever changing sets of ideas, practices, and artistic expressions, rather than a systematic formula of a perfected society. Moreover, a number of Lawrence's works involves an effort to imagine and provide alternative utopias, an effort founded upon his critical distance from the limits and problems of the conventional genre.

THE CONCEPTION OF UTOPIA—RANANIM

According to Jessie Chambers, as early as his seventeenth or eighteenth year Lawrence dreamed of taking a house where he and all the people he liked could live together (Zytaruck 166). This youthful aspiration kept recurring for a while until sometime in his forties, in varying forms, and with varying sentiments and connotations. In 1913 when Lawrence appeared to be happy with his married life and with his work in Fiascherino in Italy, he insisted others should join him in this paradisal milieu, as evidenced in a number of letters he sent to his friends such as Edward Garnett, John Middleton Murry, and Katherine Mansfield. This longing to live with a small group of people on an isolated island developed into a vision of utopian society, Rananim, formulated by an odd combination of escapist impulse, socialist fervor for the reformation of society, and a complex, at times misanthropic, response to the war-torn world and the hostile reading public.

As I shall show below, rather than being a coherent ideal, Lawrence's idea of Rananim kept changing according to his personal, social, and psychological circumstances. Appearing at times as a psychological compensation for his trying days, at times as an expression of his political drive to reform the world, Lawrence's vision of Rananim society discloses his inconsistent views of class, and patriarchal assumptions about gendered roles, along with his misanthropic leanings. Rananim appears most frequently in Lawrence's letters written during the years between 1915 and 1916; from the end of the 1910s onwards, however, the number of Lawrence's mentions of Rananim in his letters progressively diminishes. Finally, in 1926, Lawrence declares that his vision of Rananim has gone.

At the outbreak of the First World War, the insecure economic condition and the gloomy vision of the world in general outraged Lawrence. Letters written in 1914 make clear his sense of desperation and hatred of "everything"(*The Letters of D.H. Lawrence* 2: 211) in the face of the "miserable world" shattered by the war (*Letters* 2: 212). During this period, Lawrence's exposure to communism added a political fervor for social reformation to his somewhat personal dream of utopia. In his letters to his friend, S. S. Koteliansky, Lawrence keeps mentioning a utopian society, Rananim— named after one of Koteliansky's Hebrew songs at a 1914 Christmas party at the Chesham cottage (Moore 272). On January 3, 1915 Lawrence writes: "What about Rananim? Oh, but, we are going. We are going to found an

Order of the Knights of Rananim" (*Letters* 2: 252). And again on January 15, 1915 he writes to W.E. Hopkins: "I want to gather together about twenty souls and sail away from this world of war and squalor and found a little colony where there shall be no money but a sort of communism as far as nec-essaries of life go. . . . What do you think of it? I think it should be quite fea-sible" (*Letters* 2: 259).

During the period from 1915 to 1916 when Lawrence most frequently brought up his idea of Rananim in his letters, his remarks on Rananim reveal some problems and changes in his views of class, gender and mankind. In his letter written on January 28, 1915 to E. M. Forster, Lawrence states his con-viction that the ideal society should be composed of "class-less individuals" (*Letters* 2: 265). "In my Island," he observes, "I wanted people to come with-out class or money. . . . I wanted a real community . . . built out of . . . many fulfilled individualities seeking greater fulfillment" (*Letters* 2: 266). But as his sympathy with communism fades, and after the devastating disagreement about the idea of Rananim with Bertrand Russell, who advocates "demo-cratic control," in July 1915, Lawrence argues for "an elected aristocracy" (*Letters* 2: 355–56).[2] In his letter to Russell Lawrence relates his belief that "the working man shall elect superiors for the things that concern him immediately, no more. From the other classes, as they rise, shall be elected the higher governors" (*Letters* 2: 370–71). Here, instead of a classless society, Lawrence envisions utopia founded on hierarchy. At the same time, Lawrence's idea of Rananim reveals his patriarchal assumptions about gen-dered roles. In this world, Lawrence writes, "[t]here must be a rising rank of women governors, as of men, culminating in a woman Dictator, of equal authority with the supreme Man." Despite the surface rhetoric of equality, these remarks endorse the gendered division of labor that confines women to "domestic side" while men govern the "industrial side" (*Letters* 2: 371).

Furthermore, the banning of *The Rainbow* in December 1915 and the 1916 incident in which the "anti-Lawrence crew" in the Café Royal in Lon-don was making fun of his *Amores* sapped his desire to communicate his utopian ideal to other people including the reading public (*Letters* 2: 650). In his 1916 letter to Koteliansky, where Lawrence bitterly recalls the incident in London, his idea of "Island idea—Rananim" delivers a deep sense of hatred for human beings, as well as doubt and despair; expressing his wish to "exter-minate" "the creeping multitude," Lawrence continues to reduce the number of people he wants to live with. In the same letter, Lawrence imagines the paradise of his own: "If only one had the world *to oneself*" (*Letters* 2: 650). And again, two months later, Lawrence wishes "go to Rananim, without the people" (*Letters* 3: 23).

From 1916 onwards, Lawrence brings up his ideal society less and less frequently. In his 1918 letter to Koteliansky, the name, "Rananim," appears as a psychological compensation that enables him to live through the war years rather than a plan for social revolution. "Let us have our Rananim for a month or two, if we can't for ever. One must have something to look forward to," he writes (*Letters* 3: 214). In 1922 when Lawrence stayed in Sicily Rananim has become a part of his memory of the past. And finally in 1926 Lawrence acknowledges to Koteliansky that his idea of Rananim has gone: "That Rananim of ours, it has sunk out of sight." (*Letters* 5: 367). Lawrence's giving up on the idea of Rananim, however, does not mean a total abandonment of his search for utopia.[3] Rather, it registers Lawrence's growing sense of the limits and problems of this utopian idea, the seeds of which had already been planted even during the mid 1910s when he was most attached to the idea of Rananim.

REWRITING UTOPIAS: "THE MAN WHO LOVED ISLANDS" AND "A DREAM OF LIFE"

"The Man who Loved Islands," written in 1926 and published in 1928, is a tale about a man with a peculiar passion to live in a world of his own. Finding his native isle too crowded, the man acquires an island and moves there with a couple of people to serve him. As time passes the man senses ominous violence and cruelty, instead of happiness, fuming from the island. The second part of the story sketches the islander's life on a smaller island where he has moved with a smaller number of companions. On this island too, however, the man fails to feel gratified; driven by his loveless sexual desire for a girl who has waited on him, he is married to her, and fathers a daughter for whom he feels nothing. In the face of his growing sense of disgust at everything and the existence of other people, he once more leaves for a much smaller island, this time, all alone. In the third barren island, the man undergoes a total revulsion to any kind of contact with other beings and finally dies in the midst of heavy snow.

Critics have often read the story as a critique of idealism, or a fable that warns of the danger of withdrawal from relations with other lives.[4] What is usually neglected is Lawrence's critical distance from a utopian vision that he had once shared. Written around the time when Lawrence announced that Rananim had gone, the tale is full of self-mockery that alludes to circumstances, including his own psychological state as well as problematic aspects underpinning the conception of Rananim. Echoing Lawrence's disappointment at his friends' negative attitudes toward his "Island Idea—Rananim," the islander's heart sinks when he finds that there is hardly anybody who "was pining for such an island as his" and "would pay any price for it" (*The Complete Short Stories* 732). As Lawrence himself did, the protagonist wants less and less people around him and is driven by a misanthropic, egotistic, and escapist desire to live alone on "an island all of his own"(726).

This self-diagnosis involves a critical exploration of the ideological implications and problems embedded in the age-old national image of utopia—an island founded and dictated by a benevolent King Utopos in Thomas More's *Utopia*. In a number of instances, Lawrence intimates that such a utopian yearning for an isolated society is rooted in a resentful and escapist spirit combined with megalomaniac fantasy of oneself and egotism. The islander fantasizes himself as the "Master," the "Saviour," and "the fount of this happiness and perfection" on this "Happy Isle"(726, 727, 725). From the beginning, the narrator foregrounds the danger of self-centered idealism aligned with utopianism by announcing, "this story will show how tiny it [the island] has to be, before you can presume to fill it with your own personality" (722). The story goes on to show how the islander's utopian aspiration revolves around his impulse to put himself in the center of the entire universe and how it leads to the total negation of self, other, and surroundings. To borrow Lawrence's own words from an essay, "Democracy," the dream of an island utopia is governed by an impulse to "automatize into fixed aspirations or ideals"; it is a kind of "idealism" that tempts us to set up some "fixed center in the mind, and make the whole soul turn upon this center" (*Phoenix* 714).

Notwithstanding the islander's self-deceptive good intentions, this seemingly ideal utopia is in effect governed by a tyrannical impulse for domination and homogenization in the name of the common welfare that would not allow any differences or individualities. The Master "kept his eye on everything" (726). "But anyone who wants the world to be perfect" the narrator continues, "must be careful not to have real likes or dislikes. A general goodwill is all you can afford. The sad fact is, alas, that general good will is always felt as something of an insult by the mere object of it; and so it breeds a quite special brand of malice. Surely general good-will is a form of egoism" (727).

Furthermore, the story points to the ideological limits embedded in the assumptions about space and time that this kind of utopia propagates. In the following we witness that the "danger of becoming an islander" is inseparable from a view of time, space, and being as fundamentally static and abstract, an insight that anticipates the recent indictment of utopia for denying change in space and time.

> Strangely, from your little island in space, you were gone into the dark,
> great realms of time, where all the souls that never die veer and swoop
> on their vast, strange errands. The little earthly island has dwindled, like
> a jumping-off place, into nothingness, for you have jumped off, you
> know not how, into the dark wide mystery of time, where the past is
> vastly alive, and the future is not separated off. This is the danger of
> becoming an islander. (724)

In the above, the space/time of the island seems to be evaporated into a void
where temporality, self, and the entire world are lost and meaningless. The
island is a place of the terrors of infinite time, time that denies any possibility
of change. By temporalizing space and spatializing time, the narrator once
again underscores the conjunction of abstract, static, frozen space and time:
"The moment is your little islet in time, it is the spatial universe that careers
round you" (724).

The story demonstrates that the negation of any generative space/time
involves a view of human beings as passive puppets deprived of any desire or
will to change the world. From the beginning the narrator describes the
islander as "ha[ving] reduced himself to a single point in space, and a point
being that which has neither length nor breath, he had to set off it into
somewhere else; into the other worlds of undying time" (724). For him, the
island was "no longer a 'world,'" and he arrives at "desireless levels of
Time"(734, 737). Facing "a new stillness of desirelessness," the man "dis-
solv[es]" into the all-devouring space wherein "[t]ime had ceased to pass,"
and the whole world is dead (737, 741, 743, 744). The islander is totally
estranged from the "uncanny" world that once was fabricated by his own
imagination and then ruthlessly becomes an "unrecognizable island" (744).
In these ways, the story reveals Lawrence's critical understanding of the danger of the static and abstract geography, time, being, and the world underlying the utopian idealism, marking his departure from a version of traditional
utopianism.

Further criticism of traditional utopias appears in his own utopia titled
"A Dream of Life" probably written in 1927. Composed out of the need for
something to hold on to during a period of severe illness and despair, this
unfinished essay-fiction registers a strong hope for another world that is
complicated by an implied criticism of traditional utopian vision and writing. Like More's *Utopia,* it is composed of two sections: the first, an autobiographical essay based on Lawrence's recollections of his 1925 and 1926 visits
to the English Midlands; the second, a description of the utopia into which
the native town has been transformed in the future.

The narrator begins by delivering a grim picture of his hometown named Newthorpe. An atmosphere of death, inertia, and uniformity surrounds the place which the narrator ascribes to the women's "dreams" of material affluence and emancipation under the reign of capitalism and industrialism (819, 821, 822). With these thoughts in mind, the narrator walks towards a quarry. He happens to find an aperture in a rock there, and creeps into it to have a sleep. The second section begins with the narrator's waking up a thousand years later to find the place regenerated as a new world, Nethrurpp:

> I knew, even while I looked at it, that it was the place where I was born, the ugly colliery townlet of dirty red brick. Even as a child, coming home from Moorgreen, I had looked up and seen the squares of miners' dwellings, built by the Company, rising from the hill-top in the afternoon light like the walls of Jerusalem, and I had wished it were a golden city. (829)

The narrator goes on to describe the utopian society. In this ideal world, the communication takes place at the level of touch and body. It is significant that the depiction of the ideal world here echoes Morris' utopia in *News from Nowhere*.[5] Both use the same narrative frame: a present day-dreamer waking up in the future world of utopia. As in Morris, the future society in Lawrence is agricultural in an old-fashioned English way. The division of roles between men and women seems to be firmly established in both of the utopias, and the celebration of a restored masculinity reveals the writers' anxiety about contemporary women's increasing call for independence and liberation.[6]

There are, however, notable differences between these works. In comparison with Morris' utopia, Lawrence's is replete with a sense of ambiguity and ambivalence about the utopian society itself.[7] At a first glance, Lawrence's essay-fiction is structured around the contrasting evaluation of the two worlds—the present world as the realization of women's wrong dream and the ideal future world as that of the male narrator's corrective dream. Lamenting the hopeless state of the present as an outcome of "our grandmother's dreams," the narrator wishes they were "better dreamers" (821). The entry to the dream world of utopia begins by the narrator's following his "old childish longing to pass through a gate, into a deeper, sunnier, more silent world" (824), and the "golden city" is a realization of the better dreamer.

The initial contrast between the two worlds, however, comes to expose some curious similarities, as the second section mirrors the first one. Note, for instance, the similar imagery used in the depiction of the two worlds. In both, the senses of stasis, finality, death, and unanimity are prevailing. Echoing the "decent" (but tame) people in the present, the future world is characterized by "decency everywhere" (834). The "dead" and "inert" atmosphere combined by the present people's "same" lives (822) reappears as a "curious stillness" (832) and "incalculable unison" of the people in the utopia, the world founded on "unanimous instinct"(832). Such mutual mirroring becomes even more illuminating, as the narrator reveals an anxiety about the fact that both worlds are perfected places where the dream has come true; in other words, these are the worlds where no more dreams are possible. That is to say, despite the contrast in the narrator's surface evaluation of the two worlds, the present hometown can be seen as a kind of utopia, the world where the (bad) dreamer's wish has been fulfilled. Facing the deplorable state of the present, the narrator writes that "[i]t is a terrible thing to dream dreams that shall become flesh" (821). This remark of course expresses the narrator's dissatisfaction at the disastrous realization of his "grandmothers' dream." But at the same time, it also reveals a profound aversion to the very realization of dream—the construction of the perfected world—prefiguring an anxiety regarding another utopia frozen in stasis and eternity in the second section.

There are a number of instances in the text that reveal an antipathy toward the changeless utopia. At a transitional point from the present to the future the narrator brings up his childhood fascination with a "legend" of "little caves or niches in the rocks" called "everlasting wells"(824). He then relates how the enchanting legendary wells where nothing would decay became "disgust[ing]" when he finally found that the wells' association with permanence issues from their turning things to be "petrified" (824). Inserted in the moment before the narrator's confrontation with the everlasting utopia, the legend of the everlasting wells intimates the double side of utopia—the beautiful state of perfection constructed in the nightmarishly ossified time and space that precludes any human agency or possibility for change.

Significantly, the narrator's entrance into the utopia is delivered through a process of infantilization, intimating both regression and passivity without giving it any positive values such as innocence. Driven by the oedipal impulse to return to the mother's body, the narrator crawls into the little "cavity in the rock," or the "womb of quartz," sleeps in it in a fetal position (824), and wakes up into the new world in the year of 2927.[8] Looking at the transformed hometown, the narrator expresses his delightful surprise accompanied by a sense of losing his strength: "Now it had come true. But the very realization, and the very intensity of my *looking* had made me lose my strength and my buoyancy" (829). As the story goes on, it becomes clear that the narrator feels uneasiness at the disparity between the infantilized self and the grown-up consciousness. Instead of realizing the masculinity predicted by Morris' utopia, the narrator finds himself born/awaken naked and treated like a baby. Like a toddler, he is washed, clothed, and fed. And he needs an adult's help to walk. He fights against this situation, crying, "I can walk alone," and again, "I can go alone!" (828). But the people with "unanimous instinct"—who are "at once terrifying and magnificent" do not seem to listen to his request (832). He feels "afraid" in front of the people whose "stillness and the completeness of plants" deprive them of an air of "human beings" (833). These phrases register the narrator's divided feelings about the utopian world and its inhabitants; while they are magnificent and delightful, the world is threatening in its atmosphere of deadly stillness, its inhabitants oppressive in their unanimity and inhuman perfectedness. Driven by the desire at once to mingle with and be separated from them, as well as simultaneous love and anger (833), the narrator finally says: "I am like a butterfly, and I shall only live a little while. That is why I don't want to eat" (836). We don't know whether Lawrence intended to end the story here or not. But this is the last line we have.

Noting the fact that Lawrence wrote this piece while fighting with his incurable illness and likely death, Howard J. Booth contends that the abrupt ending originates from the writer's final confrontation with the issue of his frailty and death. In Booth's view, Lawrence's habitual reluctance to approach his illness in his works throughout his life makes the writer attempt to imagine a distant utopian future, using a Lawrence-figure transcending the present world of mortality. Even in this imagined world, however, Lawrence is forced to confront an unsettling awareness of his imminent death, and thus he abruptly breaks off the piece, Booth maintains. To some extent, Booth's explanation about the possible motivation that propelled Lawrence's creation of utopia sounds persuasive. But I think that the writer's anxiety and ambivalence toward his imaginary travel to utopia also derives from his constitutional aversion to the vision of the perfected, static, changeless world embedded in conventional utopianism, a tendency found in his critical approach to conventional utopias, as we have seen, and in his alternative vision of utopia, as we shall see. In this respect, I would read the ending as Lawrence's final affirmation of life, rather than as an indicator of his final encounter with death and the attendant sudden breaking off of writing. The narrator's loss of appetite—"I had little desire to eat" (834)—and his eventual conscious refusal to eat act out his disinclination to live in the dangerous world—the world that may paralyze agency, change, and human history. In this sense, paradoxically, the narrator's suicidal gesture can be seen as a profound assertion of life—the vibrant world perpetually reformulated and restructured through diverse desires, dreams, and practices. Once such desires are petrified and dreams are homogenized, the world can be deadly.

"INSURGENT NOW"

Lawrence's longing for a better world was at times combined with his apocalyptic vision, especially during his most trying days—World War One and his last years of illness and isolation. During the war period when Lawrence was attached to the idea of Rananim mixed with his misanthropic impulse, he also indulged in an apocalyptic vision for the imminent destruction of all things by supernatural intervention. In his letter to Catherine Carswell, Lawrence writes: "All the time, one seems to be expecting an arrival from the beyond, from the heavenly world. The sense of something, someone magnificent approaching, is so strong, it is a wonder one does not see visions in the heavens" (*Letters* 3: 125). During the most painful last years, the apocalyptic longing comes back to Lawrence, now seasoned by much experience, fighting with death. Instead of pouring out a wish for a total destruction of the entire world along with fuming anger at the deteriorating world and his personal tragedy, Lawrence at this time advances another vision of apocalypse, a vision that overlaps with his alternative utopia in its affirmation of "living space," cosmic relations between beings and things, and "life, here and now."

In his introduction to Frederick Carter's *The Dragon of the Apocalypse* written in 1929, Lawrence explores his unique conception of space, time, and being. Making clear that his concern is not with "theories" or the "meaning of the Apocalypse" but with the release of the imagination" (47), Lawrence maintains that Carter's previous version of the book is better than the current one, for the former succeeds in delivering a "great imaginative world" through grand astrological imagery of space, imagery that enables the reader to experience the new world not as something that takes place in a distant space and time but as a "living space" of here and now (50, 51). What is notable in Lawrence's argument is his insight into the interrelation between space, time, and being, which is crucial to his formulation of utopia. Differentiating astronomical space from astrological space, Lawrence associates the former with the mechanical quantitative expansion of space and the latter with a "live" or "living" space. Both spaces are infinite but there are significant differences in the ways in which beings formulate and experience space, time, and the relations with other beings and things. Compared with the former "illimitable space," which is no better than a "hollow void of space" where every relation is "isolat[ed]" and "homogeneous" (46), the latter is an equally vast but non-terrifying space peopled with "meaningful motions" and connections between individuals (43). Making similar points in his last book, *Apocalypse*—the first, un-revised, longer version of his introduction to the Carter's book—Lawrence states that what really matters in apocalyptic writing is its capacity to put us in momentary contact with the "living body" of the cosmos (77). In addition to privileging of living space over mechanical, abstract space, Lawrence's statement also reveals his own search for writing that reflects, realizes, and initiates the experience of a living space and connections.

Lawrence's concern with "living" space and connections between beings and the entire cosmos involves his conception of time and history as well. And this point enables us to look at Lawrence's apocalyptic vision in line with his criticism of other versions of traditional utopianisms such as the Christian belief in the advent of the millennium or the liberal belief in historical progress that also promises the final arrival of an ideal world. Lawrence inserts his antipathy to the stasis implicit in Christian utopianism in the very text of apocalypse and restructures its utopian promise from within. He criticizes the vision of New Jerusalem "where flowers never fade, but stand in everlasting sameness" (144). He also puts his anti-teleological strain as follows: "[w]e have to drop our own manner of on-and-on-and-on, from a start to a finish, and allow the mind to move in cycles, or to flit here and there over a cluster of images. Our idea of time as a continuity in an eternal straight line has crippled our consciousness cruelly"(97). This statement locates Lawrence in the contemporary modernists' attack on the belief in progress and the linear development through time as well.[9]

Indeed, while the young Lawrence was inclined to imagine the apocalypse as a necessary precursor to the advent of utopia in a traditional sense, Lawrence in his final days does not seem to follow this model. Rather than being a signifier that heralds the arrival of the blissful new world, the apocalypse itself surfaces as a radical experience of the present that Lawrence wishes to see take place both in actual human life and in literary experience. Lawrence's temperamental antipathy to changeless, homogenized, and deterministic space and time drove him to imagine his apocalypse not as a mere precondition for the realization of utopia but as a significant part of the realization of a new "life, here and now" (84). Similar to Lefebvre's moments, Lawrence's apocalyptic vision of the radical destruction of the established self and relations followed by a revelation of connection with the living cosmos is momentary, but it has an enormous impact; it presents a vision of dynamic utopia that happens "now" in its disruption of the status quo.

Lawrence's alternative utopia aligned with his stress on the radical experience of the present moment finds another expression in his essay "Democracy" where he contends that "life-activity" must "never be degraded into a fixed activity" following a "fixed direction" (*Phoenix* 715). "There can be no ideal goal for human life," Lawrence writes, in the same way as "[t]here is no pulling open the buds to see what the blossom will be" and thus, we shall and should not "preconceive" the "unrevealed blossom"; all that we know is "the flower of today" (715). Lawrence's endorsement of the present unfolding toward infinite possibilities derives from his rejection of any tendency that may displace the present "life-activity" with the pre-determined goal or the compensatory imagined space/time rather than from a pure agnosticism or Epicureanism. In a number of instances, Lawrence expands the definitive and functional boundary of utopia by replacing this rather trite term with various terms such as "life-activity," "creative reality," "life," and so forth. What commonly governs Lawrentian utopias is the urge to reconfigure the notions of space, time, and being to ground the momentum of constructing a better world within the vibrant texture of everyday life that has been obscured or repressed.

In his preface to the American edition of *New Poems* posthumously published, Lawrence makes an interesting case to this effect. Distinguishing the poetry of perfection from the poetry of the immediate present, Lawrence associates the latter with the very texture of life and self in process. Unlike the poetry of perfection, which belongs to "all that is far off" in its completeness and finality, the poetry of the immediate present has "no perfection, no consummation, nothing finished" (*Phoenix* 218–19). Reminiscent of Lefebvre's utopian moments, the poetry of the present takes place through "a revelation," an "incarnate moment," "the Now" that is at once permanent and momentary: its "very permanency lies in its wind-like transit" (219, 220). In this realm of "never-pausing, never-ceasing life itself," "inclusiveness," and "immediacy" "without denouement or close" (220), Lawrence suggests, the exquisite moment of the present is accompanied by the birth of a new sense of self. The poetry of the present is what "we have never conquered: the pure present. One great mystery of time is terra incognita to us: the instant. The most superb mystery we have hardly recognized: the immediate, instant self" (222).

The experience of the revelatory now is a crucial component for Lawrentian utopia. Another essay, "Morality and the Novel" written in 1925, clarifies this point further. Arguing that it is the task of art to "reveal the relation between man and his circumambient universe, at the living moment," Lawrence shows how a work of art enacts utopian time and space—the "fourth dimension." This fourth dimension takes place in no-place in the sense that it "has no existence" "in dimensional sense" (*Phoenix* 527). And yet, rather than pointing to a purely mystic, transcendental, unreal realm, it corresponds to Lawrentian utopia—utopia as an on-going process that at once carries us "beyond" the routinized everyday reality and makes us experience and restructure "life itself" (527).[10]

According to Lawrence, both life and artwork have a fourth dimensional quality in that they bring us the experience of the revelatory present moment wherein we undergo a total restructuration of our self and relationship with others and reality in general. Taking Van Gogh's painting of sunflowers as an example, Lawrence observes that the sunflower is a "third thing" that exists "between everything, in the fourth dimension" (527). In this fourth dimension one keeps reformulating one's self through the experience of the ever-changing, dynamic connections with others without being "bond[ed]" (531) at "the living moment" (527). For Lawrence, this fourth dimension does not belong to a transcendental, mystic, or abstract realm. On the contrary, it constitutes an important part of life that he seeks to restore throughout the essay.

To return to Lawrence's observation about the poetry of the present, the utopian moment is an occasion of "the rapid momentaneous association of things which meet and pass on the for ever incalculable journey of creation" (220). In these respects, the fourth dimension comes to be coterminous with other images of Lawrentian utopias—the "ever-present life," the "rainbow," "the trembling instability of the balance between me and my circumambient universe" opposed to "a stable equilibrium"(528). All these utopias embody "mutation," "come-and-go, not fixity, inconclusiveness, immediacy," and "fluid relationship with the rest of things" (220).

Lawrentian utopias reside neither in a remote space/time nor in a romanticized everyday life. It emerges as a kind of no-place in the sense that it is not a fully established, fixed place but a living space that is coming into being through the radical reconceptualization and restructuration of self, its relation to others, and space in the "urgent, insurgent Now" (220). In this utopia, nothing is frozen, but everything is alive, free to move in new directions, interrogating "the status quo" (531), resisting any lure of closure, opening and reopening the present to infinite possibilities and changes. As Lawrence puts it, "[t]he living plasm vibrates unspeakable, it inhales the future exhales the past, it is the quick of both, and yet it is neither. There is no plasmic finality, nothing crystal, permanent"(219). According to Lawrence, the morality of the novel is achieved by enabling the reader to see and experience "life"—life which is "something that gleams," something that "has the fourth dimensional quality" (529) wherein the self undergoes a per-petual "process of forming a new relationship" with other people, things, or the universe (527) through which the self also "change[s]" (530) in this at once "momentaneous" and eternal moment (527). In the following I will show how Lawrence achieves his conception of the novel as an apt genre for enacting his utopias.

EMERGING UTOPIA HERE AND NOW: *THE RAINBOW*

Although Lawrence at times, especially in his early career, expressed his long-ing for a better world by drawing upon conventional utopian thinking or writing, his works often make implicit or explicit critical comments on previ-ous and contemporary utopian tradition. Even when Lawrence was fasci-nated with the idea of Rananim, the other side of his mind began to conceive his own vision of utopia. For example, *The Rainbow*—composed when Lawrence's dream of Rananim is still burgeoning—testifies to the fact that the seed of his later utopian vision has already been planted from the early years. As I discussed in Chapter One, the novel dramatizes women's struggle to create and occupy their own place by interrogating male-dominant spatial discourses and practices and thus heralds the birth of a new world founded on new social relations. The vision of the new world culminates in the famous rainbow episode at the end of the novel.

It may be useful to discuss the depiction of the hideous mining town of Wiggiston in the "Shame" chapter, for it carries an interesting criticism of the utopian society that Morris portrays in *News from Nowhere*. In this chap-ter, we see Ursula's momentary homoerotic affection for and final rejection of her class mistress, Miss Inger. Secretly wishing for Inger to marry her uncle Tom, a colliery manager, Ursula invites her to Tom's house, located in Wiggiston, Yorkshire. In Morris, most of the dwelling places in the utopia are built of red brick and surrounded by long walls. And the whole town and people of the utopia evoke a certain sense of homogeneity and uniformity.[11] Similarly, in Lawrence, Yorkshire is full of redbrick houses circumscribed by long walls. Unlike in Morris, however, the prevailing tone is critical of indus-trialism. And more importantly, the passage evokes Morris' description of utopia in negative connotations—the overwhelming uniformity, the result of a wrong utopian dream realized in an abstract space and meaninglessly repet-itive time that would not allow any hope or possibility for change.

We are told that the place is crowded with "a flat succession of wall, window, and door, a new-brick channel that began nowhere, and ended nowhere." Here, "[e]verything was amorphous, yet everything repeated itself endlessly." The "homogeneous" atmosphere is prevalent and the "red-brick confusion" "rapidly spread[s]"(345) here. The whole place "was just unreal" as if it were "some gruesome dream . . . [that has] become concrete." The people seemed to have "no more hope." They live "within some utterly unloving shell" and "[i]t was as if a hard, horny shell enclosed them all" (346). Deprived of any "actuality," the place seems like "hideous abstraction" (346). In this abstract space, Lawrence intimates, the experience of creative, revealing moments is impossible. For Tom—a kind of manifestation and producer of such a space—"each moment was like a separate little island, isolated from time, and black, unconditioned by time," anticipating the islander's experience of frozen time in "The Man Who Loved Islands." He embodies "a stability of nullification" (344). In short, the passage once again reveals Lawrence's temperamental opposition to the perfected vision of utopia as a static space/time.

Lawrence's rejection of traditional utopianism enables him to propose an alternative utopia in the last chapter "The Rainbow," where Ursula wakens to a new knowledge and experience of the self and reality. As I discussed in Chapter Four, Ursula's longtime struggle to create her own space and independent self directs her relationship with her boyfriend, Skrebensky into a new phase. After the trip with Skrebensky Ursula returns home, setting her mind to part with home and him. However, the possibility of pregnancy and the cultural demand of motherhood engrained in her momentarily shatter her resolution. But her sickness and recovery ultimately reforge her will to independence. Gradually realizing the false "bondage" to Skrebensky imposed on her in the name of family and maternity, Ursula "fought and fought and fought all through her illness to be free of him and his world, to put it aside, to put it aside, into its place" (492). She asserts her break with any familial, cultural, and national ties in Joycean spirit: "I have no allocated place in the world of things, I do not belong to Beldover nor to Nottingham not to England nor to this world" (493).

This moment then leads to Ursula's awakening to a new world. She begins to see the "rift" "between her[self] and the shell"—the shell used as the metaphor for the "unreal," "unliving" and "abstract" place the people live in, as we have seen in Lawrence's description of Yorkshire. This awareness of the rift enables her to move beyond the shell and "create a new knowledge of Eternity in the flux of Time (493)." She looks into the "undiscovered land," which was "the unknown, the unexplored upon whose shore she had landed, alone, after crossing the void, the darkness which washed the New World and the Old" (494). Utopia emerges through this revealing moment that is not purely imaginary and abstract but grounded in the "flux of Time," in the "urgent, insurgent Now," that shatters the seemingly stable ego and the world.

This revealing moment brings Ursula a new communal vision. She begins to see the people in the street and the place from a new perspective. The fatalistic touch of passivity and inertia surrounding the people in the rapidly industrialized mining town gives way to a sense of possibility for change found in both people and their surroundings:

> She saw the people go by in the street below, colliers, women, children, walking each in the husk of an old fruition, but visible through the husk, the swelling and the heaving contour of the new germination. In the still, silenced forms of the colliers she saw a sort of suspense, a waiting in pain for the new liberation; she saw the same in the false hard confidence of the women. . . . She saw the stiffened bodies of the colliers, which seemed already enclosed in a coffin. . . . She saw the hard, cutting edges of the new houses, which seemed to spread over the hillside in their insentient triumph . . . the expression of corruption triumphant and unopposed, corruption so pure that it is hard and brittle. (494–95)

The "stiffened" and "hard" things—whether they are the people's psychic states, their bodies, their dwelling places, or the entire place—turn out to be the very condition of collapse and change, instead of being a symptom of inertia and hopeless fixity. Through the juxtaposition of stiffness and motion, death and birth, and sturdiness and fragility ("hard and brittle"), the passage reveals a belief that nothing can last as it is. Locating the seemingly despairing present in a new terrain of possibilities, the passage illustrates how the Lawrentian utopia is built on an awakening to something that has always been inherent but repressed in the ossified structure, an awakening accompanied by a new formation of self, time, and the world.

It is at this revelatory moment that Ursula sees a rainbow: "The colour steadily gathered from nowhere, it took presence upon itself, there was a faint, vast rainbow" (495). The image of the rainbow once again suggests that utopia here is rooted in the present, actual social world. Instead of hanging over the sky, it "stood on the earth" across the heaven bridging between "nowhere" and now-here. We read: "She saw in the rainbow the earth's new architecture, the old brittle corruption of houses and factories swept away, the world built up in a living fabric of Truth, fitting to the over-arching heaven" (496). Ursula's quest for her space, identity, and emancipation goes hand in hand with her creation of utopia, utopia that embodies the "impending sense of transformation" of the self and the world (Jameson, *Postmodernism* 312). Repudiating any closure embedded in classical utopian blueprints, Lawrence's utopia is envisioned as a perpetual journey and on-going process experienced in the radical interruption of now into everyday life, as we shall see further in *Women in Love.*

All of Lawrence's rage at the Great War, the sense of public isolation, and the longing to be far away from England went into the texture of *Women in Love.* This drama of two couples—Ursula and Birkin, and Gudrun and Gerald—revolving around lurking catastrophe, danger, and conflicts that permeate not only individual psyches but also the entire society, was origi-nally planned as a part of one book titled "The Sisters" along with the story of the sisters' grandparents that had come out as *The Rainbow.* The novel was also written during the time when Lawrence frequently turned to the idea of Rananim with a growing sense of doubt about its possibility mixed with a misanthropic impulse and apocalyptic vision of the imminent destruction of the entire world. This personal and cultural background and Lawrence's deepened disenchantment in the face of the putrefying "civilization" set a darker tone in the novel than in *The Rainbow.*

A PERPETUAL JOURNEY: *WOMEN IN LOVE*

Critics' interpretations of the world vision that *Women in Love* offers have been divided. Some critics have contended that *Women in Love* denies any redeeming utopian vision glimpsed at the end of *The Rainbow* by focusing on the tension-charged relationship between Ursula and Birkin in the midst of the disintegrated and decomposed socio-cultural milieu. Others have stressed the positive aspects of the Birkin-Ursula relationship as a sign of a better world, or at least, have viewed the conflict between the positive and the negative vision as being unresolved.[12]

In my view, *Women in Love* can be read as offering another variation of Lawrentian utopia. Unlike the utopia in *The Rainbow,* the utopia of this novel finds a much more complex expression, as it comes out of continual conflicts with other tempting versions of utopia and dystopia. While he was composing this novel, Lawrence was at once drawn and resistant to escapist, misanthropic, and totalitarian drives, as his concern with the utopian society of Rananim suggests. At the same time, his critical response to contemporary discourses of apocalypse and socialist utopianism, along with his constitu-tional antipathy to a static, deterministic vision of humanity and the world compelled him to seek a dynamic, open-ended vision of utopia, rather than a confining *enoncé* of a perfect society.

In a number of instances, the conversations between Birkin and Ursula test out possibilities and limits of various utopias. In a chapter entitled "Excurse" Birkin expresses to Ursula his wish to leave his job and the world for a remote place, revealing a hermetic desire that Lawrence himself currently expressed through his idea of Rananim. Birkin begins, "I should like to go with you—nowhere. It would be rather wandering just to nowhere. That's the place to get to—nowhere. One wants to wander away from the world's somewheres, into our own nowhere" (355). To some extent, the wish to abandon the present "somewheres" for "nowhere" indicates escapist utopianism tangled with a fascination with an unreal other world. Perplexed by this "nowhere" Ursula replies: "I'm so afraid that while we are only people, we've got to take the world that's given—because there isn't any other" (355). But Birkin's remark involves another element of utopian longing; what is really tempting to Birkin seems not so much the destiny itself as the idea of journey and wandering, a theme that haunted Lawrence throughout his life. To the still doubtful Ursula, he states, "Somewhere—anywhere. Let's wander off. That's the thing to do—let's wander off." And it is to this clearer stress on the idea of travel that Ursula is finally willing to consent: " 'Yes–' she said, thrilled at the thought of travel. . . . 'To be free,' he said. 'To be free, in a free place, with a few other people!' "(356). Birkin then proceeds to observe, adding another aspect of his idea of utopia—utopia as a psychological state: " 'It isn't really a locality, though," he said. "It's a perfected relations between you and me, and others—the perfect relation—so that we are free together'" (356).

Birkin's idea of utopia is hard to pin down. It reveals the impossible dream of living in a remote and isolated world and yet, it is attached to the journey itself rather than the goal. At the same time, it tends to define utopia in terms of the individual psychological state, which some critics have viewed as the major characteristic of Lawrentian utopia. Rather than merely indicating contradictions, these complexities point both to difficulties that Lawrence's search for utopia faced at that time, and to various aspects of the utopian visions with which it interacted. Ursula's response to Gudrun's skepticism of utopia is another example that reveals this difficulty, and especially the difficulty of articulating utopia through conventional language. When the now-married couple, Ursula and Birkin, join Gudrun and Gerald in a hotel in Austria they find both the spirit of the place and the artistic company—especially Loerke—unbearably frightening and finally decide to leave this place to go south. When Ursula tells her about this plan, Gudrun immediately catches the couple's impulse to break with the past to find a utopia, a wish that she believes unrealistic and illusive. "One wants a new space to be in, I quite agree," Gudrun says to Ursula, "[b]ut *I* think that a new world is a development from this world, and that to isolate oneself with one other person isn't to find a new world at all, but only to secure oneself in one's illusions." Facing this challenge, Ursula feels the inadequacy of conventional vocabulary and mindset in articulating her/Birkin's view of utopia and the overwhelming power of reification such language has achieved. We are told: "Ursula looked out of the window. In her soul she began to wrestle, and she was frightened. She was always frightened of words, because she knew that mere word-force could always make her believe what she did not believe"(492). Yet Ursula's "struggle for verbal consciousness" forces her to keep trying to express her idea of the new world. " 'Perhaps,' she said, full of mistrust, of herself and everybody. 'But,' she added, 'I do think that one can't have anything new whilst one cares for the old—do you know what I mean?—even fighting the old is belonging to it. I know, one is tempted to stop with the world, just to fight it. But then it isn't worth it'" (492).

The implication that Ursula shares Birkin's utopia here may seem to contradict my previous discussion about Birkin's observations of utopia and Ursula's response to them, an analysis that implies the difference between Ursula's and Birkin's utopias. Throughout the novel, however, both Ursula and Birkin keep modifying their views through dialogue, rather than representing firmly established ideas or principles. Instead of conveying utopia through a particular character reduced to a mouthpiece of fixed principles, the novel presents the utopian idea as an open discourse subjected to ongoing modifications and dialogues.

Indeed, despite the recognition of the difficulties in expressing the vision of utopia through conventional language that Ursula's response to Gudrun suggests, the novel seeks to articulate the idea of utopia through continuous dialogues. The idea of utopia shows contradictions and keeps changing even in individual characters. In the scene that depicts Ursula and Birkin's departure for Austria, for example, Ursula voices a traditional cliché about utopia. On the ship, Ursula experiences "the sense of the unrealized world ahead," the "effulgence of a paradise unknown and unrealized." She feels like going towards "the unknown paradise," "a sweetness of habitation, a delight of living quite unknown"(437). This rather conventional picture of utopia is immediately followed by Birkin's challenge. He instinctively refuses Ursula's conventional frame that locates utopia in the unreal, distant space/time, in the realm of pure dream and expectation. He does not share "the ecstasy of bliss in fore-knowledge that she knew." For him, the more overwhelming sensation was the "wonder of this transit," a "gulf of infinite

darkness, like a meteorite plunging across the chasm between the worlds."
And "[t]he world was torn in two, and he was plunging like an unlit star
through the ineffable rift" (437), echoing Ursula's vision of utopia in *The
Rainbow* founded on her awakening to the "rift" between the existing world
and her newly blooming self.

Birkin's musings rekindle and push a step further Ursula's former
utopian vision that we have seen at the end of *The Rainbow*. They present
an alternative utopia, a utopia that is coming into being within the "rift"
between reality and dream, between old and new self and world, in the
in-between space. To put it differently, utopia in the novel emerges
through the "sense of being in the present," a sense of "being poised
between the known and the unknown, in a transitional stage between
pattern and chaos"(Kalnins, "Introduction" 26), an occasion that entails a
new formulation of self and the entire universe in the ever-changing
chronotope.

The utopia that surfaces through the revealing moment of the here-
and-now brings about a new sense of self and connections with others as
well. The image of the "paradisal entry" in the chapter entitled, "Moony,"
confirms this point. This vision derives from Birkin's rigorous fight with the
fatalistic temporality, a grim apocalyptic vision of the modern world under
the reign of the "omen of the universal dissolution," an omen that is personified by Gerald (286–87). Birkin's gloomy speculation and fear give way to a
vision of "the paradisal entry into pure, single being . . . a lovely state of free
proud singleness, which accepted the obligation of the permanent connexion
with others, and with the other, submits to the yoke and leash of love, but
never forfeits its own proud singleness, even while it loves and yields" (287).
In Lawrence's words, the newly formulated selfhood is "different but not separate" in its "living continuum of all the rest of living things" (*Phoenix* 761).
The long dialogue between Ursula and Birkin concerning utopia in the
"Excursion" chapter proceeds to materialize utopia in one of Ursula-Birkin's
most successful moments of relationship. In Sherwood Forest they reach
consummation brought by the experience of the "unthinkable" "star-equilibrium" (360), "a palpable revelation of living otherness" (361). It is a Lawrentian utopia, the poetry of the present. This "forever-unfolding creative spark"
(*Phoenix* 219) brings a new dimension to the self and the world; it is a
moment of "contact" between the self and the other, and the universe that
takes place through the "rapid momentaneous association of things which
meet and pass on the for ever incalculable journey of creation" in the "insurgent Now." To reiterate my point here again, what constitutes the utopian
moment in the above episode is not so much the momentary consummation

per se as the dynamic process with which this revealing moment is pregnant—the realization and experience of the self, its relations with others, and
the world open to never-ending changes and journey.

This idea of journey and possibilities, however, should be distinguished
from the suicidal and nihilistic journey and fascination with the present of
anarchistic infinities embodied by the Gudrun-Gerald couple. Around the
end of the penultimate chapter, "Snowed Up," the narrative is ridden with
the image of journey leading to death, first expressed through Gudrun's psyche and second, through its ominous reenactment by Gerald's physical
death. In Gudrun's eye, today was the "iridescent threshold of all possibility,"
and she wanted to "to be wafted into an utterly new course, by some utterly
unforeseen event, or motion" (526). She enjoyed with Loerke the moment in
"pure amusement careless and timeless" (527). But the text suggests that
Gudrun's vision of the present charged with infinite possibilities is actually
driven by profound despair at impending death; "underneath" her false
excitement of the vision of a new life "was death itself." All was possible for
her "because death was inevitable" (526). Indeed, Gudrun and Loerke "never
talked about the future" except for a "mocking dream of the destruction of
the world" (510). Gerald's wistful surrender to death is delivered through a
similar language: "He only wanted to go on, to go on whilst he could, to
move, to keep going, that was all, to keep going, until it was finished."

In a sense, a great deal of Birkin's morbid meditations on the world and
life is driven by this kind of death impulse. However, Gudrun/Gerald's
attraction to perpetual journey is profoundly different from Birkin's.
Whereas Gudrun's fascination with perpetual journey and the infinite possibility of the present issues from the fantasy of her own death along with the
end of the entire world, Birkin's stems from the fantasy of the birth of the
new world to which he himself feels mysteriously connected. In the final
chapter entitled "Exeunt," Birkin muses on the end of human beings. But
his musings lead to a vision of the ever-lasting creation of new beings that is
already taking place within his newly burgeoning flesh in the present
moment: "To have one's pulse beating direct from the mystery, this was perfection, unutterable satisfaction. Human or inhuman mattered nothing. The
perfect pulse throbbed with indescribable being, miraculous unborn species"
(539). This thought challenges Gudrun's anthropocentric fixation upon
humanity as the being on whose birth and death the fate of the rest of the
universe depends. Furthermore, Gudrun's and Birkin's journey operates at
different temporalities. For example, the image of Gudrun in thrall to the
"tick-tack of time" and the comparison of her face to "a clock dial" intimate
that the trajectory of her life is perpetually bound to the mechanical advance

of time; enslaved by a deterministic view of time, the rigid logic of linearity, her life can never deviate into or encounter any meaningful, creative present, any subversive utopian chronotope. To put it differently, Gudrun's vision of perpetual journey and the infinite possibilities of the present shares affinities with "astrological space," a space whose infinity Lawrence regards as "mechanical," as we have seen before. In contrast, Birkin and Ursula's journey is itself a goal, as illustrated by their experience of eruptive and transformative present moments and their visions of "permanent connexion with others." Their utopia therefore belongs to "astrological space," or "living" space, which Lawrence associates with the ever-changing dynamics of self and relations between beings and things.

From this perspective, *Women in Love* is not a nihilistic abandonment of the rainbow promise. Although the novel is heavily touched by a sense of despair and anxiety in the midst of the writer's personal and social crisis, it still seeks to perform utopia in its own way. The novel offers utopia as an ongoing process whereby one loses the illusive continuity and stability of one's self, place, and social relations and constructs more fluid, ever-changing, and dynamic social being, time, and space. It presents utopia as a continuous psychological, ontological, epistemological, as well as physical journey that leads not so much to inevitable finality as to ever-flowing multi-linear futures.[13]

Chapter Six

Unlike Lawrence, whose longing for an ideal world at times expresses itself in visions of a hierarchal, male-chauvinistic society, Woolf would never have dreamed of such a utopia. And yet, there are also moments when Woolf's longing for a better world is hampered by ideological limitations. Ironically, these limitations are most visible in her explicitly political writings. However, the more important link between Woolf's utopian visions and those of Lawrence can be found in her concern with epiphanic moments that dismantle the status quo in envisioning a more fluid and dynamic structures of social being, time, and space. In some instances, Woolf's utopian spaces push Lawrence's "living space" one step further. Grounded in her own experience of London, her penetrating depictions of the modern cityscape offer a more concrete and dynamic utopian chronotope engaged in the simultaneously oppressive and liberating texture of everyday life.

WOOLF'S UTOPIA IN THE 1930s

As critics have noted, Woolf's growing interest in and sympathy with socialism affected the ways in which she deals with and articulates her feminist concerns.[1] As early as 1904, Woolf read *The Life of William Morris* with much interest, and in 1915, Woolf showed enthusiasm for Morris' narrative poem, "The Pilgrims of Hope," in which Morris' early socialist standpoint merges with a defense of the 1871 Paris Commune[2] (*Letters* 2: 60). Woolf's sympathetic understanding of socialist agendas is found in her later works as well, as illustrated in "Memories of a Working Women's Guild" (1930)—an essay based on Woolf's notes that she made in 1913 when she and Leonard attended a meeting of the Women's Cooperative Guild. In this essay, Woolf admires the invigorating power of such figures as Morris and Shelley in educating and broadening working women's concerns into more social and political ones.

Written in the 1930s, a time of great international turmoil, and for Woolf, of closer involvement with political activists, her two essays, "The Memories of a Working Woman's Guild" and *Three Guineas* provide instances where her visions of utopia seem to be somewhat dissociated from the present. Addressing a former officer of the Women's Co-operative Guild, "The Memories" begins with Woolf's refusal to write a preface to collected letters written by working-class women, a refusal which partly derives from Woolf's reluctance to frame others' works into her words, and partly from her acknowledgment of the difficulty in imagining cross-class empathy and knowledge. In the face of the task of explaining "how women whose hands were full of work . . . [could] remodel the world according to the ideas of working women," Woolf considers whether her writing can legitimately frame the writings of working class women, of whose life she has only a limited understanding.[3] Wary of assuming an all-knowing position to evaluate working-class women, Woolf attempts to demonstrate their potential contribution to building a utopia. To do this, she notes how some working women's occupation of discursive space—"a certain space" called the "Woman's Corner" in the *Co-operative News*—at length took the physical shape of an actual room in Co-operative Mothers' Meetings in 1883 (145). Woolf proceeds to state how this room functions as a ground for building a better world:

> It [The Guild] gave them in the first place a room where they could sit down and think remote from boiling saucepans and crying children; and then that room became a place where one could make, and share with others in making, the model of what a working woman's house should be. Then as the membership grew and twenty or thirty women made a practice of meeting weekly, that one house became a street of houses; and if you have a street of houses you must have stores and drains and postboxes; and at last the street becomes a town, and a town brings in questions of education and finance and the relation of one town to another town. And then the town becomes a country; it becomes England; it becomes Germany and America; and so from debating questions of butter and bacon, working women at their weekly meetings have to consider the relations of one great nation to another. (146)

At one level, the passage conveys a political call for a need to improve the living conditions of working class women. According to Woolf, working women's bondage to daily needs (and by implication, their lack of private space and time) denies them the ability to go beyond the boundary of the self and develop a sense of connection or sympathy with other people, or any socio-political desire to improve society (146–47). The lack of "baths and money" fuels their "lust for conquest" and their "desire for possession"; as long as they are confined to "the borders of their own parishes," they are unable to "enter into the lives of other people" or to think about larger socio-political issues (140, 147). It is no wonder that their meeting has "something military" about it (135).

As I have suggested in previous chapters, Woolf's desire for a more open and inclusive society crucially informs her aesthetic and political aims. Given this, the living conditions of working-class women presented her with difficult artistic, ethical, and political questions. In Woolf's view, the present conditions that prevent working women from reflecting on themselves, "the lives of other people," or "life as a whole," also prevented them from becoming great writers. Woolf states: "It is not from the ranks of working-class women that the next great poet or novelist will be drawn" (147). In a sense, this observation reveals Woolf's desire to vindicate her own class status, a desire to recuperate politically positive aspects of her class standing by shifting the focus from her limited knowledge of the working class (because of her being "shut up in the confines of the middle classes" [141]) to her relative independence from the daily need for labor and preoccupation with capital, an independence which enables her to "enter into the lives of other people." But at the same time, Woolf's concern with the aesthetic and political limitations that working women experience as a result of their living conditions invites us to look at the political implications embedded in the passage cited above. For the underlying argument of the passage is that the development of working-class-women's potential to "remold the world" depends upon their emancipation from incessant toil.

Despite Woolf's carefully articulated political fervor, the critical potential of Woolfian utopia does not seem to work well in this essay. The vision of utopia—the dynamic, ever-expanding "sisterhood of nationhood" constructed through continuous processes of "disarmament" and of blurring borders and boundaries between people and nations—does not fully bloom. The utopia that the essay imagines seems to evaporate into the realm of unaffordable dreams. Its realization is prevented by the ubiquitous class barriers that Woolf declares "impassable" (141). The difficulty that Woolf has in transcending such barriers makes her feel like an outsider to the world of working-class women.[4] Recalling her attendance at the meeting in 1913, she writes: "If every reform they demand was granted this very instant it would not matter to me a single jot. . . . However hard I clap my hands or stamp my feet, there is a hollowness in the sound which betrays me. I am a benevolent spectator. I am irretrievably cut off from the actors. I sit here, clapping and stamping, an outcast from the flock" (136). Woolf's rigid sense of a barrier between classes undermines or contradicts her political concern, and particularly the subversive potential of her utopian vision, which valorizes, however momentarily or provisionally, the demolition of borders.

Utopia in this essay seems to be reduced to a dream: a dream of building connection with others of which Woolf believes working women to be incapable, and of which Woolf is herself incapable in this essay. It seems to reside in an imaginary future (as illustrated by the image of the expanding room of working class women in the future, of which Woolf cannot be a part). The utopian moment of "meet[ing] them [the working class] not as sympathizers, as masters or mistresses . . . but casually and congenially as fellow beings with the same ends and wishes" does not take place (141). Like those working class women who have "never been beyond the borders of their own parishes," Woolf fails to transgress barriers imposed by society, and as a result, her vision of utopia retreats into a Never-Never Land (147).

In *Three Guineas* (1937), an essay written with a heightened pacifist and feminist fervor stirred by Woolf's concern with events in Spain at war and the death of her nephew Julian there, Woolf proposes that women can prevent war by holding on to their positions as members of what she calls "The Outsiders' Society." In contrast with "The Memories," where the undercurrent of longing for a better world was thwarted by Woolf's sense of the insurmountability of class barriers, Woolf's call for change in *Three Guineas* offers a strong vision of an Outsider's Society, in which women from different classes are united by their common resistance to the egotistical desire for dominance that drives men to wage war. Noting that this oppositional society has been operative "since the professions were opened to the daughters of educated men," Woolf attempts to show how "a passive experiment" in socio-political activities can effectively work to "abolish or modify other institutions of which they disapprove" (119). Woolf's contention is that women's search for a more liberating and peaceful society should start by "maintain[ing] an attitude of complete indifference" to male activities, "absent[ing] themselves from them," in a way that corrects their corrupt psychology (119, 107). This passive experiment, which Woolf claims is in fact "active," includes a massive destabilizing reinterpretation of conventional discourses of patriotism, nation, or nationalism (118).

In *Three Guineas*, Woolf makes a compelling call for women to "remain outside" of the man's world. Here the image from "The Memories" of an ever-expanding working women's room that sweeps away borders to become a "sisterhood of nationhood" is revived in a more powerful vision of an alternative community. In a famous passage, Woolf states: "As a woman I want no country. As a woman my country is the whole world" (109). And yet, the Outsiders' Society is still a class-stratified society: women are "working in their own class" here (106). Moreover we are left with a picture of a society fundamentally divided between the insider and the outsider.

In a sense, "Memories" and *Three Guineas* point to Woolf's leaning toward socialist utopianism, which reflects the impact on her of the immediate socio-political milieu: the rise of socialism, fascism, and war. While Woolf's feminism shares much of the socialist yearning for a better world of freedom and equality, her acute self-consciousness about her own class privilege and complicity with the social system, and more importantly, the aversion to the "didactic demonstrative" strain of narrative that resulted from her insight into the connection between the impulse to preach, the will to dominate, and fascism, make her polemical writings especially difficult, complex, and somewhat less than fully successful (*Diary* 4: 145).

It is illuminating to take a brief look at Woolf's ambivalence toward socialist utopianism. Woolf's mixed feelings about Morris, for example, reveal her antipathy to any rigid dogma or authoritarian prescription about an ideal society. She found Morris' life "great" and "superior" and yet, "curiously inhuman" (*A Passionate Apprentice* 221). A 1906 diary entry, where Virginia Stephen writes about her trip to a country village named Giggleswick, in Yorkshire, is another indicator of her objection to Morrisean utopia, which was frequently portrayed as a cluster of country houses set against a timeless agricultural landscape. In the cottage in this quiet countryside—a place that almost seems to embody Morris' vision of an ideal society—her initial delight gives way to a rather ominous sense of a freezing of time that seems to preclude any change, depriving life of rich texture and variety. Here, she found unattractive the cottagers who live up to "their creed, in red ink on a trip of brown paper over the hearth"—the creed being quoted from William Morris (*Diary* 1: 304). In her eyes, the cottage stands for "theories" rather than a place for life. In this "cottage with a purpose," the furniture makes this entire dwelling place look "self conscious" rather than natural and comfortable (304). Ambivalent toward this peaceful but lifeless place, Woolf refuses to frame her utopia within a changeless and abstract space/time. Woolf's ambivalence registers her profound resistance to any form of ideological closure and her desire for openness and flexibility, a desire that drove her to pursue her own version of utopia by means different

from those of contemporary utopian writings. As we shall see, a more powerful vision of Woolfian utopia—utopia built through a radical disruption of
the socially imposed self and social relations—is to be found in her other
writings.

UTOPIA IN A CITY: *MRS. DALLOWAY*

In *Mrs. Dalloway* (1925), Woolf portrays the lives, memories, and dreams of
several characters using free indirect discourse. Set in London on a single day in
the middle of June 1923, the novel conveys a sense of impending disaster that
lurks beneath the city's glistening and vigorous façade, haunting both individual
psyches and the community as a whole. At the same time, it presents Woolf's
attempt to reflect and invigorate the contemporary hope for a better world in
the wake of the First World War.[5] Throughout the novel, fears and anxieties are
interwoven with utopian fantasies and dreams. Fighting the temptations of
escapist fantasy on the one hand and helpless despair on the other, the novel
seeks a different vision of utopia, one which emerges mainly through epiphanic
moments experienced within the dynamic social space of the city.

  Woolf's portrayal of London in *Mrs. Dalloway* plays a central role in
advancing the politics of alternative utopia in the novel. In a sense, the novel
sets itself against the urbanist utopianism of figures like British sanitary
reformer Edwin Chadwick (1880–1890), Austrian architect Otto Wagner
(1841–1918), Swiss architect Le Corbusier (1887–1965), and New York
state and municipal official Robert Moses (1888–1981). Although there is
no evidence to indicate that Woolf was writing in self-conscious opposition
to these figures, it is important to note how her approach to the city differs
from theirs. For this can help us understand the political implications of her
alternative utopia. As James Donald notes in his article "This, Here, Now.
Imagining the Modern City," the utopian dream of the urban planners mentioned above can be characterized as the wish to realize the dream of Enlightenment rationality with its attendant view of space as a transparent territory
to be mapped, occupied, and exploited, and thus as a place where a population is easily manipulated. Woolf's depiction of London in *Mrs. Dalloway*
complicates and challenges this kind of urbanist utopianism. Where the
urban utopian dream that is founded on the Enlightenment belief in rationality is doomed to "reproduce and repeat the anxieties, repressions, and censorship that provoke the dream" through its wishing away of conflicts,
contradictions, and heterogeneity (Donald 182), the subversive politics of
Woolfian utopia in *Mrs. Dalloway* derives from the very dynamism and
openness of the city in all its multifaceted ambiguity and contestation.

In this respect, Lefebvre's view of urban space as a ground for utopia becomes suggestive in reading Woolf. As we have seen before, in Lefebvre's theory, the ambiguity and heterogeneity of the city—the city that is simultaneously regulative, oppressive, conflicting, and liberating—is crucial to the construction of utopia. Refusing to regard the city merely as a site of ideological reproduction, manipulation, and domination, Lefebvre views space as a terrain of infinite possibilities and changes wherein political intervention, resistance, and reconstruction, namely, the construction of utopia, can always take place. As we shall see, London in the novel features as a public realm governed by a huge social system and power, as well as a communal ground where people with the shared trauma of the War build a deep bond. At the same time, London is also a highly heterogeneous place lived and conceived differently according to gender, capital, national origin, and class. The latter aspect of the city is especially notable in that it foregrounds the fundamental ambiguity of the city as a simultaneously oppressive and liberating social space.

In addition, Lefebvre's theory helps to illuminate the temporal dimension of Woolf's vision of utopia in *Mrs. Dalloway*. For Lefebvre, the production of utopian space involves a new conceptualization of time as well. As I have noted before, Lefebvre suggests the connection between "oppressive and repressive" space and "abstract" time (391), both of which function as tools for power in their blindness to the dynamics and contradictions of time and space. Lefebvre thus sees the politics of social space as inseparable from the reconceptualization of time that "comes back into its own as privacy, inner life, subjectivity." In other words, an alternative utopian space is a realm in which another temporality prevails, a time that embraces perpetual changes and differences in individual perceptions and experiences. As I shall show, in *Mrs. Dalloway*, as in Lefebvre's theory, utopian space is generated through a dynamic chronotope: the ambiguous and dynamic social space of the city that produces and is produced by disruptive "moments" that destabilizes the status quo.

Mrs. Dalloway enacts a lived and creative urban chronotope of utopia. Woolf renders London heterogeneous and dynamic through the depiction of multiple, conflicting temporalities that are resistant to the dominant social system, as well as through the characters' distinctive spatial perspectives and experiences of the city. In this way, London emerges as a Woolfian utopia that at once occupies and creates a new terrain of spatio-temporal territory that differs from socialist, urbanist, or other traditional utopian assumptions of space, time, and being, a generative chronotope that is open to on-going restructuration for a more inclusive yet hybrid society.

The novel depicts London as a simultaneously oppressive and resisting place. Far from being a homogeneous place, London is rent by various experiences, emotions, and imaginations that differ according to the inhabitants' class, nationality, gender, and so forth. For Lucrezia, the Italian girl who is married to Septimus, the city is an indifferent or even hostile place of isolation and agony. Miss Kilman, a poor tutor of Clarissa's daughter, Elizabeth, loses her selfhood and agency in the midst of the overwhelming commodities of the urban environment.[6] These episodes contribute to presenting a complex urban texture that does not fit into other upper or upper middle-class characters' joyful experience of the city. This does not mean, however, that the novel reduces the city to a site of oppression and inequalities by depriving these less privileged people of any possibility of resistance. The much-noted motorcar scene supports this point. On the one hand, the car materializes "the voice of authority" that demands everybody's gaze and attention (20). It is a symbol of the fetishized power that controls the city space and its inhabitants' psyche. Its appearance immediately evokes "the thought of the dead; of the flag; of the Empire" that encourages people to throw themselves into "the cannon's mouth" in the name of the "membership of a society" (25, 41). The name, "Bond Street," at the beginning of the novel aptly intimates Woolf's double-edged idea of the social bond—the idea of community interlinked to the coercive social and ideological bondage. On the other hand, however, London does not entirely deprive its inhabitants of room for resistance and freedom. As critics have noted, the narrative inscribes the disturbing counter-power that challenges this control and manipulation as vividly and effectively as it indicts oppressive power. The motorcar scene in the novel embodies and then radically disrupts the existence of the center by delivering it through multiple perspectives. Rather than entirely controlling the urban space and its inhabitants, the motorcar turns out to be an object of individual interpretations and responses. Through this device, London comes out as a flexible and ambiguous space lived and interpreted differently by different individuals.

The novel presents London as flexible and ambiguous by revealing heterogeneous experiences of time as well. Note the connections that the text builds between Harley Street, the significance of the clocks of the street, and Sir William Bradshaw, the "nerve specialist" to whom Septimus goes for treatment—a symbolic representative of this area.[7] As the place where doctors attended to the richest patients in London, the street in the novel functions as a metaphor for the oppressive city, institution, or the entire social system in general.[8] Based on Woolf's own terrible experience, it is the place where Sir William—a picture of "a sense of proportion"—wields his power.

He relentlessly puts "unsocial impulses" under control and "shut[s] people up" in the name of "the good of society" by relying on "police" and his scientific authority (154).

Rather than normalizing regulation and oppression, however, the novel depicts Harley Street as a contradictory and potentially resisting social space by exposing conflicts and interrogating the legitimacy of the power structure. The novel does this by showing conflicting perspectives; for the upholders of this order—the "relations of his [William's] victims" who needs to suppress social misfits (154)—Sir William is acceptable and even endearing. But, for Septimus, he is the horrible enemy and monster. These divided sentiments expand to distinct spatio-temporal experiences of the city. In the view of Lucrezia, the marginalized, poor, foreign other, the clocks of Harley Street are associated with sinister forces of division, domination, and gnawing exploitation. For her, they are "shredding and slicing, dividing and subdividing." They "nibbled at the June day," "counseled submission, upheld authority, and pointed out in chorus the supreme advantages of a sense of proportion" (155). On the contrary, the sound of "a commercial clock" reverberating from Oxford Street through Harley Street is pleasing to a privileged person such as Hugh Whitbread—who enjoys a surplus of time and money, dallying in front of the shop window (155). Through these differences in spatio-temporal perspectives, the text unmasks the conflicts and inequalities existing in the city, thus inscribing a subversive potential within this oppressive territory.

Woolf's juxtaposition of the sound of Big Ben—signaling control, masculinity, and coercive collectivity—with that of St. Margaret's—symbolizing individuality, femininity, and embrace—further contributes to her rendering of London as a contradictory, variegated, and resisting utopian space. Anticipating Lefebvre, Woolf detects the time-space conjunction; throughout the novel the sound of Big Ben, the central and authoritative timekeeper, permeates the city:

> The sound of Big Ben striking the half-hour struck out between them
> with extraordinary vigour, as if a young man, strong, indifferent, inconsiderate, were swinging dumb-bells this way and that. (71)

By likening this authoritative time to a "young man, strong, indifferent, inconsiderate" (71), Woolf intimates that the city is a male-dominant, manipulative space. At the same time, the image of the "dumb-bell" under the control of an indifferent masculine power can be seen as suggestive of what Lefebvre calls "abstract time" that works as "a tool for power."

And yet, Big Ben is not the only temporality that governs the city life. Coming a bit later than Big Ben but still claiming its own accuracy, the bells of St. Margaret's represent a rebellious temporality that challenges the authority of the masculine, central time and space:

> Ah, said St. Margaret's, like a hostess who comes into her drawing-room on the very stroke of the hour and finds her guests there already. . . . It is half-past eleven, she says, and the sound of St. Margaret's glides into the recesses of the heart and buries itself in ring after ring of sound, like something alive which wants to confide itself, to disperse itself, to be, with a tremor of delight, at rest—like Clarissa herself, thought Peter Walsh. . . . (74)

In contrast with Big Ben, St. Margaret's is associated with femininity; it refuses to "inflict" its "individuality"(74). Rather than dividing and subdividing, this feminine temporality, "like Clarissa herself" seems to "confide itself, to disperse itself, to be, with a tremor of delight, at rest" (74). This personified image of time also accords with Clarissa's experience of being dispersed to be connected with other beings, as we shall see later.

The historical background of St. Margaret's endows its bell with a political significance that is worthy of note. Since being built in 1064, St. Margaret's has been ignored and forgotten under the shadow of Westminster Abbey—a longtime political and cultural center.[9] In this respect, the church can be seen as a metaphor for the existence of the marginalized, excluded urban inhabitants in male-dominant history and society. More importantly, on November 11, 1918, when World War One was over, members of both Houses of Parliament attended a service at St. Margaret's. The Archbishop of Canterbury read the lesson from Isaiah, Chapter 61: "He hath sent me to bind up the brokenhearted, to proclaim liberty to the captives, and the opening of the prison to them that are bound. . . . And they shall build the old wastes, they shall raise up the former desolations, and they shall repair the waste cities" (Wilkinson 262). The secondary but challenging bells of St. Margaret's fit well into its spatial significance—a metaphor for the marginalized other within the city as well as for a curing, emancipating, and restoring force. It points to utopian 'other' space and forces that have been oppressed but have always persisted, resisting, healing, and rebuilding.

The opposition of another temporality to the authority of Big Ben becomes clearer when the sound of another clock coming later than Big Ben is introduced in association with the maternal power of inclusion and the ethics of love. This sound is heard at the very moment when Clarissa finally overcomes her snobbish prejudice against her poor relatives and decides to invite them to her party. Note the following:

> Love—but here the other clock, the clock which always struck two minutes after Big Ben, came shuffling in with its lap full of odd and ends, which it dumped down as if Big Ben were all very well with his majesty laying down the law, so solemn, so just, but she must remember all sorts of little things besides—Mrs. Marsham, Ellie Henderson, glasses for ices—all sorts of little things came flooding and lapping and dancing in on the wake of that solemn stroke which lay flat like a bar of gold on the sea. Mrs. Marsham, Ellie Henderson, glasses for ices. She must telephone now at once. Volubly, troublously, the late clock sounded, coming in on the wake of Big Ben, with its lap full of trifles. (193–94)

Building a connection between Clarissa's decision to include her poor relatives among the guests for her party and the maternal image of the late clock "with its lap full of trifles," this passage epitomizes the politics of the temporal 'other' that shatters the dominant social order and social relations by challenging Big Ben's law of exclusion, suppression, and forgetfulness.

Through its ambiguity and conflicting temporalities, London emerges as a dynamic terrain for an opposing politics: a Lefebvrean utopia. The perspectives of characters like Elizabeth and Peter on London further confirms my point. In her escapade into the Strand, Elizabeth confronts a revealing moment that brings her a new perspective of the mundane space/time. In her eyes, buildings and crowds of people in the city seem to have more power than religion or historical books to "stimulate what lay slumberous, clumsy, and shy on the mind's sandy floor to break surface. . . . It was . . . a revelation, which has its effects for ever, and then down again is sent to the sandy floor" (208). This revelatory moment does not, of course, negate the power imbalances and injustices existing in the city. Rather, the uproar of the street, "this life," "this procession" opens Elizabeth's eyes to social inequities (unemployment) and sufferings (dying people) in the midst of the festive mood of the street (209). It is in the midst of the profoundly ambiguous space of the city, a place of regulation, exploitation, and inequalities, but also of a resistance that "break[s] the surface" that Elizabeth encounters a vision of the "sisterhood, motherhood, brotherhood" that penetrates the city, a vision that has the potential to generate different practices, changes, and resistances within the seemingly solid surface of mundane reality.

This vision of the city as an alternative utopia filled with an infinite potential for change and movement comes to Peter as well. On his way to

Clarissa's Party, he thought, "[w]hat with these doors being opened, and the descent and the start, it seemed as if the whole of London were embarking in little boats moored to the bank, tossing on the waters, as if the whole place were floating off in carnival (249). Despite his limits as a thinker of Woolfian utopia, as I shall show later, his enjoyment of "absorbing, mysterious, of infinite richness, this life" that comes with his recognition of the fluid, carnivalesque vision of the city, echoes the revealing moments that are akin to the spatial experiences of Clarissa and Elizabeth (248).

To reiterate, Woolf's depiction of London goes against urbanist utopianism, by underscoring, rather than suppressing, heterogeneity, ambiguity, and contestation of the city. As Elizabeth and Peter demonstrate, such a vision of a dynamic city can be found in the psyches of individuals as well. Anticipating Certeau's view of utopia based on his application of Lefebvre's spatial theory, the novel offers a vision of a utopia that emerges through a reconceptualization of space. From this perspective, Woolf's treatment of London in *Mrs. Dalloway* has an affinity with David Harvey's notion of "dialectical utopianism" as well. Indicting the traditional utopianism of stasis, Harvey defines his utopianism in terms of a different imagination or conceptualization of a city that is in perpetual motion. Clarissa's story further illuminates the political implications of the Woolfian approach to utopia, which provides a vision of an alternative utopia that maintains a critical distance not only from urban utopianism but also from other reactionary aspects of other conventional or socialist utopianisms. Furthermore, Clarissa's experience of "moments" foreshadows Woolf's envisioning of alternative utopia in disruptive moments, which appears in her writings in her last years, as we shall see.

Although many critics have drawn attention to Clarissa Dalloway, scholars have seldom explored the significance of her abandonment of social utopian thinkers with reference to the politics of Woolf's alternative utopia. As a matter of fact, the novel suggests that Clarissa had at once been an ardent admirer of socialist utopian thinkers such as Plato, Percy Bysshe Shelley, and William Morris, under the influence of her close friend, Sally. At first glance, Clarissa's desertion of these figures and her marriage to a Conservative politician seems to suggest her inability to transcend the limitations of her class position; it also can be seen as an indicator of the oppressive "social system," wherein even once-radical youngsters become conservatives, trapped within the benefits of the privileged. [10] There are, certainly, a number of instances where the novel mockingly points to Clarissa's limited class-consciousness, lack of social concerns, and snobbish self-complacency. However, Woolf's ambivalence toward Morrisean socialist utopianism and her fascination with flexibility and openness (which is suggested in her London Scene essays that I discussed in Chapter Two, as well as by the depiction of London that I have examined above), invites us to look at Clarissa's abandonment of socialist utopian fervor from a new angle, as suggesting a truth toward her own vision of a utopia that emerges through the ever-changing, dynamic here and now. [11]

Anticipating Certeau's association of the city with a text, narrative with travel, or utopia with pedestrian's spatial experience and practices, Woolf writes in her diary entry, "London itself perpetually attracts, stimulates, gives me a play and a story and a poem" (*Diary* 3: 186). Beyond providing rich material for her writing, London became a crucial physical and symbolic geography for the utopian vision of this devoted streetwalker. In *Mrs. Dalloway*, much of the Woolfian utopia is delivered through Clarissa's encounter with revelatory moments while she is walking through the London streets, moments when she imagines herself going beyond the boundary of her self and entering into others' lives without obtruding upon or manipulating them.

Looking at the omnibuses in Piccadilly, for instance, Clarissa "sliced like a knife through everything; at the same time was outside, looking on. She had a perpetual sense . . . of being out, out, far out to sea and alone" (11). Here, the sense of being alone is intertwined with an opposing sense of connection with surroundings things and other human beings near and far. She imagines herself to "b[e] part" "of the trees at home, of the house there," "part of people she had never met; being laid out like a mist between the people she knew best" (12). This is an instance of what Félix Guattari and Gilles Deleuze called a "good schizo dream," a moment of "be[ing] fully a part of the crowd and at the same time completely outside it, removed from it" (*A Thousand Plateaus* 29), that is to say, a realization of utopia where the self turns to "becoming" in its rhizomatic connection with others, as in Lawrence.[12]

Clarissa's "theory" elaborates this point further. When she is "sitting on the bus going up Shaftsbury Avenue," she "feel[s] herself everywhere." In these moments, she feels "odd affinities . . . with people she [has] never spoken to, some woman in the street, some man behind a counter—even trees, or barns" (231). In Peter's view, this theory "ended in a transcendental theory which, with her horror of death, allowed her to believe, or say that she believed (for all her scepticism), that since our apparitions, the part of us which appears, are so momentary compared with the other, the unseen part of us, which spreads wide, the unseen might survive, be recovered somehow attached to this person or that, or even haunting certain places after death"

(231). Peter's rather dismissive view of her "transcendental" theory induced by her fear of death rings true to some extent, but Clarissa's theory also designates her utopian space where her selfhood yields itself to a non-being, awakening to the knowledge of interrelatedness with others.

In an essay written in 1927, "Street Haunting: A London Adventure," Woolf again returns to this vision of a utopia that surfaces through a reconceptualization of one's self and relations with others.[13] "As we step out of the house" she writes, "[w]e are no longer quite ourselves. . . . We shed the self our friends know us by and become part of that vast republican army of anonymous trampers"(*Collected Essays* 4: 155). This delightful sense of becoming part of other people bears a political and aesthetic significance. Rather than leading toward that entire loss of selfhood against which Woolf always warns, walking enables her to forge a new creative writing subjectivity. For Woolf, "[w]alking home through the desolation one could tell oneself the story of the dwarf, of the blind men, of the party in the Mayfair mansion. . . . Into each of these lives one could penetrate a little way, far enough to give oneself the illusion that one is not tethered to a single mind, but can put on briefly for a few minutes the bodies and minds of others. . . . And what greater delight and wonder can there be than to leave the straight lines of personality and deviate into those footpaths that lead beneath brambles and thick tree trunks into the heart of the forest where live those wild beasts, our fellow men?" (*Collected Essays* 4: 165).

The vision of utopia that both Clarissa and Woolf in "Street Haunting" experience cannot be reduced to a transcendence of the panoptic conditions of the modern city. No less than Lawrence and Certeau was Woolf keenly aware of her ambivalent position as an inhabitant, user, producer, and product of an at once repressive and liberating cityspace. In Certeau's phrase, "[t]he long poem of walking manipulates spatial organizations, no matter how panoptic they may be: it is neither foreign to them (it can take place only within them) nor in conformity with them (it does not receive its identity from them). . . . It inserts its multitudinous references and citations into them" (101). To put it differently, as both insider and outsider, the pedestrian at once produces and is produced by the social space of the city that works as at once "an origin"—the place of manipulation—and "the nowhere"—"dreamed-of-place" of utopia (103).

As in Certeau, "to walk" in the city in Woolf is "to lack a place," to experience an "indefinite process of being absent" (102). Through this walking, the city comes to be "haunted by a nowhere"—the utopian space where the self undergoes a new sense of self and relationship with others (102). In both "Street Haunting" and *Mrs. Dalloway*, the walker's body is produced and produces the utopian no-place through its on-going travel; losing and redrawing their places, Woolf's walkers remap urban space as they connect with others across different socio-geographical strata. In other words, we witness the emergence of utopia as the dreamed "nowhere" that deconstructs the seemingly regulative space from within (107).

Reading Clarissa's utopian vision side by side with the perspectives of other characters like Peter Walsh or her double figure, Septimus Warren Smith, can help us to understand more clearly the multi-layered political significance of the vision of utopia that the novel seeks to offer. The episode of Peter's dreaming at Regent's Park, for example, exposes a problematic desire to evade reality that is buried in his utopian vision of escaping and merging, a desire to which Clarissa's utopian vision critically responds. Clarissa's former lover, Peter, recently returned from India to London to arrange his current lover's divorce. Dozing off in the park, he dreams of being a solitary traveler who confronts a maternal giant tree (85). At the sight of the tree, the traveler is "taken by surprise with moments of extraordinary exaltation" (85), feeling a simultaneous desire to be merged with and escape from this tree. Curiously reenacting Clarissa's and Septimus' vision of being one with a tree, this moment registers various desires such as an escapist impulse, pre-Oedipal drive, and death instinct that characterize a conventional utopian vision.

Peter's moment is triggered by an escapist impulse, "a desire for solace, for relief, for something outside these miserable pigmies, these feeble, these ugly, these craven men and women" (85). At the same time, it reveals an Oedipal desire to be unified with the encompassing maternal body. With his eyes upon sky and branches, the traveler rapidly endows them "with womanhood; see with amazement how grave they become, how majestically, as the breeze stirs them, they dispense with a dark flutter of the leaves charity, comprehension, absolution" (85–86). These "visions" retain elements of traditional utopian fantasy in their tendency to displace the actual and to subsume differences to comforting unity. They "put their faces in front of the actual thing . . . taking away from him the sense of the earth, the wish to return, and giving him for substitute a general peace, as if . . . all this fever of living were simplicity itself; and myriads of things merged in one thing" (86). This vision of total abandonment of the actual world leads to an ominous signal of death. To "walk straight on to this great figure" will have him "blow to nothingness with the rest" (87). The immediately following passage likens the traveler to a son killed "in the battles of the world." As he advances the village street, every figure there "seems ominous" "as if some august fate . . . were about to sweep them into complete annihilation" (87). The subtext of the memory of the Great War here is interwoven with the deadly power embedded in a dangerous side of utopian longing, the danger to annihilate selfhood without forming a new one, and the abandonment of this life, adumbrating Septimus' suicidal plunging into his fantasy world and death.

At times Clarissa's utopian moments also register her wish to withdraw, her pre-Oedipal impulse, and her preoccupation with her death. Her vision of merging with the other involves the death of her conventional self, but it does not mean an entire annihilation of the self. Like Birkin in Lawrence, Clarissa imagines her death—whether it is a symbolic death of the culturally imposed self in the present or literal death in the future—in light of a beginning of the new self as a part of the universe, as evidenced by her belief in her rebirth through constituting a part of the universe. For Peter, unlike Clarissa, the vision of fusion, provokes a profound fear of the annihilation of the self. In a sense, this fear suggests that his utopian longing for fusion is entirely dictated by his escapist and even suicidal impulse to escape from life in the first place. Not surprisingly, his utopian moments never develop into a new vision of social relations built upon fundamental connections and interdependence between things and beings. Instead, Peter's moments must be confined to a dream world, lest they should take over the masculine, imperial self. This fatal union must be submerged beneath the consciousness in the form of a dream, a dream that he must awaken from and forget. Thus, even when his vision of the present comes very close to that of Clarissa, it fails to break his egotistic self-sufficiency. Echoing Clarissa's attachment to "London; this moment of June" (5), "this, here, now, in front of her; the fat lady in the cab" (12), the novel reports Peter's affection for "[l]ife itself, every moment of it, every drop of it, here, this instant, now" (119). But, unlike Clarissa, whose revelatory moments always embrace the existence of other things and beings, Peter's moment ends by confirming his conviction that "one scarcely needed people any more" (118, 119).

The daydreaming of Septimus, a shell-shocked war veteran, is a most powerful version of Clarissa's vision of utopia. Clarissa's feeling of herself as being a part of a tree is reenacted through a vision of rhizomatic connections in Septimus' "schizo dream." As he watches the skywriting airplane, he feels connected to the tree and even to the entire universe. "A marvelous discovery indeed," he thinks, "that the human voice . . . can quicken trees into life!. . . . But they beckoned; leaves were alive; trees were alive. And the leaves being connected by millions of fibres with his own body, there on the seat, fanned it up and down" (32).

In a sense, Septimus' fantasy discloses the dark dystopian underside in which Clarissa's seemingly self-indulgent utopian reveries are anchored. Challenging Peter's dismissive view of Clarissa's sense of connection with things and beings (which she imagines as surviving her death) as a mere reflection of her fear caused by her recent recovery from near-fatal illness, Septimus' vision invites us to look at Clarissa's vision of utopia in relation to the memory of the Great War that haunts the contemporary psyche. At the same time, recalling the experiences of Lucrezia and Killman, Septimus' vision of London that "has swallowed up many millions of young men called Smith" points to the oppressive and dehumanizing experience of the marginalized urban populace (127). Juxtaposed with Septimus' vision of utopia, which is grounded in his profound despair and anger at the oppressive social system, inequalities, violence, and war, Clarissa's vision of radical connection thus gains a clearer socio-political bearing; both Septimus and Clarissa's visions of utopia retain a subversive potential to disrupt the dominant social system in its impulse to desert the socially established selfhood and social relations. In a sinister echo of Clarissa's "plunging" into the past at the beginning of the novel, Septimus eventually throws himself out of the window of his lodging house onto the iron spikes of the railing below. But Clarissa is to inherit his legacy of utopia, as intimated by her sense of identification with Septimus, whom she has never met. Having heard of Septimus' suicide, Clarissa leaves her guests behind and withdraws into a little room. Here, musing on Septimus' death, Clarissa confronts a curious sense of identification with him mixed with a sudden recognition of her own complicity with the social system that drove the man to death: "Death was defiance." Her thought continues:

> Somehow it [Septimus' suicide] was her disaster—her disgrace. It was her punishment to see sink and disappear here a man, there a woman, in this profound darkness, and she forced to stand here in her evening dress. She had schemed; she had pilfered. She was never wholly admirable. (282)

At this moment of recognizing her culpability, Clarissa envisions another exquisite moment of connection; looking at a neighboring old woman going to bed over the window, Clarissa feels a sudden sense of connection with the woman. As the reciprocal gaze of the old women (whether imaginary or not) suggests, this moment of connection is built upon the equal standing of self and other: "Oh, but how surprising!—in the opposite room the old lady stared straight at her!" (283). Reaching such a genuine sense of connection with others, Clarissa feels "somehow very like him—the young man who had killed himself." Clarissa's feeling of identification with Septimus points once again to the fundamental affinity between Septimus' vision of utopia and her own. Or, to put it differently, it points to the survival of an alternative vision of utopia through Clarissa's remarkable capacity to anchor her utopia in the perpetually generative chronotope of "here and now."

In conclusion, *Mrs. Dalloway* offers a vision of an alternative utopia by locating the city in the dialectics between regulation and resistance. The novel exposes the heterogeneity of the city through distinct experiences and perceptions of the city as well as through multiple temporalities, both of which defy the oppressive social system, the power structure that seeks to materialize the dominant social order within the urban space. London emerges not so much as a pre-existing fixed setting as an alterable, kinetic utopian space open to different uses and practices. Utopia in the novel occupies a paradoxical locus—at once unlocatable and deeply mundane; it is "atopical" in the sense that it does not reside in an identifiable place but happens through the very reconceptualization and reimagination of the present time/space in the form of contradictions and flexibilities. It comes through moments of throwing off culturally imposed selfhood and setting up a new connection with others, moments that Woolf found one of the most significant political experiences of sympathy and a starting point for building a better community. It also comes through the image of the ambiguous, heterogeneous social space of London where control, regulation, and exclusion are consistently exposed, interrogated, and challenged. Initiating a radical restructuration of here and now, utopia in the novel shatters the bourgeois ideology that posits the illusionary full self-presence of self, reality, time, and space. In Certeau's phrase, utopia in the novel "displaces the analytical, coherent proper meanings of urbanism. It constitutes a 'wandering of the semantic' produced by masses that make some parts of the city disappear and exaggerate others, distorting it, fragmenting it, and diverting it from its immobile order" (Certeau 102). Through these devices, the novel achieves a remarkable affirmation of and opportunity for restructuring space, time, being, and society by offering utopia in a process that is located in the generative chronotope of the here and now.

EPIPHANIES REFIGURED: "MOMENTS OF BEING," "THE MOMENT: SUMMER'S NIGHT," AND *BETWEEN THE ACTS*

According to Lefebvre and other theorists of space and utopia, I have discussed in the introduction, the politics of utopia necessarily has a temporal dimension. For Lefebvre, as we have seen, the reconceptualization of both social space and time is integral to the challenging of the status quo. Shattering the abstract and mechanical notion of time, the subjective, private dimension of time awakens us to immense possibilities contained in daily existence. For Lefebvre, therefore, utopian "moments" do not so much designate a group fantasy of an ideal world as an individual experience of transformative space and time, an experience that can be triggered by both actual social revolutions and daily life.

Anticipating Lefebvre, Woolf envisions a utopian moment as a remarkable occasion for reformulating the self, social relations, time, and the vision of the world. This moment, which Woolf at times called the "moment of being," has a curious affinity with Lawrence's "insurgent Now" as well. Like Lawrence and Lefebvre, Woolf conceives of utopia as a dynamic process that brings about a sense of the self as "becoming" and "in touch" with the vast whole; it comes into being through an abrupt interruption of the "now" that exposes one to formulations of selfhood and social relations that are different from the dominant ones. Far from being a mere retreat into an ahistorical and purely personal realm, utopian space/time thus engages with everyday life through its disruption of the illusory stability of the self and the social order.

Woolf writes of her "moments of being" in her autobiographical piece, *A Sketch of the Past*. She proposes that life is composed of moments of non-being ("that is not lived consciously," thus not remembered) and "moments of being." Stating that "the real novelist can somehow convey both sorts of being," Woolf describes "three instances of exceptional moments." Each of these moments of being came to her like "a sudden violent shock" that she remembers all her life (71). The first one, she recalls, happened through her sudden realization, "why hurt another person," when she was about to raise her fist to hit her brother (71). The second instance, which critics have often cited, took place when she was looking at a flower bed in the garden of St. Ives:

> "That is the whole," I said. I was looking at a plant with a spread of leaves; and it seemed suddenly plain that the flower itself was a part of the earth; that a ring enclosed what was the flower; and that was the real flower; part earth; part flower (70).

The third example of a "moment of being" happened when she overheard her father say that a man named Mr. Valpy had killed himself while she was walking by an apple tree in the garden. Suddenly, she felt that "the apple tree was connected with the horror of Mr. Valpy's suicide" (71). The first and the third moments, Woolf writes, brought her a deep sense of "despair," "powerlessness," and "horror" (72, 73). Whereas these two instances somehow "paralyze[d]" her, the second one "ma[de] [her] a writer" (72). Woolf writes that she felt that she "had put away [the vision of the flower] in [her] mind" that she should "go back [to], to turn over and explore" (71). This is not the place to delve into the complex psychological aspects and the relation between memory and the act of writing that Woolf's descriptions of these "moments of being" reveal. What is notable about these moments with regard to the issue of utopia is that despite Woolf's differentiations, all of these moments are marked by a sudden realization of profound connections between beings and things, a realization that comes through a radical abandonment of the conventional sense of the self and its relation to others.[14]

For Lawrence, as we have seen, alternative utopia comes into being through the revelatory vision of connection with others at the moment of the "insurgent Now." Lawrence regards art as a medium that generates such a vision of utopia, as exemplified by his observations concerning "the poetry of the present" or Van Gogh's paintings. In similar way, Woolf associates her vision of utopia based on the sense of connection with artistic achievement. Noting how she integrates her moments of being into her writing, Woolf writes:

> From this I reach what I might call a philosophy; at any rate it is a con-
> stant idea of mine; that behind the cotton wool is hidden a pattern; that
> we—I mean all human beings—are connected with this; that the whole
> world is a work of art; that we are parts of the work of art. Hamlet or a
> Beethoven quartet is the truth about this vast mass that we call the world.
> But there is no Shakespeare, there is no Beethoven; certainly and emphat-
> ically there is no God; we are the words; we are the music; we are the
> thing itself. And I see this when I have a shock. (*A Sketch of the Past* 72)

To borrow Deleuze and Guattari's terms, the moment illustrates a realization of the rhizomatic connections or interdependence of things that involves "spatiotemporal revelations" (*A Thousand Plateaus* 263).[15]

The above passage points to several important aspects that help us to connect Woolf's "moments of being" with her vision of utopia.[16] Woolf's "moment" appear here as experiences of wholeness and unity that are born out of violent ruptures of the continuum of time. They register the instant of danger and rupture of the unexpected rips in the cotton wool, shattering the lure of stasis and the status quo. It is a peculiar experience of the here and now, an experience that enables the self to transgress ideological boundaries of self-present identity of being and time, an experience that alters the whole terrain of the self and its relation to other things and beings, as well as the experience and conception of time and space.[17]

As in Lawrence, Woolf's utopia emerges out of the radical reimagination and restructuration of the present time, space, and being, rather than residing in a remote time and space. Woolf's examination of an exquisite present moment in an essay, "The Moment: Summer's Night," written in 1938, illuminates this point further. Delineating surrounding things seen, heard, and imagined at nightfall, the narrator ponders over what constitutes the present moment:

> The night was falling so that the table in the garden among the trees grew whiter and whiter; and the people round it more indistinct. An owl . . . crossed the fading sky with a black spot between its claw. The trees murmured. An aeroplane hummed like a piece of plucked wire. There was also, on the roads, the distant explosion of a motor cycle, shooting further and further away down the road. Yet what composed the present moment? (*The Moment and Other Essays* 3)

What is Woolf's answer to this question and how is it related to her vision of utopia? As the opening description suggests, the moment for Woolf is composed of a collection of visual, aural, and imagined experiences of things near and far rather than being confined to the narrow and isolated scope of one's immediate circumstances. Moreover, the present moment is not a homogeneous experience but varies from individual to individual. It is intermingled with the past or the future. We are told, "[i]f you are young, the future lies upon the present, like a piece of glass, making it tremble and quiver. If you are old, the past lies upon the present, like a thin glass, making it waver, distorting it" (3). As we shall see further later, this view of the present moment challenges the ideological construction of time, a view that is critical to the politics of Woolf's utopian chronotope.

The essay shows that the present moment is composed of two different ways of conceiving and experiencing—a unit of the mechanical process of time, on the one hand, and a fluid, dynamic, and subjective instance, on the other. To apply Lefebvre, the latter can be seen as a subversive temporality, time that "comes back into its own as privacy, inner life, subjectivity," thus challenging the former—abstract, mechanical time. In other words, the latter is akin to Lefebvre's moments that shatter the status quo by awakening us to new senses of self and relations with other beings and things. At the beginning, we confront the present moment "composed of visual and of sense impressions," a moment when everything "open[s]," "expand[s]" and "change[s]" (3). But this sense of the fluid moment is followed by another sense of the moment; the moment here is merely a part of an "order," a part which is subsumed to the "inevitable" process of time (4).

The rest of the essay is structured by alternations between the two kinds of the present moment connected to different ways in which we conceive and construct our self and reality. They imply distinctive ideological implications or politics; where the first is linked to the conventional view and experience of the present moment that sustains the ideological vision of the stability of being, its relations, and everyday life in general, the second is aligned with a radical, subversive utopian one that disrupts the illusion of the status quo and potentially initiates a different formation of selfhood and social order. For example, the first appears as a moment when the self sets up the border between oneself and other, and fails to imagine differently or change the given world. This conventional time for division and "self-assertion" is associated with the egotistic "desire to be loved," the refusal "to be jumped into extravagance," and the inability to "believe in miracles" (6). This conception and experience of the present moment is a time of fixed selfhood and of repetitious, predictable, and conventional behaviors and practices. Changes are no more than variations ultimately subsumed to a larger unchangeable "order." This is the time when "[o]ne becomes aware that we are spectator and also passive participants in a pageant. And as nothing can interfere with the order, we have nothing to do but accept, and watch" (4). It is interesting to recall, at this point, that in "The Memories" Woolf imagines herself as a "benevolent spectator" at the working-class women's meeting. In a sense, we may say that "The Memories" seems to be trapped in this first kind of moment—the conventional temporality that maintains the status quo. The prevailing sense of being "cut off" from the actors in "The Memories" forestalls a vision of utopia built through a radical demolition of boundaries and a construction of connections. Given the complicity of this conventional temporality with the dominant social order, it is no wonder that in "The Moment: Summer's Night" the present moment surfaces as a terrain where the tedious repetition of daily hardships and violence takes place. An anonymous voice reports a domestic violence in a cottage, violence issuing from the unchanging succession of everyday and despair at the lack of any possibility or of will to change: "'He beats her [his wife] every Saturday; from boredom, I should say, not drink; there's nothing else to do'" (7).

One of the most dramatic interruptions of the second kind of the present moment takes place at this moment, out of which a vision of utopia emerges. We are told, "Let us do something then, something to end this horrible moment, this plausible glistening moment that reflects in its smooth sides this intolerable kitchen, this squalor; this woman moaning; and the rattle of the toy on the flags, and the man munching. Let us smash it by breaking a match. There—snap" (7). Suddenly, the scene turns to a vision of the

natural world coming into the human one, blurring and redrawing boundaries of self, other, and reality. Here "comes the low of the cows in the field;
and another cow to the left answers." In this moment "no order is percepti-
ble; there is no sequence in these cries, these movements; they come from no
bodies." Similar to Woolf's "shocking" but delightful moments of being in *A
Sketch of the Past,* this moment marks the instant when the self becomes
blended with the universe, a moment of simultaneous fear and bliss in the
face of the loss of the old I/eye and the birth of a new one: "Then comes the
terror, the exultation; the power to rush out unnoticed, alone to be con-
sumed; to be swept away to become a rider on the random wind . . . to be
part of the eyeless dark" (8). Echoing another revealing moment when the
narrator and the owl turn to "one wing; all embracing, all gathering, and
these boundaries . . . be all swept into one colour by the brush of the wing"
(5), this abrupt moment puts the self in the "domain of *symbiosis*" (Deleuze
and Guattari, A Thousand Plateaus 238), challenging the oppressive vision
of order, sequence, and socially constructed selfhood, and affirming the
moment of connection, movement, and change.[18]

As we have seen so far, "The Moment: Summer's Night" envisions a heterogeneous, dynamic, living moment of reality that brings about a reformulation of the self—as a perpetual becoming "poised on the brink between past and
future" (Richter 39)—and a sense of connection with other beings and indeed
the entire universe. Opposing with the conventional belief that places a false
trust in a stable reality and selfhood, at the cost of the desire and capacity for
change, Woolf offers a subversive here and now that disturbs the seemingly solid
surface of everyday life and thus "shake[s]" the "whole universe" (5).

Woolf's diary first refers to what would become her last novel, *Between
the Acts* on April12, 1938: "Last night I began making up again: Summer's
Night: a complete whole: that's my idea" (*Diary* 5: 133). This diary entry
suggests the relation between "The Moment: Summer's Night" (which was
probably written a little later than this diary entry suggests) and *Between the
Acts* (Hussey, *Virginia Woolf: A to Z* 27). A more compelling relation between
these writings is to be found in a phrase cited above:"[o]ne becomes aware
that we are spectator and also passive participants in a pageant. And as nothing can interfere with the order, we have nothing to do but accept, and
watch."[19] Another significant motif that *Between the Acts* develops from "The
Moment: Summer's Night" is the interruption of the natural world (the
sound of the cows), which leads to the vision of the absent "order,"
"sequence," and "bod[y]" and finally, of "movements" and connections.

This is not, of course, to reduce the thematic complexity of the novel
to a few motifs that had appeared in "The Moment: Summer's Night." And

yet, my reading of "The Moment" in terms of the two kinds of the moment, one of which I associate with a vision of alternative utopia in Woolf's writing, enables us to look at the vision of utopia in *Between the Acts* from a new perspective.

The novel begins with the gathering of people for an annual village pageant on a summer evening in a remote village in England. The rest of the story presents episodes from the life of the village people in alternation with scenes from the pageant that tell the history of England from Old England to the present. As the narrative unfolds, we come to see that what the characters of the novel suffer as a result of their sexual orientation, gender, class, or from their memories of better days in the past, or their shared fears of the impending war.

Compared with *Mrs. Dalloway,* the prevalent mood of *Between the Acts* is much gloomier, despite its occasional tone of playfulness and humor. As biographical studies have shown, Woolf's direct experience of the Second World War, her growing sense of isolation from the public, and her loss of London life brought her an awareness that a way of life that she had known was disappearing. Based on Woolf's keen observations of her own and others' responses to this moment of socio-historical crisis, the novel explores the desires, memories, despairs, and hopes that pervaded contemporary society. The book's complex array of tones and themes has triggered divided readings regarding the social vision the novel offers. Some critics have read the novel as a gloomy portrait of social collapse. For example, Susan Squier maintains that the novel marks Woolf's loss of utopian vision resulting from World War II and the attendant deprivation of city life (189). Others read the novel in light of a politically charged optimism focusing on a new sense of community that embraces multiplicity and fluidity.[20]

When we read *Between the Acts* side by side with "The Moment: Summer's Night," we come to see that the novel puts two kinds of temporalities and the political implications of each into the complicated socio-historical and psychological contexts of the Great War.[21] The domestic violence (wife-beating) in "The Moment" returns in various forms of violence within and outside the home/nation, as illustrated by allusions to fascism.[22] In the face of rampant violence at home and abroad, the passive posture of a spectator bound to mechanical temporality becomes all the more politically dangerous as it threatens to support the perpetuation of socio-historical and psychological evil. The fight with chronic violence in *Between the Acts* is therefore inseparable from a call for an alternative utopia, a utopia that repudiates closure, a nowHere that perpetually opens and reopens in eruptive moments.

Like "The Moment: Summer's Night," *Between the Acts* problematizes the ideological limits embedded in conventional temporality, a temporality which is incompatible with a utopian chronotope due to its association with a fundamental passivity and consequent complicity with the continuous reproduction of violence, inequality, and dominance throughout history. For example, despite the differences in their sufferings and temperaments, Isa, her husband, Giles, and the homosexual William Dodge are depicted in the novel as passive spectators enslaved to what Lefebvre calls "abstract" time, which is opposed to "moments" that beget subversive utopia. Woolf's treatment of Isa is especially telling in that it invites us to see how the novel interrogates the ideological limits of a conventional vision of utopia by associating it both with abstract temporality and with the image of a passive spectator. For Isa, who suffers from imprisonment in domesticity and a loveless married life, utopia is fundamentally located in an unattainable space/time, which is shut off from the here and now. Easily "slipping into the cliché conveniently provided by fiction," Isa envisions her utopia either in the image of an isolated island or another unknown place (14). Her realization of the lack of affection between her husband and herself gives way to a romantic reverie of "a green island, hedged about with snow drops, laid with a counterpane of puckered silk, the innocent island floated under her window"(14). Later, Isa's musings further point to the ideologically problematic aspects of her conventional utopianism, such as an escapist impulse intertwined with a death drive and a desire for stasis. In an interval after the act, titled "The Victorian Age," as Isa literally "escape[s]" from other people, her musings lead to a vision of timeless utopia, where "there grows nothing for the eye." She continues: "No rose. To issue where? In some harvestless dim field where no evening lets fall her mantle; nor sun rises. All's equal there. Unblowing, ungrowing are the roses there. Change is not; nor the mutable and lovable; nor greetings nor partings; nor furtive findings and feelings, where hand seeks hand and eye seeks shelter from the eye'"(154–55).

Isa's utopian longing has limits and dangers in its fundamental loss of connection with everyday life. It fails to lead to activities and practices that may initiate a move toward a better world, for her vision of a remote island displaces existing reality with a static world of mechanical equality in frozen space/time. Just like William Dodge's helpless despair at "the doom of sudden death hanging over us," Isa's dream of utopia points to her passivity and evasion (114).[23] It is no wonder that Woolf regards both Isa and Will as "passive participants in a pageant." (*Collected Essays* 2: 293). Isa and Will "were all caught and caged; prisoners; watching a spectacle" (*Between the Acts* 176). As suggested in "The Moment: Summer's Night," the passive spectator cannot embrace a subversive temporality that destabilizes the dominant order. Both Will and Isa find the intervals of the pageantry—occasions when alternative utopian moments take place, as we shall see later—unbearable and meaning-less; they are unable to fill the gaps of the stage of history and of the present time through imagination and their own practices. For them, the seemingly suspended present moment of intervals, the void between the acts, does not produce any meaning: "[n]othing happened. The tick of the machine was maddening" (176). In the eyes of Isa, who is subject to a mechanical tempo-ral order, "one thing" simply "led to another" (47).

Isa's husband, Giles is another figure who is depicted as a passive onlooker "manacled to a rock," a spectator "forced [to] passively [to] behold" the horrible performance of history (60). Unlike Isa, he totally rejects utopia. In his passivity, however, he shares Isa's inability to accept or experience "a moment" that breaks the established sequence of time and order of life. He is a much more dangerous accomplice of the ruthless dominant social order, as illustrated by his stamping on a snake choking on a toad. What he finds really intolerable about the sight of the snake "unable to swallow" the toad and the toad "unable to die" is the moment of suspension that may bring about a violation of the established social order. The predator must devour the victim without any difficulty or delay. Otherwise, the moment signals a "birth the wrong way round—a monstrous inversion" (99). His killing of both presents his determination not to allow the advent of any new or inverted order. His notion of "we" would never include the homosexual Dodge (111). Where Isa's escapist utopian yearning, aligned with a static time and unreal space, can be dangerous in its potential complicity with the perpetuation of the routine violence materialized in the war, Giles's passivity turns out to be a more threatening force that upholds the drama of history that repeats dominance and subjugation.

As we have seen, in "The Moment: Summer's Night," the anonymous narrator's urging, "Let us do . . . something to end this horrible moment" of routinized oppression and violence, is followed by a subversive temporal dimension (signaled by "snap"), a moment charged with "movement" that disrupts "order" and "sequence," which is integral to a reformulation of self and relationships with others. Similarly, the politics of an alternative utopia in *Between the Acts* operates in eruptive moments that shatter conventional selfhood and belief of progressive history, as enacted by the intervals of the pageantry—the symbolic and literal "break" with the drama of English his-tory. Throughout the novel, the intervals function as a time when the specta-tors become actors in their own drama, while pointing to the fundamental performativity and constructedness of selfhood and history. They are also the time when the spectators are released from the act of watching and receiving meanings on the stage and made to produce their own interpretations of both the play on the stage and of their own lives. They are transitional instants, moments of being which are simultaneously stripped of established selfhood and social order, and made pregnant with new ones. For instance, during the interval preceding an act titled "The Victorian Age" in *Between the Acts,* the audience confronts utopian events when they experience what Phillip E. Wegner calls "the deterritorialized ungroundedness and loss of self-hood" (*Imaginary Communities* 90): "Somehow . . . felt . . . a little not quite here or there. As if the play had jerked the ball out of the cup; as if what I call myself was still floating unattached, and didn't settle. Not quite themselves, they felt" (149). This vision of the I/eyeless self then leads to that of a new "bodiless" community founded on less deceptive narratives of unity and forced "one-making" (175). The scene is reminiscent of the moment in "The Moment: Summer's Night" when the narrator envisions the loss of her older self (founded on divisions) followed by the constitution of new one (founded on connections) through the image of the wing, the audience.

Another moment of an alternative utopian restructuration of self and community takes place in an interval that precedes the final act, "The Present Time." Here again, the audience "were neither one thing nor the other; neither Victorians nor themselves. They were suspended, without being, in limbo (178). It is at this paradoxical moment of suspension and dynamics that the final act, "the Present Time" begins. As the title suggests, the final act of the pageant is about the present that sits uneasily on a perplexing moment of demolition/construction:

> That was a ladder. And that (a cloth roughly painted) was a wall. And that a man with a hod on his back. Mr. Page the reporter, licking his pencil, noted: "With the very limited means at her disposal, Miss La Trobe conveyed to the audience Civilization (the wall) in ruins; rebuilt (witness man with hod) by human effort; witness also woman handing bricks. Any fool could grasp that. Now issued black man in fuzzy wig; coffe-coloured ditto in silver turban; they signify presumably the League of. . . ." (181–82)

The passage underscores that a new community is built through the non-hierarchal "League" of people with different race, nationality, and gender (182). As the novel proceeds, it becomes clear that the final act is a culmination of the utopian politics of the novel operative at the subversive moment of "the present." The final act reflects the collective yearning for survival on the eve of World War II with the envisioning of a new home free of war, exploitation of labor, and dominance (183): "Homes will be built. . . . Each of us a free man; plates washed by machinery; not an aeroplane to vex us; all liberated; made whole . . ." (182–83). However, the novel refuses to frame this vision of a new emancipatory home in a conventional utopian space/time. Indeed, it is significant to note that the novel insists that a vision of a new world emerges through a new culture of space and time that "assail[s] the traditional hierarchies and sanctuaries of privilege, power," and "the entire dominant social order" (Kern 154, 180). Reenacting the eruption marked by a "snap[ping]" sound of the subversive present moment in "The Moment: Summer's Night," the final act about the present envisions an alternative utopia emerging through the eruptive moment. The tune that tells the audience about the King and the Queen at the present time in England is abruptly interrupted by a moment that leads to a vision of a new community, a "whole" which is constituted less by (forced) harmony and linear temporality than by heterogeneity and dynamic temporality resistant to closure:

> The tune changed; snapped; broke; jagged. Fox trot, was it? Jazz? Anyhow the rhythm kicked, reared, snapped short. What a jangle and a jingle!. . . . What a cackle, a cacophony! Nothing ended. So abrupt. . . . What is her [Miss La Trobe's] game? To disrupt? (183)

This vision of an alternative community of fragmented, unfixed beings in process is followed by a scene where various kinds of mirrors come out of the bushes. The appearance of mirrors creates another moment of limbo, an in-between space where the divisions between actor and spectator, reality and fiction dissolve; the audience is caught, their images reflected in the mirrors on the stage. In the midst of this scene, another significant interruption takes place: "The very cows joined in. Walloping, tail lashing, the reticence of nature was undone, and the barriers that should divide Man the Master from the Brute were dissolved. Then the dogs joined in" (184). Remember again how the entrance of the sounds of the cow into the human world in "The Moment: Summer's Night" marks a moment symbolic of the breaking of the dominant order, a moment that that heralds a rhizomatic connection between human beings and the universe. Bringing this motif into a specific socio-cultural context, the final act ends with a moment of simultaneous suspension and movement: "The hands of the clock had stopped at the present moment. It was now. Ourselves" (186). This "now" is a subversive moment; it is a dynamic moment of utopia of the here and now, pregnant with infinite possibilities moving toward multiple directions. As in *Mrs. Dalloway*, the present moment of here and now in *Between the Acts* is intertwined with the future as well as with the past. Indeed, at the last scene, the curtain rises on the future that turns itself into the pre-history when roads or houses were yet to be made, pointing to a emergence of another new world:

> Isa let her sewing drop. The great hooded chairs had become enormous. And Giles too. And Isa too against the window. The window was all sky without colour. The house had lost its shelter. It was night before roads were made, or houses, it was the night that dwellers in caves had watched from some high place among rocks. Then the curtain rose. They spoke. (219).

Here, we confront a disturbing utopian chronotope that would correct "the fetishism of a linear historicity of progress" (Shields 61). Taking place in transitional moments of crisis, this utopia retains a deep sense of anxiety as much as it generates optimistic anticipations. The present is pregnant with a dark vision of the end of the world, with concerns about the future that might turn out to be a nightmare, as well as expectations for a birth of a new world. In this sense, it obliquely echoes the abrupt interruption of Woolf's moments by a vision of disintegration and death and the prevalent sense of fear and death hanging over Clarissa's blissful here and now.[24] In both cases we witness the ultimate affirmation of life gained through an ongoing fight with death and closure.

* * *

As we have seen so far, Lawrence and Woolf's antipathy to the static, institutional, and totalitarian formula of classical utopias drove them to seek visions of alternative utopias. Utopias in their work emerge through a radical reformulation of the present wherein the self frequently abandons its socially constructed selfhood and confronts its fundamental interdependence and connection with other things and beings. To put it differently, the production of utopian spaces in these writers comes through the radical eruption of the "now" that breaks through the ideological façade of stable reality. The experience of these disruptive moments therefore cannot be reduced to simply an unreal transcendence of or withdrawal from actual social life. On the contrary, it actively interacts with, reverses, and changes everyday life. Presenting selfhood, space, time, and social relations as being heterogeneous, ambiguous, and dynamic, and thus open to changes and possibilities instead of being subjugated to ideological and mystified sets of abstractions, these writers locate utopia in the dynamic and ever-changing present time and space, interrogating the logic of historicism, linear temporality or progress, and dismantling the status quo. Rescuing utopias from any kind of closure, Lawrence and Woolf propose utopia as a dynamic process operating in the generative chronotope of the here and now.

Conclusion

In this study I have sought to explore the political implications of literary discourses about space. To do this, I have examined works of Lawrence and Woolf as exemplary texts that simultaneously reflect, reverse, and disrupt dominant spatial discourses and practices. As I have discussed, despite the numerous differences in their temperament, background, and relationship with modernist experimentalism, both Lawrence and Woolf developed a keen sense of the constructedness and changeability of self, space, and social relations through their experience of an era that saw epistemological, physical, and psychological changes in spatio-temporal perspectives and experiences. More importantly, their marginality, due to class and gender respectively, often drove them to question the ideological implications embedded in the contemporary symbolic, physical, and discursive spatial *topoi* of the oppressive socio-spatial order, and to seek a more liberating and inclusive human geography.

Combining recent interdisciplinary concerns with social space and modernity with scholars' attempts to redefine utopian writing, my study has explored how the works of Lawrence and Woolf deal with three dimensions of social space: private and public spaces; home and nation; and utopian spaces. For Lawrence and Woolf, I have argued, space plays a central role in developing their subversive politics, instead of serving merely as background or setting for events. Lawrence and Woolf treat spaces such as dining rooms, drawing rooms, houses, schools, and streets in ways that challenge place myths that have functioned to maintain class and gender hegemonies. As I have shown, domestic spaces in these writers are multifaceted social spaces charged with oppression, resistance, and conflicts between different genders and classes. In this respect, their depiction of domestic space works to shatter the Victorian ideological picture of domestic space as a purely personal, feminine, ahistorical, and harmonious haven, a picture which sustained the dominant socio-spatial order by obscuring or naturalizing unequal power relations. At the same time, the complexity and ambiguity of public space in these writers not only interrogates the Victorian ideology of separate spheres, but also disrupts the myth of public spaces as a place for emancipation and self-fulfillment. The critical renderings of public space in the works of Lawrence and Woolf lay bare the illusions of the social system that govern the dominant production of public space, a system that seeks to eradicate integral selfhood and individuality in the name of "the Whole" or "manliness" so as to raise subjects who serve imperialism, patriotism, and violence. As we have seen, characters' perspectives on public space in these writers' works often advance a subversive critique of the cultural fantasy of public space that reveals how that fantasy harms both women and men. Women's search for independence in Woolf and Lawrence (at his best) involves a fundamental social criticism that calls for the reformulation of both domestic and public spaces, instead of being confined to an effort to achieve equal access to the man's world. A focus on spatial politics, thus, helps us to understand the complex social criticism of both Lawrence and Woolf, while inviting us to look at the gender politics of Lawrence's works from a new angle as well.

Lawrence's and Woolf's challenges to the Victorian ideology of home, an ideology that has propagated the cultural fantasies of the superior middle-class self and nationhood, are integral to their critiques of class and imperial hegemonies. As I have demonstrated, both writers disrupt the Victorian ideal of home and its mirror image of the nation by exposing the process of domestication, stigmatization, or exclusion of the female, poor, foreign, racial, colonized, and/or homosexual Other that has buttressed the conceptual and physical building of the home/nation. In a number of instances, the works of Lawrence and Woolf deconstruct the imperial home and nation by uncovering a will to dominate and anxiety of the insider/intruder/oppressor embedded in the Victorian rhetoric of home and nation, a rhetoric that stresses safety, exclusiveness, and the desire to set up and guard borders against the vengeful and dangerous invasion from outside. Inviting and celebrating the demolition of the exclusionary wall of the house, the writings of Lawrence and Woolf search for more permeable and inclusive homes and nations.

In their desire to build a better world, however, Lawrence and Woolf do not simply succumb to a nostalgic longing for a lost Eden or to a romantic dream of an ideal future world, both of which threaten to deprive time and space of the potential for dynamic change through their mystification of the past and the future, respectively. Although Lawrence and Woolf at times turn toward traditional utopian visions that tend to locate a better world in a remote time and space dissociated from the present, their insight into space as heterogeneous, contested, alterable, and thus fundamentally resistant to closure enables them to envision subversive utopias. Epiphanic moments like Woolf's "moments of being" or Lawrence's "insurgent Now" often mark a transformative chronotope wherein one abandons the socially imposed self and embraces new visions of flexible, open, and ever-changing selfhood and social relationship, a generative and dynamic space/time that is deeply engaged with everyday life. To put it differently, the works of Lawrence and Woolf provide alternative modernist utopias that are perpetually coming into being through eruptive moments of the here and now that shatter the illusory stability of the self, space, time, and the social order.

By focusing on social space, I have attempted to illuminate a new way of addressing the complex political implications of the works of Lawrence and Woolf. There have been several studies that have examined similarities between Lawrence and Woolf. But the focus has usually been on the issue of the self and its relationship with the m/other, or of the subjective rendering of the exterior world. When it comes to politics, scholars have explicitly or implicitly assumed differences or oppositions between these writers. By reading against the grain, I hope to have demonstrated the less noted instances where the politics of Lawrence's work converges with that of Woolf's. While recognizing Lawrence's male chauvinistic drive and Woolf's (self-conscious) upper-middle-class reservations, I argue that the multiple meanings of physical, conceptual, and utopian spaces in these writers play a central role in advancing their critiques of the patriarchal, class-stratified, imperial social system. Refusing to subsume space to any homogenizing authoritative spatial code, Lawrence and Woolf generate subversive spatial codes that constantly destabilize the dominant socio-spatial order.

As I have suggested, Lawrence's and Woolf's treatment of space anticipates Lefebvre's observations concerning the concepts of social space and spatial politics. The aim of my study, however, is not simply to show the points of contact between theory and literature. Rather, a more important goal of my study has been to show how we might redress the tendency of some recent spatial theories to underestimate the political significance of literary discourses about space. One of the central findings in my study is that literary texts perform the subversive work of intervening in the production of social space through their critical interaction with dominant spatial codes.

As I conclude, I am conscious that my study has many limitations. The space of my study itself turned out to be a highly selective space: space structured by deliberate or unwitting neglect of other issues or works. For example,

I was not able to include Lawrence's travel writings, *or The Plumed Serpent,* or Woolf's *Voyage Out,* or *Orlando,* or to place their works in the context of other contemporary Western or non-western writers' treatments of space, all of which would have helped me to further explore the significance of spatial politics, such as the politics of home and elsewhere, or of colonized or eroticized landscape. Nor has my study been able to explore the issues of body, the uncanny, sexual politics, and/or imperialism, which loom over these British writers' discourses of space and utopia. I also recognize that I have not considered how the attempts of Lawrence and Woolf to break with a Victorian past they found suffocating sometimes led them to misrepresent the complexities of their Victorian precursors. But even as I note these limitations, I am encouraged by the thought that the space of my study is not closed; rather, it is open to continuing change and growth.

Notes

NOTES TO THE INTRODUCTION

1. For further discussion about Lawrence's relation with modernism, see Anne Fernihough's introduction to *Fantasia of the Unconscious* and Michel Bell's "Lawrence and Modernism" in the same book.

2. See, for example, Sandra M. Gilbert's discussion of the different approach to transvestism in male and female modernists. According to Gilbert, Lawrence, like other male writers such as James Joyce and T. S. Eliot, withdraws from a final commitment to an androgynous self and endorses the "established paradigms of dominance and submission associated with the hierarchies of gender," whereas Woolf makes the vision of an "intermediate sex" free and powerful ("Costumes of the Mind" 416).

3. Of course, there have been a few scholars who have noted affinities between these writers by illuminating more complex aspects of their work: their ambivalence towards the m/other; their complex relations with modernism; Lawrence's exquisite moments of male bonding, his self-knowledge of his own problematic ideas, and his linguistic complexities, all of which to some degree complicate or belie the writers' explicit claims or beliefs. In his book, *Beyond Egotism: The Fiction of James Joyce, Virginia Woolf, and D. H. Lawrence,* for example, Robert Kiely puts Lawrence and Woolf together in light of the shared awareness of the inadequacy of the legacy of the nineteenth-century literary conventions and the subsequent attempt to cast about for new forms of fiction to express new notions of literary character and modern experience. According to Barbara Ann Schapiro, although Lawrence stresses boundaries and separateness whereas Woolf emphasizes unifying connections, both writers are similar in their ambivalence toward the intrusive m/other that threatens the integrity of the self. In this view, both Lawrence and Woolf display a "simultaneous yearning for and terror of dissolution of self boundaries" (*Literature and the Relational Self* 83). Rosemary Sumner notes Lawrence and Woolf's common concern with the

unknown and the unconscious and their shared effort to create new forms of fiction based on a "tension between harmony and chaos" that provides "irreducible uncertainty" (13,169).

4. To quote further, Woolf writes: "I am also reading D. H. L. with the usual sense of frustration: and that he and I have too much in common—the same pressure to be ourselves: so that I don't escape when I read him: am suspended: what I want is to be made free of another world" (*The Diary of Virginia Woolf* 4: 126).

   In a posthumously published article, "Notes on D. H. Lawrence"— probably written in 1931—Woolf expresses a more favorable assessment of Lawrence. Admitting that "until April 1931" she knew him "almost solely by reputation and scarcely at all by experience" (*Collected Essays* 1: 352) she praises Lawrence's "great power and penetration." In her view, Lawrence's "remarkable strength" in *Sons and Lovers* issues from his class standing that enabled him to approach writing differently from a writer such as Proust, who was a member of "a settled and satisfied society" (355). At first glance, the remark indicates the class distance that Woolf felt toward Lawrence combined with her envy of Lawrence's ability to cross over different classes, an ability she felt her refined and decorous upbringing had deprived her of. (See Zwerdling for further discussion of Woolf's self-conscious class snobbishness and her wish to transcend her class enclave while acknowledging the class benefit—such as the capital—that guaranteed her freedom as a writer). But at the same time, given her lifelong sense of being an outsider as a woman and her attempt to turn this disadvantage into a critical and artistic force, the remark also points to Woolf's sympathy with Lawrence as a less privileged member of society and even seems to allude to her own strength and capability for a "different approach to writing" (355).

5. See Bradbury and McFarlane's discussion of modernist spatial form (19–56).

6. "The patchwork continuity" seen from the aeroplane, Beer states, "undermines the concept of nationhood which relies upon the cultural idea of the island" as well as the notion of narrative "held within the determining contours of land-scape" (*Virginia Woolf* 150).

7. See Kern.

8. For Lefebvre's definition of "social space," see Chapter Two titled "Social Space."

9. Here, Lefebvre's phrase, "being-there," certainly alludes to Heidegger's essay, "Building, Dwelling, Thinking," but without sufficiently acknowledging Heidegger's concern with the interrelation between cognitive, linguistic, and physical space.

10. For this contention, see the introductory chapter of *The Production of Space.*

11. At the same time, Lefebvre's view of semiological "reading" does not seem to fully recognize the semiological effort to redefine reading, representing, and

reality, an effort that elucidates subversive aspects of literary language. To elaborate on this further, Roland Barthes' task in *S/Z*—to which Lefebvre himself refers—is to address the notion of reading and literature from a new perspective, that is to say, to open a new possibility to read/write the text by blurring the division between reading and writing, reality and representation, reader and writer. Significantly however, Lefebvre's references to semiology consistently stick to the idea of "reading" in a conventional sense of decoding meanings of the text without recognizing that the semiological act of reading interrogates the traditional view of reference in the first place. In my view, this tendency derives from the fundamental division in Lefebvre between language and reality, wherein the latter is presumed to exist prior to the former, hence privileging the latter in the name of truth/materiality. Lefebvre's limited understanding of language is manifested in his consistent neglect of the subversive aspects of language that he might have learned from Barthes and Julia Kristeva. Instead, he draws selectively on their critique of the ideological function of language as a transparent vehicle for representation, without attending to these theorists' observations about other aspects of language or textuality. Borrowing Phillip E. Wegner's contention that Barthes's semiosis can be viewed as a part of the activity of making the world through language, I would suggest that Lefebvre's spatial politics is not necessarily incompatible with Barthes's semiotic approach to text and space. My later discussion of spatial code and the politics of literature will clarify this point further.

NOTES TO THE PART ONE INTRODUCTION

1. The terms, "public" and "private" have multiple meanings that vary according to society, culture, and history. In addition, many social theorists and critics have used these terms in different theoretical and/or political contexts. However, detailed investigation of definitional and political complexity of these words goes beyond the scope of my study. For the discussion of the issue of "public" and "private" see Jeff Wientraub and Krishan Kumar's *Public and Private in Thought and Practice: Perspectives on a Grand Dichotomy,* Dorothy O. Helly and Susan M. Reverby's *Gendered Domains: Rethinking Public and Private in Women's History,* Nancy Fraser's "Rethinking the Public Sphere," and Anna Snaith's *Virginia Woolf: Public and Private Negotiations.*

2. Thus, a critic such as Billy T. Tracy argues that Lawrence believed the domestic sphere to be the appropriate place for women to use their talents (15).

3. See Sharon Marcus (89–101) for the ideological imports of the worship of the family and domestic space in the discourse of Victorian intellectuals.

4. Lefebvre proposes the notion of "appropriated space" in order to argue for the possibility of resistance and change in social space instead of reducing

space to an autonomous determinant (165). According to him, every social space has been produced by dialectical relations between the production of appropriated space produced by the "demands" of its users and the production of dominated space produced by "commands" of the state (116). Unlike dominated space subjugated to state power, Lefebvre contends, appropriated space is independent of the latter, since it is constantly recreated and reproduced by interests and activities of actual users. In Lefebvre's view, the state constantly seeks to repress the subversive potential of appropriated space by obscuring its very existence. Lefebvre's political project of relocating social space in the realm of political practice, therefore, involves the attempt to recuperate this appropriated space.

NOTES TO CHAPTER ONE

1. The poem cited here originally appears in the Clarke college notebook, not as a single poem, but as part of a long poem or sequence of poems titled "A Life History: In Harmonies and Discords." In 1916, Lawrence took the poem from this notebook sequence and made some small changes for publication (e.g., "she-delirious" for "delirious," "male thong" for "thick lash") on its own in the collection *Amores*. (Lockwood 28–29).

2. M. J. Lockwood, for example, states that the poem illustrates an early conception of Lawrentian philosophy of a "duality of opposites" (27).

3. Critics have hardly noted the rewriting of the mythic image of home in the poem through the ironic evocation of the ash tree, a symbol of stability, the image of the ideal home. According to one of the most prevailing mythic accounts, the ash tree, "yggdrasil," is known as the great cosmic tree or the world-tree in Norse mythology. Scholars cite a description by the thirteenth-century Icelander Snorri Sturluson: "the ash is the biggest and best of all trees; its branches extend over the whole world, and spread out over the sky . . ." (*Dictionary of Northern Mythology* 186). The ash gives shelter to diverse creatures from gods to animals. It is also related to the Germanic myths of man's creation from a tree-trunk. The manifold symbols that fall together in Yggdrasil as the world-tree, the protective tree, the world-axis, and so forth have often lead to attempts to associate this myth with Christian characteristics as well (c.f., the legend of the Rood). Other scholars interpret the ash tree as a tree of terror, observing the base word *yggr* 'terror,' an etymology that fits the passage from the novel. For further explanation about the significance of the ash tree see *Encyclopedia of World Mythology and Legend*.

4. Taking this phrase as one of Lawrence's most typical symptoms of womb envy, Kate Millett contends that this kind of morbid worship of the matriarch is simply an obverse side of misogyny that is to be developed in his later works (258). Instead of assuming that the Brangwen man's perspective is Lawrence's own as Millett does, I read the passage as the writer's self-conscious mocking

of the male discourse. This is not the place to discuss in detail Lawrence's use of narrative point of view in the novel. But let me briefly mention that many critics have already problematized the Millettian identification of the narrative voice with Lawrence's own, arguing for the writer's ambivalences towards, complexities about, or critical distance from the perspective of the narrator. Or, to put it more precisely, throughout *The Rainbow,* the narrative perspective frequently shifts rather than belonging to a single persona, reflecting various characters' perspectives and thoughts, and thus obscuring the writers' own view.

5. See Sharon Marcus for a historical background of the statement, "an Englishman's home is his castle"—from the context of the original version to the shift of meanings throughout the nineteenth century (91–92). According to Marcus, when Edward Coke first uttered a version of this statement, "a man's house is his castle," in a seventeenth-century legal treatise, the castle was a metaphor for the legal right to be free from invasion of one's home. Throughout the nineteenth century, however, the phrase was commonly modified to stress its national component—"an *English*man's home is his castle"—paralleling the current discourse that began to view the English architectural form in association with national identity, combined with a gradual emphasis on male authority and power over domestic space (home and nation).

6. One thing to be added here is that although the essay speaks exclusively about a man's mastery, the idea of mastery can be appropriated by a feminist agenda as well when it is understood as an expression of self-fulfillment and independence, a kind of mastery over oneself rather than as domination over others.

7. Cynthia Lewiecki-Wilson also suggests the historical and social context of domestic space in the novel through her observations concerning the class and gender conflicts in the Morel house.

8. To understand the socio-cultural bearings of the new home to Mrs. Morel, it may be helpful to take a brief look at the opening scene in *The Rainbow.* Here the depiction of the houses and surroundings indicates the Brangwen women's confinement within the symbolic and geographical boundary of domesticity and the social yearnings that make them restlessly seek an alternative outlet. "Her house," we are told, "faced out from the farm-buildings and fields, looked out to the road and the village with church and Hall and the world beyond. She stood to see the far-off world of cities and governments and the "active scope of man," while men relish a sense of fulfillment both in the small town and in the world of cities (9). In this scene, the house and its surroundings signify at once the deprivation of social activities for women and a symbolic psychological compensation for their disadvantages. From this point of view, the location of the new house in *Sons and Lovers* intimates that the new dwelling place denies Mrs. Morel even such a tiny little symbolic and literal space, space that might allow room to cultivate or at least release

social instincts, more strictly confining her to a narrow orbit of home both psychologically and physically.

9. Lawrence's antipathy to the confinement of women in the home can also be found in his 1913 letter to Edward Garnett, where Lawrence writes, "I don't want to bury Frieda alive" (*The Letters of D .H. Lawrence* 1: 501).

10. For an excellent discussion of Lawrence's ambivalence towards his father figure, Mr. Morel, see H.M. Daleski. As Daleski notes, despite the prevailing hostile comments about the father, Lawrence does not fully suppress his sympathy for and bonding with the father, revealing the Oedipal feeling mixed with Lawrence's valorization of vitality, warmth, and exuberance of the working class father.

11. In the same letter where Lawrence expresses his feminist objection to Frieda's being buried in the home he writes as follows, revealing the complex perspective on gender and class, developed in part by his marriage to Frieda: "Wherever I go with her [Frieda] we shall have to fall into the intelligent, as it were upper classes. . . . I am common. . . . I find a servant maid more interesting than a Violet Hunt. . . . But Frieda is a lady and I hate her when she talks to the common people. . . . [S]he makes . . . class distinctions felt—even with my sister" (Letters 1: 502).

12. In a similar vein, in *The Rainbow*, Lawrence portrays how domestic space works as a site where one forms his/her selfhood while erasing the inferior other in terms of class: "Anna treated the serving woman as one of an inferior race. Tom Brangwen did not like it. . . . Then gradually she accepted Tilly as belonging to the household, never as a person" (69).

13. Reading the novel in terms of a "definitely Freudian" "Oedipal" drama, (246) Millett problematizes Lawrence's gender politics by contending that "the Oedipus complex is rather less a matter of the son's passion for the mother than his passion for attaining the level of power to which adult male status is supposed to entitle him" (247–48). In this view, the final chapter aptly epitomizes sexism: finally getting rid of a "devouring maternal vampire," Paul the conqueror launches into the brave new world awaiting him (246, 252). Although the last scene certainly reveals Paul's ambivalence toward his mother that runs through the novel—his Oedipal feelings for the mother and the desire to escape from her—Millett's reading is problematic in that it assumes a binary division between home/mother/feminine and city/masculine, a division that the novel itself dismantles. Daleski advocates what Millett condemns; in his view, the final scene registers Paul's resistance to capitulating to his mother, an act of self-liberation based on his decision to leave women and home for the liberating and masculine world of the city. Despite the difference in their assessments of the significance of the ending scene, both critics equate home, domesticity, and mother.

14. The terms "space" or "spatial" in Kiely's discussion refer to several things: at the beginning, the issue of space is evoked from a formalist perspective, as

suggested by his argument about how the novel's forward motion—temporality—is counteracted by spatial components, that is, the stability of symbolic
language and the repetition of peculiar linguistic structures. This view
echoes Joseph Frank's notion of spatial form. As the essay goes on, however,
the referents of "space" include a concrete domestic space ("bed" 99; "the
house" 101), "narrative space" (99), or the space as absence—whose equiva-
lent is silences and gaps between words (111). Kiely's concern with the multiple meaning of space could be more illuminating, I think, if he provided
some explanations about how these meanings are related to or distinct from
one another instead of using them somewhat at random.

15. For Millett, "the place of the female" in the Lawrentian scheme cannot be
    clearer than in *The Rainbow.* "This novel's real contrasts," she writes, "are
    between the older women . . . who know their place, and the newer breed
    . . . who fail to discern it" (250).

16. Note another example where Anna detects and mocks the masculine
    impulse in Will to establish a god-like power by belittling woman—a
    symptom of the fundamental insufficiency of his ego. Jeering at Will's
    wood-carving work, Eve, Anna says, "She is like a little marionette. Why
    is she so small? You've made Adam as big as God, and Eve like a doll"
    (174).

17. For Millett the chapter is further evidence of Lawrence's "womb envy" disorder
    (258) combined with his amazement at the late Victorian woman's inhibited
    sexuality and fertility. This reading, however, does not take into account Anna's
    seething frustration at the cultural demands of feminine duties.

18. Reading the battle between Anna and Will in the cathedral in light of a
    "journey from the old tribal consciousness to the mental awareness and
    individuality of the Christian era" (74), Virginia Hyde associates Anna's per-
    spective with a negative stage of Christianity that seeks individualization
    and differentiation. Here again Anna is related to a "rationalistic mind" that
    brings out the sacrifice of Will, the Christ figure (76).

19. For further explanation of abstract space see Chapter Four in *The Produc-
    tion of Space.*

20. It is interesting to note Lawrence's statement about Gothic cathedrals that
    appeared in "Study of Thomas Hardy," written probably while he was com-
    posing *Sons and Lovers.* Anticipating the Cathedral chapter in *The Rainbow,*
    Lawrence states that the architectural whole of Gothic cathedrals embodies
    a "monism" that suppresses individuality and difference. But such monism,
    Lawrence suggests, is always already challenged from within. The following
    passage confirms my argument about Anna's subversive spatial code and the
    significance of Lincoln cathedral as social space. He writes: "There was . . .
    in the Cathedrals already the denial of the Monism which the Whole
    uttered. All the little figures, the gargoyles, the imps, the human faces,
    whilst subordinated within the Great Conclusion of the Whole, still, from

their obscurity, jeered their mockery of the Absolute, and declared for multiplicity, polygeny" (*Phoenix* 454).

21. Lawrence's stress on the multiple meanings of the cathedral can also be
found in an essay "America, Listen to Your Own." Advising Americans to
find out their own history and culture instead of relying on the support of
the "perfected past" (90) of Europe, Lawrence suggests that monumental
cathedrals convey different meanings to different people. They could be
symbolic of culture and tradition for the European, but not for the American with a different history and geography. It would be "an insult to life
itself to be *too* abject, too prostrate before Milan Cathedral or a Ghirlan-
dajo," Lawrence states (90).

22. Indeed, we encounter numerous references to space in relation to Ursula's
search for independent selfhood and fulfillment. Note the recurrent phrases
such as "she *would* have a place in the house" (357); "Gradually she became
conscious that she could not go on living at home as she was doing without
place or meaning or worth" (357); "She had no place nor being there [the
school]" (376); "she could not take her place in it [the school] (387); "She
could not take her place and carry out her task. She would fight and hold
her place in this state also, in the world of work and man's convention"
(406); "Almost everything was subordinated now to this one desire to take
her place in the world. . . . She must take her place" (410). And then, note
the phrase in the last chapter to which I shall return later: "She [Ursula]
repeated. . . . 'I have no allocated place in the world of things, I do not
belong to Beldover not to Nottingham nor to England nor to this world.
. . . '"(493).

23. I will explore the significance of this third space further in terms of utopian
space in Chapter Five.

24. In Rob Shield's words, "place myths" are "discourses about place and space"
produced by "social practices." They function as a "means of framing social
performances, interactions and presuppositions about appropriate activities
in particular places" (Hetherington 24, 25).

25. Anton goes off to the Boer War, and his thought delivered in a free indirect discourse further illuminates the ideological dimension of the public
world's spatial code, the world that annihilates individuality in the name
of the whole: "He went about at his duties, giving himself up to them.
. . . What did a man matter personally? He was just a brick in the whole
great social fabric, the nation, the modern humanity. His personal movements were small, and entirely subsidiary. The whole form must be
ensured not ruptured, for any personal reason whatsoever, since no personal reason could justify such a breaking. . . . The Whole mattered—but
the unit, the person, had no importance, except as he represented the
Whole" (328).

NOTES TO CHAPTER TWO

1. Taking issue with Marcus's argument, Eve M. Lynch, for example, contends that Woolf's project to seek woman's language through the "sisterhood" between (upper) middle-class and working class women "within the house" is "problematic" in that such bonding tends to dismiss gender relations between women from different classes in the name of maternity or femininity (70).

2. The untitled story was written about 1906, and Susan M. Squier and Louise A. DeSalvo, who edited it for a special Woolf issue of *Twentieth Century Literature*, gave the title.

3. Critics have read the story as an early manifestation of Woolf's feminist concern with the confinement of women in domesticity. Louis A. DeSalvo has noted that the story deals with the tensions between the sexes and women's oppression located in the land-tenure system. Observing that this story "establishes many of recurring themes" in Woolf, Brenda R. Silver has also read it in light of women's oppression in the house (*Gender of Modernism* 651). My discussion in this section is basically in line with these readings, but I offer another reading of the story in relation to the metaphor of home and imperial ideology in Chapter Four.

4. This does not mean, of course, that no insider can be a critic. On the contrary, Woolf herself was always self-conscious about her own implication within the social system that she criticizes. Furthermore, following Jacques Derrida and others, I believe that assuming an entirely independent and transcendental critical position is illusory and itself ideological.

5. According to Woolf, the male-dominated public world has made women their accomplice in various ways by subjugating and domesticating them through marriage. For example, she argues that middle-class women have been consciously and unconsciously " in favor of war" and the British imperialism through marriage—the only profession open to them (39). That is to say, to make a good marriage they need servants and fine clothes, luxuries that bolster the capitalist and imperial social system that wage war. In this way, Woolf argues, the private houses work to endorse the militaristic society. From this perspective, her consent to be a member of the barrister's society could be a kind of symbolic marriage that may end by forging another tie to the problematic man's world.

6. For Woolf's refusal to assume an independent critical perspective, see "The Leaning Tower," a lecture given by Woolf to the Workers' Educational Association in Brighton in 1940 and published later in *Folios of New Writing* in the same year. Here Woolf indicts the poets of the thirties—whose works were overtly political and polemical—of their complicity with the very society that they condemn by pointing out their class and economic privileges. In Woolf's view, these writers' self-righteous critique of the sins of society derives from their failure to recognize their own complicity and thus, their

accusation is no better than "scapegoat beating" and "excuse finding" (*The Moment and Other Essays* 115).

NOTES TO CHAPTER THREE

1. In his influential book, *Son of Woman* (1931) John Middleton Murry argues that the weakness of Lawrence's art derives from his crippling relationship with his mother. See Dennis Jackson and Fleda Brown Jackson's "Introduction" to *Critical Essays on D. H. Lawrence* for biographical readings of Lawrence, which, despite distinct evaluations, have reduced Lawrence's works to expressions of personal experiences. See Margaret Storch for a discussion of Lawrence's antagonism towards women. Judith Ruderman in her book *D. H. Lawrence and the Devouring Mother* examines Lawrence's relentless fight with and attempt to escape from the devouring mother. Although in a different context, Paul Delany also states that "if in [*Sons and Lovers*] he had fought free of his devouring mother, in *Women in Love* he was similarly casting off the incubus of a devouring mother country" (264).
2. Leavis 39–55.
3. Influential feminist scholars who have attacked Lawrence's patriarchal assumptions and endorsement of male domination include Kate Millett, Hilary Simpson, and Cornelia Nixon, to name but a few. Some recent feminist scholars, however, have attempted to reevaluate Lawrence's gender politics in relation to the issue of home. Refusing to reduce Lawrence's fictions to an expression of the writer's personal animosity toward women, Cynthia Lewiecki-Wilson, for example, argues that Lawrence's ambivalences and contradictions concerning home and family may be profitably investigated from an alternative feminist point of view. See also Carole Siegel and Anne Fernihough for the attempts to use Lawrence's works as positive resources for feminist theories.
4. Considering its blatant social criticism, it is no wonder that the Adelphi rejected the essay for the reason of its possible offence to the reader. See Warren Roberts and Harry T. Moore's "Introduction" to Phoenix II (xii).
5. In the introduction to his book *The Silent War* Füredi notes that "the idea of white superiority" that has been shaped by "the gains aggressively acquired by the white caste at the expense of the Negro" since the Victorian era, have become a source of anxiety and fear of racial revenge along with the decline of the West from the end of the First World War onward (1).
6. That Countess Elizabeth rose from humble origins to become one of the most powerful people in the Elizabethan era invites us to look at the great house in relation to the house of Lawrence's sister—who also rose to higher social standing. Lawrence reveals his knowledge of the historical background that surrounds Hardwick Hall, when he writes: "Built in the days of

good Queen Bess, by that other Bess, termagant and tartar, Countess of Shrewsbury" (262).

7. See Joseph M. Flora for a discussion of Lawrence's critical reaction to Henley. Flora observes that Lawrence found Henley's work of more than passing interest and that Lawrence's "blood consciousness" is a deliberate rebellion against Henley's "mind consciousness" that summarizes, in Lawrence's view, Henley's famous poem, "Invictus."

8. The celebration of British imperial power permeates the entire poem, as evidenced by the recurrent images of "bugles" blown "round the world," "the worlds" that England has to "watch and ward," and the "Mother of Ships whose might" is "the fierce old Sea's delight."

9. Moore, for example, sees Egbert as a "parasitic dweller at Godfrey Marshall's family colony at Crockham" (283). Leavis states that the theme of the tale is "the impossibility of making a life with no more that this" and regards Egbert as being "irresponsible, ineffective, . . . and parasitic" (335), a character from whom Lawrence distances himself. In Ruderman's view, Winnie's father embodies the patriarchal power that Lawrence has come to espouse in contrast with the ineffective and irresponsible Egbert (86–87).

10. In my view, Lawrence's understanding of the predominance of Marshallean power prevented him from giving us a naïve romantic tale of a triumphant rebel. However, this does not mean that Lawrence makes Egbert entirely defeated. Critics have usually neglected the significance of Egbert's daughter, Joyce, who inherits her father's anti-authoritarian legacy and, together with her father, becomes a member of "some forbidden secret society" (325). Her character reappears as Yvette or Ursula in search of freedom and independence, transgressing the threshold of the house.

11. Frieda also seems to be aware of the allusion to Queen Victoria, as evidenced by the fact that one of the titles that she suggested to Lawrence for the novella was "Granny on the Throne." See *Letters from D. H. Lawrence to Martin Secker* (70).

12. Several critics have read the novella in terms of symbolic boundaries, borders, and transgressions. John Turner, for example, discusses Lawrence's exploration of the "bourgeois ambivalence toward the counterculture" (144) revolving around the boundary between hygiene and pollution (147). John B. Humma also elaborates on the theme of social pathology through the trope of "inside and outside" (78). In a similar vein, Peter Balbert sees Yvette's meeting with the gipsy as a meeting with an "as-yet-undefined dimension of time and space" (404). I generally agree with these observations. However, these critics have tended to exaggerate the mystical power of the gipsy. I think that the easy equation between the gipsy, the external world, and "the dark gods of blood consciousness"(Balbert 403) in these readings is problematic in that they are in danger of reinscribing boundaries.

13. The suggestion that part of the powerful image of the gipsy is not inherent in the man but is created through Yvette's desire and imagination runs through the novella. For example, we are told that Yvette's fascination with the man originates "not from the outside, but from the inside, from her secret female self" (45).

14. See Michel Foucault's *Madness and Civilization.*

15. In response to Cooley's claim that he fights the ant threatening the home with fire, a claim ironically delivered along with his own threat, "don't oppose me" (121–22), Harriett expresses her sense of fear in an imaginary letter to Cooley, saying that "I really don't feel safe." To quote the passage further: "Dear Kaiser Kangaroo," began Harriett, "I must thank you very much for the dinner and the violets, which are still quite fresh and blue in '*Coo-ee.*' I think you were very horrid to me, but also very nice. . . . I want to tell you that I *do* sympathise. . . . I have a holy terror of ants since I heard you. . . . I shall make myself into a Fire Brigade, because I am sure you will be kindling firers all over everywhere. . . . Being only a poor domestic female, I really don't feel safe with fires anywhere. . . ." (124).

16. See Dennis and Fleda Brown Jackson for a literary critical trend since the 1930s that has associated Lawrence's advocacy of dark gods with his fascistic disposition. In her study of British imperial fictions since the 1880s, Susan Howe concludes that characters in these works usually suffer from claustrophobia at home, become greedy for land, and then explore the vast world outside. Although Howe does not mention Lawrence directly here, critics' attacks on Lawrence's imperial ideologies have often problematized Lawrence's fascination with the dark outside, the exotic, and primitive lands. See, for example, Wayne Templeton's "Indians and an Englishman." Peter Nicholls also suggests the ideological limits of Lawrence's primitivism (118). See also Debra A. Castillo for a critique of Lawrence's primitivism, racism, and imperialism.

17. See Ruderman and Simpson. For Simpson, Lawrence's advocacy of dark gods not only reveals his masculinist impulse but also marks his displacement of social and political concerns onto religious one.

18. About Kangaroo's exclusion of women from his "home," see his claim that he is "a son of man" (121) and that his "family knows no female" (119).

19. See the following phrase: "Poor Richard Lovatt wearied himself to death struggling with the problem of himself, and calling it Australia" (28).

NOTES TO CHAPTER FOUR

1. See Jane Marcus's "Britannia rules *The Waves*," Susan Dick, Masami Usui, Judith Lee, and Robin Hackett.

2. Genevieve Abravanel also reads the novel in reference to the imperial fantasies of the racial Other. As my discussion shall show, however, my reading

challenges Abravanel's suggestion about Woolf's fundamental complicity with the imperial vision of British imperial subjectivity.

3. See Marcus for a discussion about colonial fear and guilt in the novel.

4. In this respect my reading diverges from that of Kathy J. Phillips, who contends that all the characters "allow the conformity, force, intolerance, and possessiveness which make colonization possible and oppressive" (182). Phillips identifies many persuasive instances that show the characters' complicity with imperialism, but I think she tends to neglect other examples that render these characters complicated and dynamic.

5. See Sharon Marcus for a fuller discussion about the British cultural ideal of home, architectural discourses and practices, and the cultural psyche in London during 1840 to 1880.

6. See Marcus 83–88.

7. See Füredi for a discussion about the increasing unease among western European elites about the growing masses of poor, much of which shaped their theories of social and racial hierarchy as well as the science of demography, theories that were especially prevalent during the 1930s in metropolises like London.

8. See Alex Zwerdling for a discussion about the intellectual background of the attack on the Victorian family system that influenced Woolf.

9. For example, see James Naremore and Clare Hanson.

10. See Mitchell A. Leaska for another interpretation of Rose's complex fantasy and guilty feeling surrounding the episode in terms of her strong attachment to her father.

11. Although Linden Peach does not read the episode in direct reference to the ideology of home, some of her observations concerning "bourgeois fear of the lower classes" and imperialism overlap with mine. Noting that the passage illustrates Woolf's interest in "the difficulty of separating the imaginary 'texts' of the street from their 'reality,'" Peach contends that the horrid man leering at Rose is "an index of the way in which the lower class have become a social text" (190). For Peach, the reappearance of the man in Rose's nightmare as a robber "has more to do with what the middle-class project onto the lower orders than with the latter in reality" (191). Applying Judith Walkowitz's observations on the urban explorers' "penetrat[ion]" into urban slum areas, Peach goes on to approach Rose's fantasy journey to Lamley's in light of "the imperialist mode of comprehending space" (191).

12. In a similar vein, Jane Marcus in her essay "*The Years* as Greek Drama, Domestic Novel, and *Götterdämmerung*" suggests that Woolf reveals "fear" of "violent nature" that she finds in her friend Ethel Smyth—feminist, suffragette, composer, and writer—through the figure of Rose (297).

13. It seems that it is Eleanor, not Crosby, who realizes the poor living condition that Crosby has had so far: "'I should think you'd be glad to be out of that basement any how, Crosby,' said Eleanor, turning into the hall again.

She had never realized how dark, how low it was, until, looking at it with 'Our Mr. Grice,' she had felt ashamed. 'It was my home for forty years, Miss,' said Crosby. The tears were running" (216). See Woolf's *A Sketch of the Past* for her critical observations about the unequal spatial arrangement and the inferior living conditions of the servants in her childhood family house.

14. For further discussion about the material, psychological, social, and intellectual significance that the new home in Bloomsbury carried for Virginia, see Squier's *Virginia Woolf and London* and Snaith's "'At Gordon Sq. and Nowhere Else': the Spatial and Social Politics of Bloomsbury."

15. Note, for example, the scene in the same section of the novel in which Sara speaks to Maggie about the appearance of Kitty Lasswade at the meeting: " 'Who came in?' she [Maggie] asked at length. 'Somebody very beautiful; clothed in starlight; with green in her hair,' said Sara. 'Whereupon'—here she changed her voice and imitated the tones in which a middle-class man might be supposed to welcome a lady of fashion" (187–88). Among the critics who pay attention to Sara's mocking of others' voices is Joanna Lipking. There are other instances of Sara's self-conscious performance of conventional language or behavior. See also the passage that describes her deliberate assuming of a class role in a specific place: "in deference to him [Martin] she assumed the manner of a lady lunching with a gentleman in a city restaurant" (229). This example suggests that Sara is sensitive to the constructedness of selfhood rather than naively following cultural decorum.

16. David Bradshaw, for example, reads this scene as Woolf's acknowledgment that even the outsider—Sara—is as susceptible to bigotry as those who have excluded her.

17. In a similar vein, Jane Marcus reads the scene in terms of an initiation of North by Sara. According to Marcus, "through their ritual object 'the hair of the Jew in the bath,'" Sara converts North's disgust "into a recognition of common cause with the outcasts and scapegoats of the world" ("*The Years* as Greek Drama, Domestic Novel, and *Götterdämmerung*" 284). Margaret Comstock also suggests that Sara has overcome her initial disgust and shows relative "absence of resentment or fear toward outsiders" in comparison with North (275).

18. Note Woolf's use of the language for the children's song: "Etho passo tanno hai, Fai donk to tu do. . . ." (429–30). Like the undecipherable message of the dark god in Lawrence, I would read this song as a language of the Other. The significance of the unintelligible language here is multiple. At one level, it points to the failure of communication caused by the age-old barrier between the self and the other. In this respect, like Lawrence, Woolf does not provide naïve optimism for a better society. At another, it reflects the refusal to impose arbitrary meaning on the language of the Other, since

such an imposition or translation, for Woolf and Lawrence, can be another form of domination.

19. Critics have discussed the meaning of the children's song. David Eberly reads the "shrill," "discordant" and "meaningless" song as an expression of Woolf's view of the nature of communication (150). Both Marcus and Comstock read the scene as a sign of the novel's optimistic vision of the future.

NOTES TO THE PART THREE INTRODUCTION

1. For more detailed studies of the concept, definition, and function of utopia see Frank E. and Fritzie P. Manuel, Ruth Levitas, Ernst Bloch, and Angelika Bammer.

2. According to George Beauchamp, utopia is characterized by its desire for uniformity, harmony, conformity, and stasis, and thus profoundly antithetical to a liberalism that celebrates pluralism, diversity, individualism, and the idea of progress that emerged in the eighteenth to nineteenth century along with the birth of liberalism.

3. For these arguments, see Thomas Pavel.

4. Seeking to reintegrate Marxism and utopia, Bloch stresses the pedagogic function of utopia which he calls "the education of desire." Instead of confining utopia to an ideal society or literary genre, Bloch broadens its definitional and functional range to daydreams, myths, fairy-tales, traveler's tales, and so forth. Developing Bloch's hermeneutic model of utopia—utopia as an anticipatory illumination of a "not-yet" ever existed horizon of human existence—along with Louis Marin's influential concept of utopia, Jameson attempts to suggest how "the very failure of the utopian text, its inability to offer any systematic description of an emerging society" "succeeds" in that it "enables us to conceptualize for the first time the place that such a description must one day fill" (Wegner 65). For Jameson's notion of utopia see his essay, "Of Islands and Trenches." See also Phillip E. Wegner's "Horizons, Figure, and Machines" for a positive evaluation of Jameson's view of utopia. For the Marxist/socialist view of utopianism, see Deana Knight and Levitas, among others.

5. Levitas is similar to Bloch in her attempt to broaden the concept of utopia. However, she distances herself from Bloch by labeling the latter's utopia as "unqualified optimism" (102).

6. Marin's theory issues from his poststructuralist critique of belief in mimetic representation combined with his Marxist concerns. His stress on the "construction" of utopia helps us redress a number of scholars' indictment of the totalitarian desire for homogeneity, the fear of change and diversity, in short, the fundamentally reactionary impulse in utopian writing. Disrupting the age-old divisions between reality and representation, referent and language,

history and text, and absence and presence, Marin views utopia less as an ideal model/referent that is preexisting than as a "textual product." This view highlights generative or constitutive aspects of *Utopia*/utopia as "discursive events" (41) instead of reducing the text either to a single content (a conservative desire) or a form (which would end with a textual displacement/erasure of contradictions and conflicts in the "real" world). Marin's observations concerning the genesis of this literary genre suggests also that his view of utopia as discursive and textual space does not necessarily exclude physical or cultural space. For Marin, the birth of the genre itself is tied up with a specific historical context; from the sixteenth to eighteenth century a historical break between the feudal and capitalist economies occurred (*Utopics* 10). In this view, Marin suggests, the utopian space that such a genre produces, reflects contradictions of this historical transition of that period. In other words, such contradictory space is itself utopian space. But the connection between the discursive and the actual space remains rather obscure in Marin, and I will show how Lefebvre's theory helps us to bridge these.

7. For Harvey, both the "utopianism of temporal process" and "utopianism of spatial form" are wrong. According to Harvey, the former—as evidenced by such thinkers as Hegel and Marx—expresses the social processes in purely temporal terms. Such utopias are problematic since their endlessly open project never reaches spatial closure. "Utopianism of spatial form"—exemplified by Thomas More's Utopia or Frank Lloyd Wright's Broadacre City— is equally problematic as it aims to control time through space, i.e., exclude the temporality of the social process and the dialectics of social change through a fixed spatial form. By spatiotemporal utopia Harvey proposes to build an ideal society without totalitarianism and authoritarianism, while avoiding an endless fluidity at the same time. His utopia is "rooted in our present possibilities at the same time as it points towards different trajectories for human uneven geographical developments" (196). As shall be clear, my view of utopia in this chapter also takes into account spatiotemporal aspects. However, my arguments diverge from Harvey's in that I view both time and space as being dynamic and fluid, whereas Harvey relates space to closure and time to fluidity.

8. See Lefebvre's "Space: Social Product and Use Value." Here, the realized utopia of the urban society involves the recapturing of the city by the oppressed and the primacy of use over exchange.

9. Underscoring the discursive and linguistic aspects of Foucault's notion of heterotopia, scholars such as A.J. Greimas, Gianni Vattimo, and Brian McHale advance it as a semiotic concept associated with postmodernism. Regarding a "transition from utopia to heterotopia," as "the most radical transformation in the relation between art and everyday life to have occurred since the sixties," Vattimo contends that it is heterotopia, "with its underlying principle of plurality," rather than "the unilinear, rigid organization of a utopia," that dominates

postmodern aesthetics today. For McHale, the heterotopia is not "what the text describes but what it is . . . a chronotope of coexistence" (Chernetsky 255). For more details, see Chernetsky.

10. Challenging the view of utopia as an "image or a representation" or "a definite ideology" (Marin, "Frontiers of Utopia" 412), Marin stresses the unsolvable tension and paradox in utopia. For Marin, utopia is characterized by the on-going tension between "totality and infinity, limit and transcendence, closure and liberty" (406). It is a paradoxical attempt to "define the infinite by a harmonious and rigorous totalization" (407).

11. Lefebvre advances a theory of moments in *La somme et le reste,* a work written before the well-known book, *The Production of Space.* Lefebvre's theory of moments derives from many sources: his fascination with the Dadaists' penchant for surprise, shock, and their attack on traditions; his Marxism; his interest in Romanticism (especially in the aesthetics of sublime); his joint study with Situationists about the Paris Commune. After the breach between Lefebvre and the Situationists the latter accused Lefebvre of plagiarizing their ideas. They also observed that whereas their idea of 'situation' was spatio-temporal and genuinely revolutionary Lefebvre's "moment" was purely temporal and passive. In my view, Lefebvre's idea of moments is concerned neither with an entirely temporal dimension nor with purely passive experience. Rather, it indicates the centrality of temporality to Lefebvre's spatial theory. David Harvey is one of the few scholars who mention Lefebvre's theory of moments but his observation in his afterword to *The Production of Space* is a bit dismissive. For a more detailed discussion of Lefebvre's theory of moments in relation to the utopian space see Shields.

12. This rather abrupt introduction of Bakhtin needs more explanation. I bring Bakhtin into my conceptual background of utopia because his view of space and time, especially his notion of chronotope (space-time), elucidates some significant aspects of the relationship between time, space, utopia, and social being, aspects that have interesting affinities with Lefebvre's theory. Despite the numerous differences between Lefebvre and Bakhtin, their intellectual and political backgrounds—most notably their association with Marxism and their knowledge of Emmanuel Kant, Einstein, and Henri Bergson—drove them to turn their back on the traditional view of time and space as "transcendental" (Bakhtin 85) or "mental" (Lefebvre 3) and instead, to view them as "immediate reality" (85). In addition, Bakhtin's concept of chronotope is relevant to Lefebvre's emphasis on the time-space conjunction and his concern with spatial politics. In Bakhtin's words, chronotope—a term he borrows from a Soviet physiologist—is "the intrinsic connectedness of temporal and spatial relationships that are artistically expressed in literature"(84). Reading from the Greek romance to the European novel, Bakhtin shows that distinct spatio-temporal features, namely chronotopes, reveal a wide variety of worldviews as well as "image[s] of

man" (85) as either a passive spectator or an active constructor of history. Functioning at times as a primary means for "materializing time in space" the chronotope emerges as a center for "concretizing representation, as a force giving body to the entire world" (250). One of the notable achievements of the Rabelaisian chronotope, Bakhtin contends, lies in its establishment of a new relationship of time to earthly space by presenting a "generative" time that is a terrain for "creative acts." This generative time is "profoundly spatial," "concrete," and "realistic" (208). My occasional use of the terms, a "utopian chronotope" and "generative time" in discussing Woolf and Lawrence should be understood in this complex context. For Bakhtin's notion of chronotope see his essay "Forms of Time and of the Chronotope in the Novel" collected in *The Dialogic Imagination*. See also Clark and Holquist for further explanation of it.

NOTES TO CHAPTER FIVE

1. Addressing the notion of utopia in the conventional sense of a fantasy of an ideal society, George J. Zytaruk views Lawrence's idea of Rananim as representative of his utopianism and contends that Lawrence's utopia was doomed to failure from the inception due to the political and conceptual naivety. Billy T. Tracy Jr. also argues that Lawrence's search for utopia in the real world inevitably failed, "for the destination of his search was a state of mind, not a physical habitat" (2). Taking Lawrence's writing about the Etruscan places as an example, Tracy defines utopia in Lawrence as a retreat to an imaginary invention of the ideal past (2). Reading Lawrence's novels in light of his quest for paradise, Reloy Garcia divides his works into four stages. In Garcia's view, Lawrence's search for paradise shifts its locations: from the initial location, Middle lands, the larger world of man through the Continent to the human psyche, namely from the external to the internal world. For Eugene Goodheart, despite the revolutionary implications of Lawrence's utopianism, the writer at times loses his grip on reality in his attempt to achieve transcendence by annihilating the world and individuality and thus becomes a "victim of the malaise of the modern novel" (34).
2. For more detail about the failure of Lawrence's much-anticipated visit to Cambridge in March 1915 to discuss his idea of Rananim with Russell and his friends, see Moore 274–83.
3. Here my argument diverges from Zytaruk's contention that Lawrence's abandonment of Rananim marks his final acceptance of the failure of his vision of utopia founded on political naivety and impractical economic views. In Zytaruk's view, Lawrence's dismissal of Rananim idea indicates the end of his avowed mission to "see the social revolution set going" (293).
4. For these readings see F. R. Leavis, Kingsley Widmer, and Julian Moynahan.

5. Raymond Williams briefly notes the affinity between Morris' *News from Nowhere* and Lawrence's "A Dream of Life" but he does not develop any detailed discussion. Neither does he consider differences between these works. See Chapter 22 in Williams' *The Country and the City*.

6. Women's roles and status in Morris' and Lawrence's visions of the new world might be an interesting issue to explore. For the purpose of my study, however, let me briefly note some anti-feminist aspects in these male-centered utopias. In both of the future worlds located in the past, in fact—the medieval era in Morris and sometime "ancient" in Lawrence—the modern awareness of women's rights and emancipation is somewhat ridiculed or entirely denied as undesirable. Richard Hammond, a historian who guides the narrator through the utopia in Morris' work, reveals that the central freedom restored in the ideal world in fact belongs to men. One of the characteristics of the utopia is women's abandonment of maternal anxiety about their children's future, which had hampered masculinity and overall individuality. In this ideal world, he states that such kind of motherhood no longer exists. "[W]e live amidst beauty without any fear of becoming effeminate" (74—75), he says. Speaking mockingly about the "superior women['s]" search for "emancipation" during the nineteenth century" (62), Hammond advances a retrogressive view of women as an object of desire bound to domestic duties: women as "a child bearer and rearer of children, desired as a women, loved as a companion" (64). Considering the narrator's lingering doubts about Hammond's stance that is "tied to the past" and "disrespectful" to women (63), it is difficult to estimate to what extent the text endorses the representative man of utopia, Hammond's perspective on women's rights and roles. But this issue goes beyond the scope of this chapter. In Lawrence's case, the negative rendering of women's greed and will-to-dominate and the consequent realization of nightmarish world—in contrast with the utopia in the second section—seems to confirm Lawrence's patriarchal ideology. However, a careful reading suggests another interpretation. We come to know that the female domination is a result of their reaction to their "grandfathers'" and "husbands' domination" rather than women's inherent penchant for power (818). That is to say, we might argue that what Lawrence really problematizes is the chronic repetition of domination and subordination that prevails the modern society, rather than women's emancipation *per se*.

7. Although Howard J. Booth—who exceptionally pays detailed attention to "A Dream of Life"—rightly mentions Lawrence's distance from the contemporary scientific utopia or anti-utopia, he contends that the utopia delineated in the second section "is not critiqued" by the author. He attributes Lawrence's "ambivalence" to the utopia to his mixed feelings about his hometown—his nostalgic longing to be a part of it and a sense of alienated from it. While I agree with these observations to some extent, I believe that

Lawrence's ambivalence toward the utopian society he depicts certainly
involves his critical reaction to conventional utopias.

8. The passage is an interesting example of what Frank E. Manuel and
   Fritzie P. Manuel observes concerning "creating a utopian world."
   According to them, it is "psychologically a regressive phenomenon for an
   individual," a phenomenon that Manuel rephrases as "an attempt to
   return to the womb" (Manuel 27; Levitas 159). Levitas brings up the
   Manuels to criticize their reductive approach to utopian writing. I find
   the passage interesting because Lawrence here seems to deliberately foreground psychological tendency implicated in certain conventional
   utopias.

9. For this association of Lawrence's view of time with modernist efforts to
   subvert linearity, see Anne Fernihough.

10. This is not the place to examine the notion of the "fourth dimension" at
    length, but a brief examination of Lawrence's use of the term is worthwhile
    for the purpose of my study. The idea of the fourth dimension frequently
    appeared in the aesthetic discourse of modernism—especially in the con-
    temporary Cubist, Post-impressionist, and Futurist dialogues with the cur-
    rent scientific discourse. Lawrence derived this term with significant
    modifications from the current discourse as well as from his reading of Peter
    D. Ouspensky's *Tertium Organum: A Key to the Enigmas of the World,* a
    book-length treatment of fourth dimension metaphysics. For a detailed
    study of the Cubist and Futurist adaptations of the notion of the fourth
    dimension and the attendant politicization of time and space—their attach-
    ment to nationalism, masculinity, patriotism, anti-rationalism, and the
    complicity with fascism and so forth—see Mark Antliff. Antliff explores the
    Futurists'—such as Umberto Boccioni's—incorporation of aesthetic theories
    of time and space and their attempt to transform the public consciousness
    and inaugurate a political revolt against Italy's democratic institutions, with
    a specific concern with the notion of the fourth dimension. Despite occa-
    sional similarities between Lawrence and these trends, there are notable dif-
    ferences. As my discussion shall show, in addition to Lawrence's explicit
    ambivalence toward Boccioni—see "Study of Thomas Hardy," especially
    pp. 463–64 in *Phoenix*—Lawrence's resistance to evolutionary temporality,
    for example, prevents his version of the fourth space and its space-time
    dimension from being subsumed to the logic of teleology and unification
    that prevails in the politicized concept of the fourth dimension. Lawrence's
    use of the fourth dimension has a more significant affinity with Ouspensky
    in its spatio-temporal terms, especially in his concern with the present
    where the diverse temporalities and spaces are concrete and relational. Bruce
    Clarke's "Aether and Phonograph: D.H. Lawrence's Fourth Dimension" is
    another source to refer to. Clarke makes several interesting points about
    Lawrence's adoption of the contemporary aesthetic and scientific discourses.

But his association of Lawrence's fourth dimension with "atemporal" spatiality and a "transcendental spatial movement" (par. 14) is problematic in that it tends to render Lawrence's use of term rather abstract and mystical, as evidenced by his association of Birkin's fascination with the fourth dimensional utopian "nowhere" in *Women in Love* with his "sexual mysticism" or his sense of "obscure destination" (par. 15). I will return to this issue later.

11. For example, Morris writes about "a little town" "dominated by the long walls and sharp gables of a great red-brick pile of building" (124). For further examples, see especially Chapter 2, 3, and 22.

12. See, for instance, Kinsley Widmer and Anne Fernihough. Reading the novel in light of Lawrence's "social nihilism" (22), Widmer observes that the only alternative in the novel seems to be "heightened individual consciousness and permanent flight" (23). In this view, Birkin's utopianism—his yearning for "asocial marriage" and "isolated flight" (28)—is merely the other side of Lawrence's nihilism. Anne Fernihough, while implicitly dissociating Lawrence from the nihilist camp by focusing on his persistent search for a new world and language, also states that the new world prophesized at the end of *The Rainbow* fails to materialize in this novel. Instead of reading the novel as a pure denial of hope, Harry T. Moore relates the governing spirit of the novel to the Coleridgean attempt to "achieve wholeness" through incorporation of "decay with creation" (292). For Rosemary Sumner, despite Lawrence's despair of the human race and the attendant glimpse of its possible extinction, the novel does imagine a more desirable world rather than sinking into nihilism. Reading the novel basically in light of Gudrun's rhetoric of necessity conflicting with Birkin's rhetoric of hope, Maria DiBattista states that the novel "opens itself up to the future only by insisting on a kind of blank space in time, empty yet still capable of being filled with new utterance" (89). According to Michael Bell, the saving ontology of *The Rainbow* is consistently glimpsed in *Women in Love,* but remains only "at an exotic distance" (127), for such experience is no longer conceivable in the world of increasing alienated individuation and the attendant failure of language, representation, and communication.

13. See Maria DiBattista's distinction between Gudrun's "rhetoric of finality" and Birkin's "rhetoric of futurity" (*First Love* 80).

NOTES TO CHAPTER SIX

1. As critics such as Jane Marcus have rightly noted, Woolf's works adopt much of language and spirit of the contemporary socialist concerns from her feminist point of view.

2. In the letter Virginia Stephen asks the addressee whether she could borrow the poem that she found "magnificent" on the ground of her reading of its

review. There is no evidence whether she eventually read the poem or not. However, her other diary entries, letters, and essays confirm that she showed consistent interest in and read many of Morris' works and life throughout her life.

3. In her much revised version of this essay, "Introductory Letter," that appeared in Life As We Have Known It by Co-Operative Working Women (1931), Woolf changes her original contention that the next great novelist or poet would not come from the working class into a more considered evaluation of the working class women's writings. Despite the difference in tone, the main argument in both essays conveys Woolf's self-consciousness about her own limited understanding about the working class and her subsequent refusal to idolize working class people or their political causes, or to advance a "fictitious" sympathy with them ("The Memories" 140).

4. As I have mentioned in Chapter Two, an essay such as "The Leaning Tower" (1940) suggests that Woolf's refusal to propagate a hypocritical sense of connection with the working class derives from her awareness of her own complicity with oppressive social systems. But in "The Memories," Woolf does not directly enough bring up the issue of her own complicity. Rather, the focus here seems to fall on her inability to understand their life and their causes.

5. Note the recurrent sense of an impending disaster in Clarissa's "feeling" that "something awful was about to happen" (3) and her double figure, Septimus' fear of "something tremendous about to happen" (104).

6. Note the shopping scene at the Army and Navy Stores that symbolically dramatizes Kilman's loss of body ("a soul cut out of immaterial substance" 203) and agency ("she lost her way" 201), in the midst of "all the commodities of the world" (201). In contrast, Clarissa's indulgence in the city's spectacles and commodities reveals at once her class privilege and her positive ability to evade the manipulation of the market place.

7. Woolf writes in her diary that when she went to see Dr. Harrington Sainsbury in early 1922, he said to her "Equanimity-practice equanimity Mrs. Woolf" (Diary 2: 189). In his autobiography, Leonard Woolf recalls their "fairly long odyssey through Harley Street and Wimpole Street which gave us a curious view of medical science and the tiptop Harley Street specialists." (An Autobiography 2: 222).

8. See Mark Hussey's Virginia Woolf A to Z, 171.

9. See Masami Usui for a discussion about the historical background of St. Margaret's. Usui contrasts Westminster Abbey with St. Margaret's by suggesting that they represent the masculine and the feminine tendencies in society respectively. According to Usui, while Westminster Abbey has always been a center of politics, St. Margaret's-which stands literally in the shadow of the abbey-has been ignored and marginalized. Accordingly, Usui contends, St. Margaret's in *Mrs. Dalloway* represents "a dimension of women's

history that has been ignored and forgotten within male-dominated history" (154).

10. As her diary entry shows, Woolf intended to criticize "the social system" in *Mrs. Dalloway* (*Diary 2*: 248).

11. In this regard, my reading differs from Alex Zwerdling's. Zwerdling contends that these characters' temporary concern with utopian socialists is merely a part of a youthful stage and that Woolf's interest lies in the process through which these independent and responsive women are "gradually transformed into a conventional member" of their class (136). Of course, it is not difficult to recognize Clarissa's and Sally's defects and limits. Yet I believe that Clarissa's departure from socialist utopianism provides not only an indicator of her limits, but a clue to Woolf's alternative utopian vision.

12. For Deleuze and Guattari's discussion of Woolf in light of schizo dreaming see especially Chapter 2 and 10 of *A Thousand Plateaus*.

13. For a discussion of the ideological limits of the subjectivity of the essay, see Susan M. Squier. In Squier's view, the oscillation between an insider and an outsider position finally gives way to a "male-identified perspective" (*Virginia Woolf and London* 51). As my discussion shows, Woolf's politics derives not so much from the position of a self-righteously detached outsider as from a more sophisticated awareness of her complicity and critical distance in relation to power.

14. That is to say, Woolf's sudden questioning about why she hurt her brother is related to the blurring of the division between the self and the other that serves as once of the bases for her critique of dominance and violence. The vision of the flower which is part of the earth conveys more explicitly the idea of interrelatedness between beings and things. The sudden association of the apple tree with the man's suicide is another variation of the sense of interconnection. Although Woolf writes here as if only the second type of moment served as material for her writing, I think that there are examples where the other two instances reappear. For example, the strong pacifist conviction that runs through Woolf's writings is inseparable from her deep sense of connection with others, connections founded on a desertion of the socially established ego. Another example that shows Woolf's (perhaps unwitting) appropriation of the third moment is found in *Mrs. Dalloway* through the motif of trees with which each of Clarissa, Septimus, and Peter imagines herself /himself as being identified in epiphanic moments, and also, through Clarissa's sudden sense of identification with Septimus when she retreats into her room after she heard about his suicide. The significance of these moments in relation to the issue of utopia will be discussed further below.

15. Quoting a passage from Woolf's *Flush*—"The thin dog is running in the road, this dog is the road"—Deleuze and Guattari state, "[t]hat is how we need to feel. Spatiotemporal revelations, determinations, are not predicates

of the thing but dimensions of multiplicities" (A Thousand Plateaus 263). Regarding "the principal characteristics of a rhizome," Deleuze and Guattari explain as follows: "the rhizome connects any point to any other point. . . . The rhizome is reducible neither to the One nor the multiple. . . . It is composed . . . of . . . directions of motion. It has neither beginning nor end, but always a middle (milieu) from which it grows and which it overspills . . . (21).

16. The meaning of moments of being in Woolf's writing is multiple and complex. Some critics such as Patricia Ondek Laurence stress the idea of stasis and timelessness in Woolf's moments of being. Others underscore their kinetic aspects. Harvena Richter, for example, approaches the moments in light of change, disintegration, fragmentation, or even violence. Such a moment, Richter observes, points to a "disembodied mood" in its sense of loss of personality or self (41). Jeanne Schulkind states that such an idea of a privileged moment is "a commonplace of religious experience and in particular of mystical traditions of thought, as well as a recurrent feature of idealist philosophies from Plato onwards" ("Introduction" 17).

17. In this respect, Woolf shows affinity with an influential utopian thinker, Ernst Bloch. For Bloch, "any notion of its full self-presence is ideological" (Shields 23).

18. The essay ends with a return to home from this cosmic journey: "we are boxed and housed" (297). The ending, however, does not register the final subjugation of the radical experience of the present moment to the chain of daily life. The rhythmic alternations between different temporalities that run through the essay leave us with a strong sense of perpetual movements, an expectation of the eruption of the radical now into the last scene.

19. Some critics have noted the relation between these works, but there has been hardly any detailed exploration of it. Alice von Buren Kelley observes that the pageant in *Between the Acts* embodies the metaphor that Woolf uses in the passage that I have cited in "The Moment" (241). As my discussion shall show, I think that it is only some of the characters of the novel who embody the image of the passive spectator. The entire event of the pageant, however, problematizes such passivity and makes the event more active and dynamic through the second kind of moment that "The Moment: Summer's Night" advocates.

20. For these readings, see Melba Cuddy-Keane and Michel Pridmore-Brown, for example.

21. Far from being neatly divided into the play and the intervals, on the one hand, and into spectators and actors, on the other, the novel blurs these boundaries. The pageants are frequently interrupted by actual life, as we shall see later. The ending scene of the novel most explicitly muddles the boundary between reality and drama, as it depicts the beginning of the conversation between Isa and her husband, Giles: "Then the curtain rose. They spoke" (219).

22. For readings of the novel in terms of a critique of fascism at home and abroad, see Pridmore-Brown, Elizabeth Abel, Judith Johnston, and Merry Pawlowski.

23. Note the connotation of evasion that his last name "Dodge" carries, a connotation which somewhat matches Isa's escapist impulse and the lack of will to face squarely or change life. Reminiscent of Rhoda and Louis in *The Waves*, Isa and Will feel that they are "conspirators" (114).

24. Remember that Clarissa's utopian moments that bring a radical recognition of connection with others often include her fantasy of her death. Note, for example, the episode when her revealing moment leads to her musings on her future survival as a part of surrounding things such as trees and houses, a thought that assumes her previous death (12).

Bibliography

Abel, Elizabeth. *Virginia Woolf and the Fictions of Psychoanalysis.* Chicago: U of Chicago P, 1989.

Andrews Malcolm. *Dickens on England and the English.* New York: Harper &Row Publishers, Inc., 1979.

Antliff, Mark. "The Fourth Dimension and Futurism: A Politicized Space." *The Art Bulletin* 82 (2000): 720–33.

Armstrong Frances. *Dickens and the Concept of Home.* Ann Arbor: UMI Research Press, 1990.

Armstrong, Nancy. *Desire and Domestic Fiction: A Political History of the Novel.* New York: Oxford UP, 1987.

Bachelard, Gaston. *The Poetics of Space: The Classic Look at How We Experience Intimate Places.* Trans. Maria Jolas. Boston : Beacon Press, 1994.

Bakhtin, M. M. *The Dialogic Imagination.* Trans. Caryl Emerson and Michael Holquist. Texas: U of Texas P, 1982.

Balbert, Peter. "Scorched Ego, the Novel, and the Beast: Patterns of Fourth Dimensionality in *The Virgin and the Gipsy.*" *D. H. Lawrence Review* (1993): 395–416.

Baldanza, Frank. "*Orlando* and the Sackvilles." *PMLA* 70 (1955): 274–79.

Bammer, Algelika. *Partial Visions: Feminism and Utopianism in the 1970s.* New York: Routledge, 1991.

Barron, Janet. "Equalizing Puzzle: Lawrence and Feminism." *Rethinking Lawrence.* Ed. Keith Brown. Philadelphia: Open UP, 1990.

Baxter, Gisèle Marie. "After Such Knowledge, What Forgiveness?": Exile, Marriage and the Resistance to Commitment in D. H. Lawrence's *Kangaroo.*" *The Journal of Narrative Technique* 24. 2 (1994): 127–40.

Beauchamp, George. "Changing Times in Utopia." *Philosophy and Literature* 22.1 (1998): 219–30.

Beer, Gillian. "*Between the Acts:* Introduction." *Virginia Woolf: Introductions to the Major Works.* Ed. Julia Briggs. London: Virago Press, 1994. 395–424.

———. *Virginia Woolf: The Common Ground.* Edinburgh: Edinburgh UP, 1996.

Bell, Michael. *D.H. Lawrence: Language and Being.* Cambridge: Cambridge UP, 1992.

Bem, Sandra L. and Daryl J. Bem. "Training the Woman to Know Her Place: The Power of a Nonconscious Ideology." *Beliefs, Attitudes, and Human Affairs.* Daryl J. Bem. Belmont: Brooks/ Cole, 1970.

Benjamin, Walter. *Illuminations.* Trans. Harry Zohn. New York: Schocken Books, 1969.

Berman, Marshall. *All That Is Solid Melts into Air: The Experience of Modernity.* New York: Simon and Schuster, 1982.

Blanchot, Maurice. "Everyday Speech." *Yale French Studies* 73 (Fall 1987): 12–20.

Blunt, Alison and Gillian Rose. *Writing Women and Space: Colonial and Postcolonial Geographies.* New York and London: The Guilford Press, 1994.

Booth, Howard J. "'A Dream of Life': D.H. Lawrence, Utopia and Death." *English Studies* 5 (1999): 462–78.

Bourdieu, Pierre. *The Field of Cultural Production: Essays on art and Literature.* Ed. and introd. Randal Johnson. New York: Columbia UP, 1993.

Bowlby, Rachel. "Walking, Women and Writing: Virginia Woolf as *flâneuse.*" *New Feminist Discourses: Critical Essays on Theories and Texts.* Ed. Isobel Armstrong. London and New York: Routledge, 1992.

Bradbury, Malcolm and James McFarlane, eds. *Modernism: A Guide to European Literature 1890–1930.* London: Penguin, 1991.

Bradshaw, David. "Hyams Place: *The Years,* the Jews and the British Union of Fascists." *Women Writers of the 1930s: Gender, Politics, and History.* Ed. Maroula Joannou. Edinburgh: Edinburgh UP, 1999. 179–91.

Brewster, Dorothy. *Virginia Woolf's London.* Washington Square: New York UP, 1960.

Buchanan, Ian. *Michel de Certeau: Cultural Theorist.* London: SAGE Publications, 2000.

Castillo, Debra A. "Postmodern Indigenism: Quetzalocatl and All That." *Modern Fiction Studies* 41.1 (1995): 35–73.

Caughie, Pamela L. "Virginia Woolf and Postmodernism: Returning to the Lighthouse." *Rereading the New: A Backward Glance at Modernism.* Ed. Kevin J.H. Dettmar. Ann Arbor: U of Michigan P, 1992. 297–323.

Certeau, Michel de. *The Practice of Everyday Life.* Berkeley: U of California P, 1984.

Chernetsky, Vitaly. "Travels Through Heterotopia: The Textual Realms of Patrick Modiano's *Tue des Bourtiques Obscures* and Mikhail Kuraev's *Kapitan Dikshtein.*" *Studies in the Twentieth Century Literature* 22 (1998): 253–71.

Clark, Katerina and Michael Holquist. *Michael Bakhtin.* Massachusetts: The Belknap Press of Harvard UP, 1984.

Clark, L.D. *The Minoan Distance: The Symbolism of Travel in D.H. Lawrence.* Tucson: U of Arizona P, 1980.

Clifford, James. *Routes: Travel and Translation in the Late Twentieth Century.* Cambridge: Harvard UP, 1997.

Comstock, Margaret. "The Loudspeaker and the Human Voice: Politics and the Form of *The Years.*" *Bulletin of the New York Public Library* 80. 2 (Winter 1977): 252–75.

Cuddy-Keane, Melba. "The Politics of Comic Modes in Virginia Woolf's *Between the Acts.*" *PMLA* 105.2 (1990): 273–85.

Cushman, Keith. "The Virgin and the Gipsy and the Lady and the Gamekeeper." *D. H. Lawrence's "Lady": A New Look at "Lady Chatterley's Lover.* Eds. Michael Squires and Dennis Jackson. Athens: U of Georgia P, 1985. 154–69.

Daleski, H. M. *The Forked Flame.* London: Faber and Faber, 1965.

Daly, Macdonald. Introduction. *Kangaroo.* By D. H. Lawrence. xiii–xxxi.

Delany, Paul. *D. H. Lawrence's Nightmare: The Writer and His Circle in The Years of the Great War.* New York: Basic Books, 1978.

———. "*Sons and Lovers :* the Morel Marriage as a War of Position." *The D.H. Lawrence Review* 21 (1989): 153–65.

Delavenay, Emile. *D. H. Lawrence: The Man and His Work. The Formative Years, 1885–1919.* London: William Heinemann, 1972.

Deleuze, Gilles and Félix Guattari. *Anti-Oedipus: Capitalism and Schizophrenia.* Trans. Robert Hurley, Mark Seem, and Helen R. Lane. Minneapolis: U of Minnesota P, 1983.

———. *A Thousand Plateaus: Capitalism and Schizophrenia.* Trans. Brian Massumi. Minneapolis: U of Minnesota P, 1987.

Derrida, Jacques. *Specters of Marx: The State of the Debt, the Work of Mourning, and the New International.* Trans. Peggy Kamuf. Introd. Bernd Magnus and Stephen Cullenberg. New York: Routledge, 1994.

DeSalvo, Louise A. "Shakespeare's *Other* Sister." Ed. Jane Marcus. *New Feminist Essays on Virginia Woolf.* Lincoln: U of Nebraska P, 1981. 61–81.

———. *Virginia Woolf: The Impact of Childhood Sexual Abuse on Her Life and Work.* Boston: Beacon, 1989.

DiBattista, Maria. *First Love: The Affections of Modern Fiction.* Chicago and London: U of Chicago P, 1991.

———. *Virginia Woolf's Major Novels: The Fables of Anon.* New Haven: Yale UP, 1980.

Dillon, Michael. *Politics of Security: Towards a Political Philosophy of Continental Thought.* Routledge, 1996.

Doherty, Gerald. "The Dialectics of Space in D.H. Lawrence's *Sons and Lovers.*" *Modern Fiction Studies* 39.2 (1993): 327–43.

Donald, James. "This, Here, Now. Imagining the Modern City." *Imagining Cities: Scripts, Signs, Memories.* Eds. Sallie Westwood and John Williams. London and New York: Routledge, 1997. 181–201.

Douglas, Mary. "The Idea of a Home: a Kind of Space." *Social Research* 58 (1991): 287–307.

———. *Purity and Danger: An Analysis of the Concepts of Pollution and Taboo.* London: Routledge and Kegan Paul, 1966.

Draper, R. D. "The Defeat of Feminism: D. H. Lawrence's *The Fox* and "The Woman Who Rode Away." *Critical Essays on D. H. Lawrence*. Eds. and introd. Dennis Jackson and Fleda Brown Jackson. 158–69.

Duncan, Nancy, ed. *BodySpace: Destabilizing geographies of gender and sexuality.* London and New York: Routledge, 1996.

DuPlessis, Rachel Blau. "Woolfenstein." *Breaking the Sequence: Women's Experimental Fiction*. Ed. and introd. Ellen G. Friedman and Miriam Fuchs. Princeton: Princeton UP, 1989. 99–114.

Eysteinsson, Astradur. *The Concept of Modernism*. Ithaca and London: Cornell UP, 1990.

Fernihough, Anne. *D. H. Lawrence: Aesthetics and Ideology.* Oxford: Clarendon Press, 1993.

Ferns, Chris. *Narrating Utopia: Ideology, Gender, Form in Utopia Literature.* Liverpool: Liverpool UP, 1999.

Fleishman, Avrom. *Virginia Woolf: A Critical Reading.* Baltimore and London: Johns Hopkins UP, 1975.

Flora, Joseph M. *William Ernest Henley.* New York: Twayne Publishers, 1970.

Foucault, Michel. *Madness and Civilization: A History of Insanity in the Age of Reason.* Vintage, 1988.

———. "Nietzsche, Genealogy, History." *The Foucault Reader*. Ed. Paul Rabinow. New York: Pantheon Books, 1984.76–100.

———. "Of Other Spaces," *Diacritics* 16 (Spring 1986): 22–27.

———. "Questions on Geography." *Power/ Knowledge: Selected Interview and Other Writings 1972–77.* Ed. C. Gordon. Trans. Colin Gordon, Leo Marshall, John Mepham, Kate Soper. New York: Pantheon, 1980. 146–65.

———. "Space, Knowledge and Power." Interview. Rizzoli Communications, March, 1982. Rpt. *The Foucault Reader* Ed. Paul Rabinow. New York: Pantheon, 1984. 239–56.

Frank, Joseph. *The Idea of Spatial Form.* New Brunswick and London: Rutgers UP, 1991.

Fraser, Nancy. "Rethinking the Public Sphere." *Postmodernism and the Re-reading of Modernity.* Eds. Francis Baker, Peter Hulme, and Margaret Iversen. Manchester & New York: Manchester UP, 1992. 197–231.

Friedland, Roger and Deirdre Boden, eds. *NowHere: Space, Time and Modernity.* Berkeley and Los Angeles: U of California P, 1994.

Friedman, Susan Stanford. "Bodies and Borders, Nations and Narrative: Spatial Poetics and the Case of Arundhati Roy's *The God of Small Things*." A paper delivered at Narrative Conference, April 2000.

———. "Definitional Excursions: The Meanings of Modern/Modernity/Modernism." *Modernism/Modernity* 8.3 (2001): 493–513.

———. *Mappings: Feminism and the Cultural Geographies of Encounter.* Princeton: Princeton UP, 1998.

Füredi, Frank. *The Silent War: Imperialism and the Changing Perception of Race.* New Jersey: Rutgers UP, 1998.

Geoghegan, Vincent. *Utopianism and Marxism.* London: Methuen, 1987.

George, Rosemary Marangoly, ed. *Burning Down the House: Recycling Domesticity.* Ed. Rosemary Marangoly George. Colorado: Westview Press, 1998.

Giddens, Anthony. "Action, Subjectivity, and the Constitution of Meaning." *The Aims of Representation: Subject/ Text/ History.* Ed. Murray Krieger. Stanford: Stanford UP, 1993. 159–74.

Gilbert, Sandra M. *Acts of Attention: The Poems of D. H. Lawrence.* Carbondale and Edwardsville: Southern Illinois UP, 1990.

———. "Costumes of the Mind: Transvestism as Metaphor in Modern Literature." *Critical Inquiry* 7 (1980): 391–417.

Goldman, Jane. *Feminist Aesthetics of Virginia Woolf: Modernism, Post-impressionism and Politics of the Visual.* Cambridge: Cambridge UP, 1998.

Goode, John. "Individuality and Society in *Sons and Lovers* ." *Sons and Lovers* . Ed. Rick Rylane. New York: St. Martin's Press, 1996. 125–32.

Goodheart, Eugene. *The Utopian Vision of D. H. Lawrence.* Chicago: The U of Chicago P, 1963.

Gottdiener, Mark. *The Social Production of Urban Space.* 2ⁿᵈ ed. Austin: U of Texas P, 1994.

Gottlieb, Laura Moss. "*The Years:* A Feminist Novel." *Virginia Woolf: Centennial Essays.* Eds. Elaine K. Ginsberg and Laura Moss Gttlieb. Troy: Whitston, 1983.

Grossberg, Lawrence. "The Space of Culture, The Power of Space." *The Postcolonial Question: Common Skies, Divided Horizons.* Eds. Ian Chambers and Lidia Curti. London: Routledge, 1996. 169–88.

Grosz, Elizabeth. *Space, Time and Perversion.* New York: Routledge, 1995.

Guiguet, Jean. *Virginia Woolf and Her Works.* Trans. Jean Steward. New York: Harcourt, Brace & World, 1965.

Habermas, Jürgen. *The Structural Transformation of the Public Sphere.* Trans. Thomas Burger. London: Polity, 1989.

Hall, Stuart and Paul du Gay, eds. *Questions of Cultural Identity.* London: Sage Publications, 1996.

Hanson, Clare. *Virginia Woolf.* New York: St. Martin's Press, 1994.

Harvey, David. *The Condition of Postmodernity.* Oxford: Blackwell, 1989.

———. Afterword. *The Production of Space.* By Henri Lefebvre. Trans. Donald Nicholson-Smith. Oxford: Blackwell, 1991. 425–34.

Heidegger, Martin. "Building, Dwelling, Thinking." *Basic Writings.* Ed. David Farrell Krell. New York: HarperCollins, 1993. 343–64.

Henig, Suzanne. "D.H. Lawrence and Virginia Woolf." *The D.H. Lawrence Review* 2 (1969): 265–71.

Henke, Suzette. "*Mrs. Dalloway:* The Communion of Saints." *New Feminist Essays.* Ed. Marcus. 125–47.

Hetherington, Kevin. *The Badlands of Modernity: Heterotopia and Social Ordering.* New York: Routledge, 1997.

Howe, Susanne. *Novels of Empire.* New York: Columbia UP, 1949.

Humma, John B. *Metaphor and Meaning in D. H .Lawrence's Later Novels.* Columbia and London: U of Missouri P, 1990.

Hummon, David M. "House, Home, and Identity in Contemporary American Culture." *Housing, Culture, and Design: A Comparative Perspective.* Eds. and introd. Setha M. Low and Erve Chambers. Philadelphia. U of Pennsylvania P, 1989. 207–28.

Hussey, Mark. *Virginia Woolf A to Z.* Oxford: Oxford UP, 1995.

Hutcheon, Linda. *The Politics of Postmodernism.* London and New York: Routledge, 1989.

Huyssen, Andreas. *After the Great Divide: Modernism, Mass Culture, Postmodernism.* Bloomington: Indiana UP,1986.

Hyde, G. M. *D. H. Lawrence.* London: Macmillan, 1990.

Hyde, Virginia. *The Risen Adam: D. H. Lawrence's Revisionist Typology.* Pennsylvania: Pennsylvania State UP, 1992.

Jackson, Dennis and Fleda Brown Jackson. "Introduction." Eds. and introd. Dennis Jackson and Fleda Brown Jackson. *Critical Essays on D.H. Lawrence.* Massachusetts: G. K. Hall, 1998. 1–46.

Jacobus, Mary. *Reading Women: Essays in Feminist Criticism.* New York: Columbia UP, 1986.

Jameson, Fredric. "Of Islands and Trenches: Neutralization and the Production of Utopian Discourse" *The Ideologies of Theory: Essays 1971–1986.* Vol.2: Syntax of History. 75–101. Minneapolis: U of Minnesota P, 1988.

———. *Postmodernism, Or, The Cultural Logic of Late Capitalism.* 8th ed. Durham: Duke UP, 1999.

Johnston, Judith L. "The Remediable Flaw: Revisioning Cultural History in *Between the Acts.*" Ed. Jane Marcus. *Virginia Woolf and Bloomsbury: A Centenary Celebration.* Bloomington: Indiana UP, 1987. 253–77.

Kalnins, Mara. Introduction. *Apocalypse & the Writings on Revelation.* By D. H. Lawrence. Cambridge and New York: Cambridge UP, 1980.

Kamuf, Peggy. "Penelope at Work: Interruptions in *A Room of One's Own.*" *Novel: A Forum on Fiction* 16 (1982): 5–18.

Kaplan, Alice and Kristin Ross. "Introduction to Everyday Life." *Yale French Studies* 73 (Fall 1987): 1–4.

Kermode, Frank. *The Sense of an Ending: Studies in the Theory of Fiction.* New York: Oxford UP, 1967.

Kern, Stephen. *The Culture of Time and Space 1880–1918.* Cambridge: Harvard UP 1983.

Kiely, Robert. *Beyond Egotism: The Fiction of James Joyce, Virginia Woolf, and D.H. Lawrence.* Cambridge: Harvard UP, 1980.

Kinkead-Weekes, Mark. *D.H. Lawrence, Triumph to Exile, 1912–1922.* Cambridge and New York: Cambridge UP, 1996.

Kirby, Kathleen M. *Indifferent Boundaries: Spatial Concepts of Human Subjectivity.* New York: Guildford Press, 1996.

———. "Re: Mapping Subjectivity: Cartographic Vision and the Limits of Politics." *BodySpace.* Ed. Nancy Duncan. London and New York: Routledge,1996. 45–55.

Knight, Diana. *Barthes and Utopia: Space, Travel, Writing.* Oxford: Oxford UP, 1997.

Kumar, Krishan. *Utopian and Anti-Utopia in Modern Times.* Oxford: Blackwell, 1987.

Latané, Bibb and James H. Liu. "The Intersubjective Geometry of Social Space." *Journal of Communication* 46. 4 (1996): 26–34.

Laurence, Patricia Ondek. *The Reading of Silence: Virginia Woolf in the English Tradition.* Stanford: Stanford UP, 1991.

Lawrence, D. H. *Apocalypse & the Writings on Revelation.* Ed. and introd. Mara Kalnins. Cambridge and New York: Cambridge UP, 1980.

———. *The Complete Poems of D. H. Lawrence.* Eds. Vivian de Sola Pinto and Warren Roberts. New York: Viking, 1964.

———. *D. H. Lawrence and Italy.* Introd. Anthony Burgess. New York: Viking, 1972. New York: Penguin, 1985.

———. "England, My England." *The Complete Short Stories.* Vol. 2. 1961. New York: Penguin, 1976.

———. *Kangaroo.* 1923. Ed. Bruce Steele. Introd. MacDonald Daly. London: Penguin, 1997.

———. *The Letters of D. H. Lawrence, Volume II: 1913–1916.* Eds. George J. Zytaruk and James T. Boulton. Cambridge: Cambridge UP, 1981.

———. *Letters from D. H. Lawrence to Martin Secker 1911–1930.* Buckingham: Martin Secker, 1970.

———. "The Man Who Loved Islands." *The Complete Short Stories.* Vol. 3. 1961. New York: Penguin, 1988. 722–46.

———. *Psychoanalysis and the Unconscious, and Fantasia of the Unconscious.* Introd. Philip Rieff. New York: Viking, 1969

———. *Sons and Lovers .* 1913. Middlesex: Penguin, 1970.

———. "The Spirit of Place." *Studies in Classic American Literature.* New York: Viking, 1961.

———. *The Symbolic Meaning: the Uncollected Versions of Studies in Classic American Literature.* Ed. Armin Arnold. Fontwell, Arundel: Centaur Press, 1962.

———. *The Virgin and the Gipsy.* 1930. Middlesex: Penguin, 1976.

———. *Phoenix: The Posthumous Papers of D.H. Lawrence,*1936. Ed. and introd. Edward D. McDonald. New York: Penguin, 1985. 92–99.

———. *Phoenix II.* Eds. and introd. Warren Roberts and Harry T. Moore. New York: Viking, 1970.

———. "The Woman Who Rode Away." *The Complete Short Stories*. Vol. II. 546–81.

———. *Women in Love* . 1920. London: Penguin, 1995.

Leaska, Mitchell. "Virginia Woolf, the Pargeter: A Reading of *The Years*." *Bulletins of the New York Public Library* 80. 2 (Winter 1977): 172–210.

Lee, Hermione. *Virginia Woolf*. 1996. New York: Vintage, 1999.

Lefebvre, Henri. *Everyday Life in the Modern World*. Trans. Sacha Rabinovitch. New Brunswick and London: Transaction Books, 1984.

———. *The Production of Space*. Trans. Donald Nicholson-Smith. Oxford: Blackwell, 1991.

———. "Space: Social Product and Use Value." *Critical Sociology: European Perspectives*. Ed. J. W. Freiberg. New York: Irvington Publishers, 1979. 285–95.

LeShan, Lawrence and Henry Margenau. *Einstein's Space and Van Gogh's Sky: Physical Reality and Beyond*. New York : Macmillan, 1982.

Leavis, F.R. *D.H. Lawrence: Novelist*. New York: Alfred A. Knopf, 1956.

Levenson, Michael H. *Modernism and the Fate of Individuality*. Cambridge: Cambridge UP. 1998.

Levitas, Ruth. *The Concept of Utopia*. New York: Syracuse UP, 1990.

———. "Utopian Literature and Literality: Nowhere and the Wanderground." *News from Nowhere* 9 (1991): 66–79.

Lewiecki-Wilson, Cynthia. *Writing against the Family: Gender in Lawrence and Joyce*. Carbondale and Edwardsville: Southern Illinois UP, 1994.

Lockwood, M. J. *A Study of the Poems of D. H. Lawrence: Thinking in Poetry*. New York: St. Martin's Press, 1987.

London, Bette. *The Appropriated Voice: Narrative Authority in Conrad, Forster, and Woolf*. Ann Arbor: U of Michigan P, 1990.

Low, Setha M. and Erve Chambers. "Introduction." Eds. and introd. Setha M. Low and Erve Chambers. *Housing, Culture, and Design: A Comparative Perspective*. Philadelphia: U of Pennsylvania P, 1989. 3–9.

Lynch, Eve M. "The Cook, the Nurse, the Maid, and the Mother: Woolf's Working Women." *Virginia Woolf: Themes and Variations*. Eds. Vara Neverow-Turk and Mark Hussey. New York: Pace UP, 1993. 68–75.

Lyotard, Jean-François. *The Inhuman: Reflections on Time*. Trans. Geoffrey Bennington and Rachel Bowlby. Stanford: Stanford UP, 1991.

———. *The Postmodern Explained: Correspondence 1982–1985*. Eds. Julian Pefanis and Morgan Thomas. Trans. Don Barry, Bernadette Maher, Julian Pefanis, Virginia Spate, and Morgan Thomas. Minneapolis and London: U of Minnesota P, 1993.

Malcolm, Janet. "A House of One's Own." *The New Yorker* (June 1995): 58–78.

Manuel, Frank E. and Fritzie P. Manuel. *Utopian Thought in the Western World*. Oxford: Blackwell, 1979.

Marcus, Jane. "Britannia Rules *The Waves*." Ed. Margaret Homans. *Virginia Woolf: A Collection of Critical Essays*. New Jersey: Prentice-Hall, 1993. 227–48.

————. "Enchanted Organs, Magic Bells: *Night and Day* as Comic Opera." Ed. Ralph Freedman. *Virginia Woolf: Revaluation and Continuity.* Berkeley: U of California P, 1980. 96–122.

————. *Art and Anger: Reading Like a Woman.* Columbus: Ohio State UP, 1988.

Marcus, Sharon. *Apartment Stories: City and Home in Nineteenth-Century Paris and London.* Berkeley: U of California P, 1999.

Marin, Louis. *Utopics: A Spatial Play.* London: Macmillan, 1984.

————. "Frontiers of Utopia: Past and Present." *Critical Inquiry* 19.3 (1992): 397–420.

Marshik, Celia. "Publication and 'Public Women': Prostitution and Censorship in Three Novels by Virginia Woolf." *Modern Fiction Studies* 45.4 (1999): 853–86.

Massey, Doreen. "Flexible Sexism." *Environment and Planning D: Society and Space* 9 (1991): 31–57.

————. "Politics and Space/Time." *Place and the Politics of Identity.* Eds. M. Keith and S. Pile. London: Routledge, 1993. 141–61.

————. *Space, Place and Gender.* Oxford: Politic Press, 1993.

McDowell, Linda. "Spatializing Feminism: Geographic Perspectives." Duncan 28–44.

McDowell, Linda and Joanne P. Sharp. *Space, Gender, Knowledge: Feminist Readings.* London: Arnold, 1997.

McGee, Patrick. "The Politics of Modernist Form: Or, Who Rules *The Waves?*" *Modern Fiction Studies* 38. 3 (1992): 631–50.

Meyers, Jeffrey. *D.H. Lawrence and the Experience of Italy.* Philadelphia: U of Pennsylvania P, 1982.

Miller, J. Hillis. *Fiction and Repetition: Seven English Novels.* Massachusetts: Harvard UP, 1982.

Miller, Marlow A. "Unveiling: The Dialectic of Culture and Barbarism" in British Pageantry" Virginia Woolf's *Between the Acts." Papers on Language and Literature* 34. 2 (1998): 134–61.

Millett, Kate. *Sexual Politics.* New York: Doubleday, 1970.

Moore, Harry T. *The Priest of Love: A Life of D. H. Lawrence.* New York: Penguin, 1981. Expanded and Rev. ed. of *The Intelligent Heart.* 1954.

Morris, Jan. *Traveling With Virginia Woolf.* London: The Hogarth Press, 1993.

Morris, Meaghan "On the Beach." *Cultural Studies.* Eds. Lawrence Grossberg, Cary Nelson, Paula Treichler. New York and London: Routledge, 1992. 450–72.

Morris, William. *News From Nowhere: Or an Epoch of Rest.* Ed. Krishan Kumar. Cambridge: Cambridge UP, 1995.

Moynahan, Julian. *The Deed of Life: The Novels and Tales of D. H. Lawrence.* New Jersey: Princeton UP, 1963.

Naremore, James. "Nature and History in *The Years." Virginia Woolf: Revaluation and Continuity.* Ed. and introd. Ralph Freedman. Berkeley: U of California P, 1980. 241–62.

Nehls, Edward. "The Spirit of Place." *The Achievement of D. H. Lawrence.* Eds. and introd. Frederick J. Hoffman and Harry T. Moore. Norman: U of Oklahoma P, 1953. 268–90.

Neilson, Brett. "D.H. Lawrence's "Dark Page": Narrative Primitivism in *Women in Love* and *The Plumed Serpent.*" *Twentieth Century Literature* 43. 3 (1997): 310–25.

Nixon, Cornelia. *Lawrence's Leadership Politics and the Turn against Women.* Berkeley: U of California P, 1986.

Peach, Linden. *Virginia Woolf.* New York: St. Martin's Press, 2000.

Phillips, Kathy J. *Virginia Woolf against Empire.* Knoxville: U of Tennessee P, 1994.

Philo, C. "Foucault's Geography," *Environment and Planning D: Society and Space* 10 (1992): 137–61.

Pinkney, Tony. *D.H. Lawrence and Modernism.* Iowa: U of Iowa P, 1990.

Pollnitz, Christopher. "'Raptus Virginis': The Dark God in the poetry of D. H. Lawrence." *D. H. Lawrence: Centenary Essays.* Ed. Mara Kalnins. 111–38.

Poole, Roger. *The Unknown Virginia Woolf.* Cambridge: Cambridge UP, 1978.

Pawlowski, Merry. "Virginia Woolf's *Between the Acts:* Fascism in the Heart of England." *Virginia Woolf Miscellanies.* Eds. Vara Neverow-Turk and Mark Hussey. New York: Pace UP, 1991. 188–91.

Pridmore-Brown, Michele. "1930–40: Of Virginia Woolf, Gramophones, and Fascism." *PMLA* 113. 3 (1998): 408–21.

Reed, Christopher. "'A Room of One's Own': The Bloomsbury Group's Creation of a Modernist Domesticity." *Not At Home: The Suppression of Domesticity in Modern Art and Architecture.* London: Thames and Hudson, 1996. 147–60.

———, ed. "Through Formalism: Feminism and Virginia Woolf's Relation to Bloomsbury Aesthetics." *Twentieth Century Literature* 38 (1992): 20–43.

Richter, Harvena. *Virginia Woolf: The Inward Voyage.* Princeton: Princeton UP, 1970.

Ricoeur, Paul. *Lectures on Ideology and Utopia.* Ed. George H. Yaylor. New York: Columbia UP, 1986.

Pinkney, Tony. "Space: The Final Frontier." *News from Nowhere* 8 (1990): 10–27.

Roessel, David. "The Significance of Constantinople in *Orlando.*" *Papers on Language and Literature* 28 (1992): 398–416.

Ronen, Ruth. "Description, Narrative and Representation." *Narrative* 5.3 (1997): 274–86.

Rooks, Pamela A. "D.H. Lawrence's "Individual" and Michael Polany's "Personal": Fruitful Redefinition of Subjectivity and Objectivity." *D. H. Lawrence Review* 23. 2–3 (1991): 21–29.

Rose, Gillian. "As If the Mirrors had Bled: Masculine Dwelling, Masculinist Theory and Feminist Masquerade." Duncan 56–74.

———. *Feminism and Geography.* Oxford: Polity Press, 1993.

Rosner, Victoria Page. "Housing Modernism: Architecture, Gender, and the Culture of Space in Modern British Literature." Diss. Columbia U, 1999.

Ross, Kristin. *The Emergence of Social Space: Rimbaud and the Paris Commune.* Minneapolis: U of Minnesota P, 1988.

Ruderman, Judith. *D. H. Lawrence and the Devouring Mother: The Search for a Patriarchal Ideal of Leadership.* North Carolina: Duke UP, 1984.

Rylance, Rick. "Lawrence's Politics." *Rethinking Lawrence.* Ed. Keith Brown. Philadelphia : Open UP, 1990. 163–80.

Sarker, Sonita. "Locating a Native Englishness in Virginia Woolf's *The London Scene." NWSA* 13. 2 (2001): 1–30.

Sarup, Madan. "Home and identity," *Travellers' Tales: Narratives of Home and Displacement.* Eds. George Robertson, Melinda Mask, Lisa Tickner, Jon Bird, Barry Curtis and Tim Putnam. London and New York: Routledge, 1994.

Schapiro, Barbara Ann. "Maternal Bonds and the Boundaries of Self: D.H. Lawrence and Virginia Woolf."*Soundings: An Interdisciplinary Journal* 69:3 (1986): 347–65.

———. *Literature and the Relational Self.* New York: New York UP, 1994.

Scheckner, Peter. *Class, Politics, and the Individual" A Study of the Major Works of D. H. Lawrence.* New Jersey: Associated UP, 1985.

Scott, Bonnie Kime. "Woolf, Barnes and the Ends of Modernism: An *Antiphon* to *Between the Acts." Virginia Woolf: Themes and Variations.* Eds. Vara Neverow-Turk and Mark Hussey. New York: Pace UP, 1993. 25–32.

Seeley, Tracy. "Virginia Woolf's Poetics of Space: "The Lady in the Looking-Glass: A Reflection." *Woolf Studies Annual* 2 (1996): 89–116.

Seidel, Michael. *Exile and the Narrative Imagination.* New Haven and London: Yale UP, 1986.

Shands, Kerstin W. *Embracing Space: Spatial Metaphor in Feminist Discourse.* Connecticut and London: Greenwood Press, 1999.

Shields, Rob. *Lefebvre, Love & Struggle: Spatial Dialectics.* London: Routledge, 1998.

Showalter, Elaine. "Killing the Angel in the House: The Autonomy of Women Writers." *Antioch Review* 32 (1973): 339–53.

Siegel, Carol. *Lawrence among the Women.* Charlottesville : UP of Virginia, 1991.

———. "Reading *Women in Love* and *Sons and Lovers* like Sisters and Brothers: Lawrence Study in the Feminist Classroom." *Approaches to Teaching the Works of D. H. Lawrence.* Eds. M. Elizabeth Sargent and Garry Watson. 106–15.

———. "With Lawrence in America, from House/ Wife to Nomad: *The Plumed Serpent."* Ed. Paul Poplawski. Connecticut and London: Greenwood Press, 2001. 119–31.

Simpson, Hilary. *D. H. Lawrence and Feminism.* Illinois: Northern Illinois UP, 1982.

Snaith, Anna. ""At Gordon Sq. and Nowhere Else": The Spatial and Social Politics of Bloomsbury." *Virginia Woolf: Turning the Centuries.* Eds. Ann Ardis and Bonnie Kime Scott. 256–66.

———. "Virginia Woolf's Narrative Strategies: Negotiating Between Public and Private Voices." *Journal of Modern Literature* 20.2 (1996): 133–48.

———. *Virginia Woolf: Public and Private Negotiations.* London: MacMillan, 2000.

Soja, Edward W. *Postmodern Geographies: The Reassertion of Space in Critical Social Theory.* London: Verso, 1989.

Solomon, Julie Rubin. "Staking Ground: the Politics of Space in Virginia Woolf's *A Room of One's Own* and *Three Guineas.*" *Women's Studies* 16 (1989): 331–47.

Spivak, Gayatri Chakravorty. "Time and Timing: Law and History." *Chronotypes: The Construction of Time.* Eds. John Bender and David E. Wellbergy. Stanford: Stanford Up, 1991. 99–117.

Springer, JoAnn. "Unhousing the Self: Virtual Space in *Between the Acts.*" *Virginia Woolf and the Arts.* Eds. Diane F. Gillespie and Leslie K. Hankins. New York : Pace UP, 1997.

Squier, Susan M. *Virginia Woolf and London: The Sexual Politics of the City.* Chapel Hill: U of North Carolina P, 1985.

———. "The Politics of City Space in *The Years:* Street Love, Pillar Boxes and Bridges." *New Feminist Essays on Virginia Woolf.* Ed. Jane Marcus. Lincoln: U of Nebraska, 1981. 216–37.

Stewart, Jack. *The Vital Art of D. H. Lawrence: Vision and Expression.* Carbondale and Edwardsville: Southern Illinois UP, 1999.

Stone, Lawrence. "The Public and the Private in the Stately Homes of England, 1500–1990. *Social Research* 58.1 (Spring 1991): 227- 51.

Storch, Margaret. ""But Not the America of the Whites: Lawrence's Pursuit of the True Primitive." *D. H. Lawrence Review* 25.1–3 (1993 & 1994): 48–62.

Sumner, Rosemary. *A Route to Modernism: Hardy, Lawrence, Woolf.* New York: St. Martin's Press, 2000.

Templeton, Wayne. "The Drift Towards Life: Paul Morel's Search for a Place." *D.H. Lawrence Review* 15.1–2 (1982): 177–94.

Thornton, Weldon. *D. H. Lawrence: A Study of the Short Fiction.* New York: Twayne Publishers, 1993.

Torgovnick, Mariana. *Gone Primitive: Savage Intellects, Modern Lives.* Chicago: U of Chicago P, 1990.

Tracy, Jr., Billy T. *D. H. Lawrence and the Literature of Travel.* Ann Arbor: UMI Research Press, 1983.

Tratner, Michael. *Modernism and Mass Politics: Joyce. Woolf, Eliot, Yeats.* California: Stanford UP, 1995.

Tremper, Ellen. *"Who Lived at Alfoxton?": Virginia Woolf and English Romanticism.* London: Associated University Presses, 1998.

Turner, John. "Purity and Danger in D. H. Lawrence's *The Virgin and the Gipsy.*" *D. H. Lawrence: Centenary Essays.* Ed. Mara Kalnins. Bristol: Bristol Classical Press, 1986. 139–71.

Usui, Masami. "The Female Victim of War in *Mrs. Dalloway.*" *Virginia Woolf and War: Fiction, Reality, Myth.* Ed. Mark Hussey. New York: Syracuse UP, 1991. 151–63.

Wallenstein, Sven Olov. "Utopia/Heterotopia." *Utopist World Championship 2001.* Soc. Stockholm. http://www.soc.nu/Utopian03/uwc2001/wallenstien.html

Watson, J. R. "The Country of My Heart: D. H. Lawrence and the East Midlands Landscape." *The Spirit of D. H. Lawrence: Centenary Studies.* Eds. Gamini Salgado and G. K. Das. New Jersey: Barnes and Noble Books, 1988. 16–31.

Wegner, Phillip E. *Imaginary Communities: Utopia, the Nation, and the Spatial Histories of Modernity.* Berkeley: U of California P, 2002.

———. "Horizons, Figures, and Machines: The Dialectics of Utopia in the Work of Fredric Jameson." *Utopian Studies* 9:2 (1998): 58–73.

Wells, H. G. *A Modern Utopia.* Lincoln: U of Nebraska P, 1967.

Widmer, Kingsley. *The Art of Perversity: D. H. Lawrence's Shorter Fictions.* Seattle: U of Washington P, 1962.

———. *Defiant Desire: Some Dialectical Legacies of D. H. Lawrence.* Carbondale and Edwardsville: Southern Illinois UP, 1992.

Wilde, Oscar. *Essays of Oscar Wilde.* Ed. Hasketh Pearson. London: Metheun, 1950.

Wilkinson, Alan. *The Church of England and the First World War.* London: SPCK, 1978.

Willbern, David. "Malice in Paradise: Isolation and Projection in 'The Man Who Loved Islands.'" *The D.H. Lawrence Review* 10 (1977): 223–41.

Williams, Linda Ruth. *Sex in the Head: Visions of Femininity and Film in D.H. Lawrence.* New York: Harvester Wheatsheaf, 1993.

———. *D. H. Lawrence.* Plymouth: Northcote House, 1997. Williams, Raymond. *The Country and the City.* New York: Oxford UP, 1973.

———. *The Politics of Modernism: Against the New Conformists.* Ed. and introd. Tony Pinkney. New York: Verso, 1989.

———. "Lawrence's Social Writing." Ed. Mark Spilka. *D. H. Lawrence: A Collection of Critical Essays.* New Jersey: Prentice-Hall, 1963. 162–74.

Wilson, Elizabeth . *The Sphinx in the City.* London: Virago, 1991.

———. "The Invisible Flâneur." *New Left View* 191 (1992): 90–110.

Wilson, Jean Moorcroft. *Virginia Woolf Life and London: A Biography of Place.* New York and London: Norton, 1987.

Wolff, Janet. "The Invisible Flâneuse: Women and the Literature of Modernity." *Theory, Culture and Society* 2.3 (1985): 37–46.

Woolf, Leonard. *An Autobiography.* Vol.2: 1911–1969. New York: Oxford UP, 1980.

Woolf, Virginia. *Between the Acts.* 1941. San Diego: Harcourt Brace & Company, 1969.

———. *Collected Essays.* Vol. IV. New York: Harcourt, Brace & World, 1967.

———. *The Common Reader.* First Series. 1925. Ed. and introd. Andrew McNeillie. New York: Harcourt Brace & Company, 1984.

———. *The Diary of Virginia Woolf. Volume 4, 1931–1935.*

———. *The Diary of Virginia Woolf. Volume 5, 1936–1941.* San Diego: Harcourt Brace & Company, 1984.

———. *The Diary of Virginia Woolf. Volume 3, 1925– 1930.* Ed. Anne Olivier Bell. New York: Harcourt Brace Jovanovich, 1980.

———. *The Diary of Virginia Woolf. Volume 2, 1920–1924.* Ed. Anne Olivier Bell. NewYork: Harcourt Brace Jovanovich, 1978.

————. "Flying over London." *Collected Essays*. Vol. 4. New York: Harcourt, Brace & World, 1967.

————. "The Journal of Mistress Joan Martyn." *The Complete Shorter Fiction of Virginia Woolf*. Ed. Susan Dick. 2ⁿᵈ Ed. San Diego: Harcourt, 1989.

————. *The London Scene*. London: The Hogarth Press, 1982.

————. *The Letters of Virginia Woolf* (.)Vol. II. Eds. Nigel Nicolson and Joanne Trautmann. New York: Harcourt Brace Jovanovich, 1976.

————. *Moments of Being*. Ed. Jeanne Schulkind. 2ⁿᵈ ed. San Diego: Harcourt, 1985.

————. *The Moment and Other Essays*. Ed. Leonard Woolf. London: The Hogarth Press, 1947.

————. *Mrs. Dalloway*. 1925. San Diego: H arcourt Brace & Company, 1981.

————. "Notes on D.H. Lawrence." *Collected Essays*. Vol. I. 352–55.

————. *A Passionate Apprentice: The Early Journals, 1897–1909*. Ed. Mitchell A. Leaska. San Diego: Harcourt, 1990.

————. *A Room of One's Own*. 1929. San Diego: Harcourt Brace & Company, 1981.

————. "Street Haunting: A London Adventure." *Collected Essays*. Vol. 4. 155–66.

————. *To The Lighthouse*. 1927. San Diego: Harcourt Brace & Company, 1981.

————. *Three Guineas*. 1938. San Diego: Harcourt Brace & Company, 1966.

————. *The Waves*. 1931. San Diego: Harcourt Brace & Company, 1959.

————.*The Years*. 1937. San Diego: Harcourt Brace & Company, 1965.

Worthen, John. "Lawrence and Eastwood." Kalnins. 1–20.

Wussow, Helen. *The Nightmare of History: The Fictions of Virginia Woolf and D. H. Lawrence*. Bethlehem: Lehigh UP: London: Associated UP, 1998.

Young, Richard O. "Where Even The Trees Come And Go: D. H. Lawrence and the Fourth Dimension." *The D. H. Lawrence Review* 13 (1980): 30–44.

Zwerdling, Alex. *Virginia Woolf and the Real World*. California: U of California P, 1986.

Zytaruk, George J. "Rananim: D. H. Lawrence's Failed Utopia." Salgado and Das. 266–94.

Index

B

Bachelard, Gaston, 12, 20–22
Bakhtin, Michael, 150, 225 12n
Beer, Gillian, 4, 210 6n
Bourdieu, Pierre, 6

C

Carlyle, Thomas, 63
Chronotope, 14, 39, 144, 152, 172, 174,
    175, 181, 192, 195, 199, 203,
    204, 207, 225 9n, 225 12n.
    See also space/time
Cultural studies, 6

D

De Certeau, Michel, 7, 147, 148, 188
Deconstruction, 6, 89
Derrida, Jacques, 90, 91, 121, 122, 217 4n

E

Eliot, T. S., 1, 209 2n

F

Fascism, 2, 67, 68, 69, 129, 179, 198, 233
    22n
Feminism, 1, 2, 61, 62, 67, 68, 69, 129,
    179
Foucault, Michel, 3, 4, 108, 145, 146, 147,
    148, 220 14n
Fourth dimension, the, See Lawrence
Frank, Joseph, 2, 3, 4, 95, 215 14n
Freud, Sigmund, 214 13n
Friedman, Susan Stanford, 7

G

Giddens, Anthony, 6
Good Housekeeping, 63, 71

H

Harvey, David, 6, 145, 146, 149, 186, 224
    7n
Heidegger, Martin, 210 9n
Henley, William Ernest, 98, 99, 100, 219
    7n; "England, My England," 98;
    A Book of Verses, 98
Here and now, 10, 14, 15, 138, 142, 144,
    152, 162, 163, 187, 192, 194,
    197, 199, 202–204, 207
Heterotopia, 145, 146, 148, 149, 224 9n
Home, 9, 12, 21, 22, 23, 85–92 *passim,*
    94–97, 100–104 *passim,* 139,
    202, 205, 212 3n, 213 5n, 217
    3n, 218 3n, 221 5n; association
    of nation with, 13, 87, 88, 117,
    206; Victorian ideology of, 13,
    27, 63, 85, 86, 88, 89, 92, 206,
    221 11n; alternative
    home/nation, 104–116; imperi-
    alism and the discourse of,
    98–100 *passim; See also* domestic
    space; Lawrence; Woolf

I

Imperialism, 24, 52, 53, 68, 72, 73, 91, 97,
    100, 109, 122, 123, 124, 125,
    126, 130, 131,206, 208, 207
    5n, 220 16n, 221 4n, 221 11n

Industrialization, 5, 24, 48, 49, 98
"insurgent Now." *See* Lawrence

J

Joyce, James, 1, 35, 54, 167, 209 2n, 219
    10n

K

Keats, John, 63, 64
Kern, Stephen, 4, 202, 210 7n

L

Lawrence, D. H.:
    Woolf and, 1–11, 19, 20, 21, 227 5n;
        and anti-feminism, 2; and
        World War I, 98, 153, 154, 155,
        156, 162, 169; treatment of
        space in, 3, 5, 20, 21, 30, 35,
        207; domestic space in, 12, 13,
        21, 23, 25, 27, 30–34, 38, 40,
        41, 42, 48, 49, 51, 53, 55, 104,
        214 12n; public space in, 24,
        30, 36, 38, 43, 49–56; spatial
        politics in, 19, 30, 47, 49,
        52–55; utopia in, 15, 154, 155,
        156, 157–168 *passim,* 169, 170,
        172, 174, 175, 194, 226 1n,
        227 7n; utopianism in, 226 1n,
        229 12n; and Christian utopi-
        anism, 163; and socialist utopi-
        anism, 163; and traditional
        utopianism, 153, 158, 161, 167,
        170; gender politics in, 19, 25,
        28, 34, 35, 38, 55, 62, 80, 206,
        214 13n, 218 3n; misogyny in,
        1, 2, 93, 212 4n, 249 4n; misan-
        thropy in, 105, 112; and Lon-
        don, 155, 175; "insurgent Now"
        in, 14, 162–166, 168, 172, 193,
        194, 207; idea of Rananim in,
        14, 51, 153, 154–156, 166,
        169, 170, 226 2n; the fourth
        dimension in, 5, 165, 228 10n;
        the moment in, 164, 167, 168;
        home in, 19, 20, 25, 27–29, 30,
        31–34 *passim,* 37, 38, 40, 41,
        42, 48, 51, 52, 54, 55, 94, 167;

        spatial politics in, 9, 19, 30, 47,
            49, 52, 53–55, 206
    Works of:
        Amores, 27, 155, 212 1n; "On Com-
            ing Home," 91, 94, 96, 97, 111,
            114; "Discord in Childhood,"
            12, 25, 27, 30; "England, My
            England," 13, 91, 94, 97–**100,**
            108; *Fantasia of the Unconscious,*
            1, 106, 209 1n; "Germans and
            English," 91, 94, 96, 97, 99;
            Kangaroo, 13, 92, 93, **104–115;**
            "Master in His House," 12, 25;
            "Returning to Bestwood," 91;
            The Rainbow, 12, 14, 23, 25,
            28, 30, **34–55,** 68, 94, 151,
            155, **166–169,** 172, 174, 213
            4n, 214 12n, 215 15n, 229 12n;
            Sons and Lovers, 12, 20, 25,
            30–38, 48, 93, 94, 210 4n, 213
            8n, 215 20n, 218 1n; "Surgery
            for the Novel—Or a Bomb,"
            103, 113; *The Virgin and the
            Gipsy,* 92, 94, **100–104,** 111,
            113
Leavis, F. R., 1, 35, 38, 39, 43, 93, 98, 218
    2n, 219 9n, 226 4n
Lefebvre, Henri, 149, 150, 181, 192, 193,
    195, 199, 211, 211 4n, 225
    11n; social space in, 6–8, 210
    8n, 211 4n. *See also* space
Lewis, Wyndham, 1
London, 221 7n. *See also* Lawrence; Woolf

M

Marx, Karl, 90, 91, 224 7n
Massey, Doreen, 6, 21
McDowell, Linda, 6
Militarism, 12, 24, 49, 52, 53, 67, 68, 96,
    126, 132
Millett, Kate, 43, 212 4n, 214 13n, 215
    15n, 218 3n
Modernism, 1–5, 209 1n, 217, 228 10n
Modernity, 2, 3, 4, 5, 22, 88, 148, 205
Moment, the, 158, 165, 172, 173, 194,
    200, 202, 232 16n, 233 24n;
    epiphanic, 11, 14, 15, 151, 175,

180, 207, 231 14n; in Marin, 147; in Lefebvre, 150, 225 11n. *See also* Lawrence; Woolf
"moments of being." See Woolf
More, Thomas, 144; *Utopia,* 144
Moretti, Franco, 7
Morris, William, 143, 159, 161, 166, 175, 176, 179, 186, 227 5n, 229 11n, 230 2n;

N

Nation. *See* home
Nationalism, 12, 24, 38, 48, 51, 53, 68, 99, 100, 129, 178, 228 10n
News from Nowhere, 143, 159, 166, 227 5n
Nietzsche, Friedrich, 90

P

Pacifism, 2
Pound, Ezra, 1
Primitivism, 110, 220 16n

R

Rananim. *See* Lawrence
Rose, Gillian, 6, 33
Ruskin, John, 12, 20, 21, 22, 85, 87; "On Queen's Garden," 85

S

Semiotic, 8, 145, 211, 224 9n
Sexuality, 1, 104, 110, 130, 136, 215 17n
Soja, Edward, 6
Space: domestic, 9, 19, 20, 21, 22, 205, 211 3n, 213 5n, 215 14n; Victorian ideology of domestic, 85, 205; public, 206, 249; social, 1, 3, 6–10, 12, 13, 15, 19, 22, 24, 33, 34, 47, 55, 57, 60, 64, 65, 66, 67, 72, 73, 77, 81, 145, 148, 149, 151, 180, 181, 183, 188, 192, 205, 207, 215 20n; politics of social, 149, 181. *See also* time; Lefebvre; Lawrence; Woolf
Spatial code, 9, 19, 23, 25, 30, 32, 39, 41, 44, 45, 46, 64, 65, 66, 67, 70, 72, 75, 76, 77, 78, 79, 80, 207, 211, 215 20n, 216 25n

Spatial politics, 8, 206, 207, 208, 211 11n, 225 12n. *See also* space; Lawrence; Woolf
Stein, Gertrude, 4

T

Temporality, 10, 145, 147, 158, 172, 181, 184, 195, 196, 198, 199, 202, 204, 215 14n, 224 7n, 225 11n, 228 10n
Time, 3, 4, 10, 14, 40, 44, 55, 68, 128, 135, 145, 147, 149, 150, 151, 158, 160, 162–164, 166–168, 173, 174, 179, 181–184 *passim,* 192, 193–196 *passim,* 199, 200, 201, 202, 207, 219 12n, 224 7n, 226 12n, 228 9n; conjunction of space and, 3, 4, 5, 10, 39, 41; time/space, 40, 149, 158, 164, 165, 167, 171, 179, 185, 192, 193, 199, 202, 207, 228 10n; space and, 3, 4, 5, 10, 39, 41, 48, 49, 147, 149, 150, 151, 157, 158, 162, 164, 175, 177, 181, 184, 193, 195, 202, 224 7n, 228 10n, 229 12n
22 Hyde Park Gate, 58, 59

U

Uncanny, 90, 118, 138, 158, 208
Urbanization, 5
Urban studies, 6
Utopia, 10, 13, 14, 15, 143–153 *passim,* 185, 223 1n, 224 6n, 225 10n, 227 6n. *See also* Lawrence; Woolf
Utopia. See More
Utopianism, 144, 145, 146, 157, 186, 223 4n, 224 7n, 226 1n; "Dialectical Utopianism," 186; socialist, 169, 179, 186, 231 11n; "spatiotemporal utopianism," 145, 146; urbanist, 151, 180, 186. *See also* Lawrence; Woolf

V

Victoria, Queen, 101, 219 11n

W

Williams, Raymond, 35, 36, 38, 86

Woolf, Virginia:

    Lawrence and, 1–11, 19, 20, 21, 227 5n;
and fascism, 1; and feminism, 1,
24, 67–71 *passim,* 179; and war,
68, 69, 117, 129, 178, 179, 180,
181, 184, 189, 191, 198, 200,
201, 217 5n; treatment of space
in, 3, 5, 19, 20, 21, 25, 207;
home in, 20, 22, 58, 63, 64, 68,
73; domestic space in, 12, 13, 21,
23, 57, 58–67, 68, 70, 120, 121,
127, 137, 205 the city and, 180,
185, 192; and London, 15, 25,
35, 63, 67, 68, 71, 72, 73, 78, 79,
80, 92, 128, 138, 151, 180, 181,
182, 183, 185, 186, 187, 190,
191, 192, 198, 231 13n; public
space in, 24, 57, 63, 67, 68, 69,
70, 71–80; spatial politics in, 9,
11, 12, 19, 57, 61, 64, 67,
68–70, 72, 77, 206; the moment
in, 185, 189, 191, 193, 194, 195,
200, 201; "moments of being" in,
14, 15, 193; utopia in, 11, 14, 15,
151, 175–184 *passim,* 186–192,
193, 194, 195, 196, 198, 199,
200, 202, 203, 204, 208, 231
14n; utopian visions in, 14; and
urbanist utopianism, 151, 180,
186; and socialist utopianism,
179, 186, 231 11n; and traditional utopianism, 199; and
suffragette, 132, 136, 221 12n;

Works of:

    Between the Acts, 151, 192, **197–203**,
232 19n; "Docks of London,
The," 12, 25, 71, 72, 78, 80;
"Great Men's Houses," 12, 25,
57, **62–64**, 71; "The Journal of
Mistress Joan Martyn," 13, 67,
92, **118–122**, 131; *The London
Scene,* 12, 25, 57, 67, 71, 187;
"The Memories of a Working
Women's Guild," 14, 151, 175;
"The Moment: Summer's Night,"
15, 151, **192–197**, 198, 199,
201, 202; *Mrs. Dalloway,* 12, 14,
25, 57, 58, 62, **64–67**, 77, 151,
180–192, 198, 202, 230 9n, 231
14n; "Oxford Street Tide," 12,
25, 71, 72, 77–**80**; *A Sketch of the
Past,* 12, 20, 22, 25, 57, **58–62**,
193, 194, 197, 222 13n; "Street
Haunting," 188; *Three Guineas,*
12, 14, 57, 67, 68, 71, 117–118,
129, 134, 151, 176, 178; *The
Voyage Out,* 208; *The Waves,* 13,
92, **122–127**, 220 1n, 233 23n;
The Years, 13, 71, 92, **127–139**,
221 12n

War, 38, 48, 50, 68, 69, 99, 100, 118, 129,
154, 155, 178, 179, 191, 198,
200, 217 5n. *See* Lawrence;
Woolf

Westminster Abbey, 70, 71, 184, 230 9n

World War I, 4, 5, 98, 153, 154, 162, 169,
180, 181, 184, 189, 191, 218 5n

World War II, 198, 201